In this book you will learn...

- How to build stronger kids and help them make smart choices.

- The dangers to children in modern Western society.

- How to choose safe, high-quality childcare and safe child minders.

- How to safeguard children in a wide variety of potentially dangerous situations, including bullying, cyberspace and the Internet.

- How to protect against child sex offenders.

- How to protect against child sexual abuse.

- Coping mechanisms for a parent's most difficult moments.

- Parenting tips for stages through adolescence.

- How to choose safe student exchanges for teenagers.

- How to protect your children in cyberspace.

Smart Parenting
for Safer Kids

Helping children to make
smart choices and stay safe

**A PRACTICAL GUIDE FOR PARENTS
AND PARENT EDUCATORS**

JoJo

PUBLISHING

Professor Freda Briggs AO

Acknowledgments

A book that covers such a wide range of topics could not be written without the assistance of a number of people. I wish to thank:

- Distinguished Professor of Child Development, Laura Berk, State University of Illinois and child psychologist Dr. Marie O'Neill, South Australia, for contributions to *Chapter 1: Getting the Balance Right.*
- Child care experts Dr. Sarah Farquhar, CHILD Forum, New Zealand and Professor Sonia Jackson, London University, for assistance in writing *Chapter 2: Choosing Safe Services for Your Child.*
- Dr. Ken Rigby and Dr. Barbara Spiers, University of South Australia and Associate Professor Mary Briggs, University of Warwick, UK, for contributions to *Chapter 3: Protecting Your Child from Bullying.*
- Holly Brennan, Family Planning, Queensland, for her advice for *Chapter 4: Promoting Healthy Sexual Development in Children.*
- Professor Caroline Taylor, Edith Cowan University, for critiquing chapters on child sexual abuse.
- Chief Superintendent Chris Gould of Avon & Somerset Police and Child-Safe, UK and Danielle Grijalva, USA, on safe student travel.
- Peter Jeans, Assistant Principal, Springvale Secondary College, Victoria; Lise Nikulinsky, (Dragonfly Foundation, WA); Amanda Robinson, former child protection police officer; and Jay Dale, teacher and publisher, for critiquing the manuscript.

- Richard Beach, Nancy Groh, Lee Chisholm cyber-safety consultants with New Zealand's NetSafe for *Chapter 10: Protecting Children in Cyberspace.*

Contents

Foreword

This unique book is a practical guide for parents and parent educators to help children stay safe. In typical Freda Briggs style, it is both explicit and realistic, as she draws on a lifetime of knowledge, research and practical experience to provide helpful information on the myriad issues that worry parents.

This book sheds light on several significant risks — the sexual abuse of children, safe use of the Internet and modern-day bullying.

The memory of sexual abuse in childhood never leaves its victims, even as adults. Many children suffer the shock and powerlessness of abuse, unable to tell anyone about what happened. Those who do tell are often further injured when adults refuse to believe them. The luckier few are immediately believed and protected.

The memory of bullying never goes away and now, with advances in technology, bullying has accelerated and become even more sinister. While the home may once have provided some relief from schoolyard bullying, the ubiquitous Web provides a 24-hour opportunity for bullying and abuse to continue.

The trauma of both these social evils can impact negatively on the maturing child and affect self-esteem and their trust in others.

People who hurt children sexually contrive a web of perverted self-belief centred on their own needs, which Professor Briggs identifies in detail. Offenders can sometimes be very clever and have extended their reach through all the advances and activities of our society, manipulating parents as well as others responsible for children's safety to access potential victims. Dr. Briggs' book provides an understanding of the behaviours of child sex offenders and their reach.

Inexplicably, people in responsible positions refuse to discuss sexual abuse, leaving child victims unprotected. The fight to get children's voices heard rests with a few advocates and Freda Briggs is the most credible and influential advocate throughout Australia. Ms. Briggs has garnered great expertise supported by research and she is now regularly called upon by the media and politicians for her insights.

Freda Briggs' advocacy extends beyond sexual abuse to improving training programs for the helping professions, which often fail to identify the fundamental building blocks in the development of children. This book provides sound information for both parents and professionals about the developing needs and experiences of children.

Dr. Sue Vardon, AO
*Former Chief Executive Officer, Child Protection
and Family Services, South Australia and former
Commonwealth CEO, Centrelink*

Why this book is needed

"Most parents want to be good parents but a hell of a lot of things get in the way."
Dr. Fiona Stanley, former Australian of the Year (2008)

Before we are allowed to drive a car unsupervised, we must undergo training and pass a proficiency test. There are government departments that examine and monitor our fitness to drive and there are punishments if we place the safety of others at risk.

Although parenting is the most important and rewarding, as well as the most difficult, frustrating and demanding responsibility that anyone can undertake, there is no systematic training or licensing required to become a parent. The challenges are such that if you Google the word 'parenting' today, you will find, at minimum, 98 million parenting articles on the Internet.

The reason for this is that parenting and childhood have become increasingly more complex than in the past and it is difficult for even the most conscientious parents to stay abreast of the changes, especially those related to technology. Most parents do their best but have little or no preparation for the challenges associated with rearing 21st century children. The most challenged of all are grandparent carers whose grandchildren exhibit very different behaviours and expectations from those of earlier generations. Furthermore, grandparent carers are usually placed in their role reluctantly, perhaps because their own children have turned to drugs, suffer mental illness or simply abandoned parental responsibilities at the time when their own parents were reaching retirement. Migrants from vastly different cultures are also challenged when their children wish to adopt Western lifestyles and values different from their own.

When babies are born, professionals weigh and measure them and instruct parents how to feed and wean them. When they are developing normally, the parents are left to their own devices to bring them up as they see fit. Every day, they make choices on how best to do this. Much depends on the information and skills acquired from one's own childhood experiences. Part of being a parent is replicating what is believed to be good while discarding the bad. Nevertheless, parenting behaviour is learned and emulated and parents often find themselves parroting the hated and potentially damaging words and actions of their own parents when they experience similar frustrating, emotional situations.

The readers of this book probably grew up in a far less stressful era than the current generation of children. We reminisce about the freedom we had — how we could walk to school and play safely in the street and the park, disappearing for hours and returning home only for meals and bedtime. The urban world has changed since then and, thanks to technology, it continues to change, even as you read this.

An additional hazard is that childhood is getting shorter. Girls as young as 9 have reached puberty; a 9-year-old African girl living in Greece has given birth. An 11-year-old British boy fathered a child, while others of the same age have been charged with rape in both Australia and the UK. Secondary school students distribute sexually explicit images of girls' genitals and breasts and, because the girls are under the age of consent, may be charged and placed on the paedophile register, thereby limiting their future careers.

Today's 11-year-olds are probably as worldly as you were at 18 but their sexual knowledge is often inaccurate and more often than not, their emotional development does not keep pace with their physical development. The effects are exacerbated if children miss out on a balance of discipline and affection, quality family time, sensible boundaries, and family rules and training alongside positive male and female role models.

Many 21st century youngsters have been reared from early childhood on a diet of television and videos, explicit commercialised sex, violent computer games and the belief that fame and celebrity bring easy money and an even easier lifestyle. They have become accustomed to eating in restaurants, watching plasma TVs, wearing designer clothes and receiving gifts of the most up-to-date, high-tech equipment. Unlike previous generations, many fail to recognise the importance of education, career preparation or working hard and saving for the future. Why should they, when everything they wanted has already been handed to them?

British research findings released by Random House publishers in March 2008 confirmed that childhood is over by the age of 11. Little girls abandon dolls at the age of 6 and demand makeup. Parents succumb to 'pester pressure' and permit privileges previously associated with adulthood at a time when children are neither socially nor emotionally equipped to cope. They are allowed to stay out late, drink alcohol, get tattoos and body piercings, wear tight, trendy, provocative clothes and watch adult movies long before the legally allowable age.

Despite Britain having the highest teenage pregnancy rate in Europe, there is no national, school-based, child protection/ personal safety programme and nearly half of the 1,170 parents interviewed for Random House said they allowed their 16-year-olds to spend the night with partners of the opposite sex. More than half of those parents (55 percent) believed that children were young adults by age 11 and almost 75 percent allowed them to drink alcohol at home. Not surprisingly, almost 75 percent admitted that their children were defiant, with no respect for authority. What became clear was that many parents had abandoned responsibility for keeping children safe. Kids have been permitted to make decisions unthinkable just a few years ago: they are the ones who decide where they go, with whom, what time they return; what, when and where to eat; and which clothes they will wear, with little or no oversight.

Children now have more decision-making power than ever before. Most parents don't want to be authoritarian but they don't know how to be authoritative, so they slip into permissiveness, depriving children of the critical guidelines and boundaries they require to avoid developing feelings of insecurity. Interestingly, some 12 to 14-year-olds in the so-called cool groups secretly envy peers who have parents who set boundaries. Although these youngsters may be labelled 'nerds' they are often envied because they are permitted to relax and act their true age, without the need to copy others. The good news is that 12 to 14-year-olds feel safest with parents who are not trying to be their best friends, but instead provide a safe environment within which they can grow up at a normal pace. Young teenagers may appear to look cool in the latest fashions but appearances belie their developmental level. Being grown up is more about the capacity to think than dress.

As parents, we need to look at how the world has changed and analyse what we need to do differently. We can't supervise our children and grandchildren all the time. We need to know how to teach them effectively to stay safe and avoid the dangerous situations they may encounter. The challenge is to get the balance right.

This book deals with real risks in a way that enables parents and carers to become better informed and make strategic, long-lasting decisions to improve the safety and development of children. It is about *preventing* problems, because crimes such as sexual and drug abuse have no cure.

Chapter 1

Laying the Foundations

I n this chapter I'll cover a range of issues which lay the foundations to keeping your children safe.

Some of the basic factors for parenting successfully included in this chapter are:

- Choosing the best parenting style.
- Building strong foundations.
- Developing a child's confidence.
- Encouraging appropriate assertiveness.
- Using preventative discipline
- Creating the best environment.

Also covered are some of the basics relating to the extra 'difficult' parenting moments:

- Surviving the 'crying baby'.
- Coping with temper tantrums.
- Dealing with sibling rivalry.
- Managing the adolescent years.

GETTING THE BALANCE RIGHT: PROTECTION VS. NEGLIGENCE

Over-protective parenting

Parenting styles can be viewed as a continuum with overprotective parents at one end and negligent parents at the other. Overreaction to the media coverage of very rare cases of child abduction and the widespread fear of drugs has led some parents to create a generation of 'bubble-wrapped' kids who seldom play outside, are escorted to and from school, sports and social gatherings and, at the age of 18, have never travelled on public transport. The adolescent's inappropriate behaviour is defended, debts and speeding fines paid and the child is not made to take any responsibility for anything.

Overprotection and excessive parental intrusion stifle a child's emotional, social and physical development and the growth towards independence. It can be seen as a form of psychological abuse. These kids grow up lacking self-confidence and the capacity to make sound decisions for themselves, having become overly dependent on parents. They remain in the family home long after they reach adulthood or, at the opposite extreme, rebel and leave before they have the maturity to handle independent living successfully. In other words, the long-term effects can be the opposite of those expected by their overprotective carers.

Referred to as 'helicopter parents', the over-protectors deny youngsters the opportunities to take risks and learn from mistakes. They believe unrealistically that, by controlling their children's every move, they can protect them from harm. The kids are denied the opportunity to develop the social skills and experience needed to stay safe in and outside their extended families.

Children beyond preschool years need opportunities to experiment and learn from mistakes, with parents acting as a safety net rather than as hovering helicopters. However, that doesn't mean allowing them to go partying, get drunk or wreak havoc. Sound parenting involves developing a child's confidence, safety knowledge and safety skills without creating excessive anxiety. Children have to learn how to experience their world at each stage of their development because if parents do all the regulating for them, they never develop the safety strategies and problem-solving skills needed to stay out of danger.

Negligent parenting

Overprotection is stifling but it is equally as dangerous to give children too much freedom before they have the skills and maturity to use it wisely. Have you ever wondered why children as young as 6 years old have been caught setting fire to schools? Or why 14-year-olds have been arrested for stealing cars at four o'clock in the morning? Did you ever wonder, "Where were their parents? Why weren't those kids in bed?"

Sadly, some parents don't seem to care where their children are as long as they are "out of the way" and the parents' own needs are being met. Some give youngsters large sums of money and tell them to get lost for the weekend. Then there are kids who say they are going to sleep at a friend's place but go to night-clubs and stay out all night. Others sneak out when parents think they are asleep. And, of course, there are the rebellious kids who defy their parents' instructions.

Although there are services to assist parents experiencing problems with young children, the community doesn't seem to know what to do with adolescents. It is illegal to lock them in to stop feral behaviour. Truancy officers no longer investigate and shame school absentees, and parents cannot rely on overloaded child protection services for support.

In Western society, there are few deterrents for antisocial and dangerous adolescent behaviour. Problems can arise wherever you live. In 2001, residents in the remote New Zealand town of New Plymouth[1] feared for their lives after a thousand drunken youths went on a rampage. Trouble erupted when police closed a party after complaints from local residents. Drunken kids turned on police and it took three hours to clear the area. Nine young people were arrested. Since that time there have been ongoing problems with random teenage groups meeting on the beach and sending text messages inviting others to join them.

Early in 2007, another thousand alcohol-fuelled youngsters engaged in more violence and damage to local properties. Several police units were dispatched to deal with the disorder caused mainly by drunken girls. There was a huge outcry from local residents who called a meeting of the entire town. Police found that, while some parents were shocked by their children's behaviour, "others couldn't care less". One parent in a BMW was caught passing alcohol to the children.[2] Meanwhile, in the even smaller country town of Levin, police dealt with 150 highly intoxicated, violent youngsters, many of whom were only 13 years old.

This problem is by no means limited to New Zealand. In April 2007, someone anonymously advertised teenager Rachael Bell's Sunderland (UK) party on MySpace. Expecting 60 guests, 200 gatecrashers arrived, some bringing suitcases later used to stash stolen valuables before trashing the house, causing massive damage.

In Melbourne, Australia, 16-year-old Corey Delaney (alias Worthington), achieved unprecedented international notoriety when, while his parents were on a weekend holiday and he was supposed to be staying with friends, he arranged a party for 100 adolescents advertised on MySpace. Five hundred drunken teenagers descended and created mayhem. They allegedly damaged not only the Delaney house but the entire street. The bill for helicopter assistance, police dogs and damage to police cars came to $20,000.

Corey Delaney's public profile grew exponentially with media interviews published worldwide. Viewers were stunned by his complete and utter lack of remorse, his assertion that it was a great party, he would do it all over again and his refusal to meet with and apologise to his parents. Talkback programmes ran hot with callers eager to suggest how to handle this juvenile. Some felt sorry for his parents, no doubt thinking "There but for the grace of God go I," and "How must they have felt, seeing their remorseless son showing off on TV?" It was reported that irresponsible promoters rewarded his unacceptable behaviour with offers of $1 million for a year's work arranging parties and participating in media interviews. He accepted an offer to appear on TV's *Big Brother* series. The publicity that followed on MySpace and YouTube gave Delaney legendary status among his peers.[3] And the smirk didn't diminish when police disclosed that they were charging him with possessing pornographic images of underage girls taken with his mobile phone in his parent's house. In 2009, it was reported that the now 17-year-old was living in a de facto relationship with an older female.

These young people represent a parent's worst nightmare. At the same time, there is something seriously wrong with a society that rewards irresponsible, immature, publicity-seeking, hooligan behaviour and excuses the sexual violence and drug habits of sports heroes, as well as the anti-social behaviour and drug- and alcohol-related antics of Hollywood personalities.

Sadly, this behaviour is not unusual. In surveys of New Zealand secondary school students, even those in elite schools, students admitted that trashing the host's home was part of the fun of partying.

In her bestseller, *He'll Be OK: Growing Gorgeous Boys into Good Men,*[4] New Zealand author Celia Lashlie emphasises the importance of good male role models to counter today's unhealthy societal influences. She recognises that, while dads are absent or exhausted from overwork, the kids are using young people as their role models — and from the least desirable sources, such as Facebook, YouTube and reality TV. They aspire to be celebrities and are unconcerned whether how they achieve it is right or wrong.

Parents face uncertainty as to when to permit their children to do things on their own and when to say, "No, not yet. You're not old enough for that." Quite clearly, Corey Delaney was not sufficiently mature to be left with friends while his parents took a weekend break. But what about the parents of the other 500 youngsters who created havoc for police and the neighbourhood? Where did those parents think their kids were? What did they think their children were doing when, in fact, late at night, they were trashing police vehicles in a normally quiet suburb? Some parents were reported to have dropped their kids off at the house without seeking evidence that they had even been invited to the party!

Such is the magnitude of the problem that Internet sites have now been set up to advise parents on how to implement 'safe partying'. The central messages are: notify police that the party will take place; employ security guards; make it 'invitation only' or, better still, consider holding it on licensed premises.

Before you leave your kids at a party, make sure that they have actually been invited and that parents will be present.

The challenge for society is what to do with tweens and teens when parents have lost control. Not so long ago they would have been labelled as "in need of care and protection" taken to court and placed in the care of the state (or, if in the UK, the local authority). Nowadays, if parents are negligent, there are little, if any, negative social or legal consequences. Adolescents can abandon school and live a lawless life for several years before encountering deterrents. They are apprehended for perhaps one to two percent of their crimes and, by the time they reach a juvenile detention centre, they have learned that they can do whatever they like. The size of this problem was revealed in 2008 by a Commissioner of Police who told the media that 10 percent of young people born after 1984 in the state of Victoria had criminal convictions before they were age 21 and that juvenile crime is increasing at the rate of 18 percent annually.[5] Violence against parents has increased and children are responsible for 20 percent of home burglaries and reported sex offences. Police blamed media violence and dysfunctional parents.[6]

Fortunately, there are still plenty of cool kids who counter the negative, stereotypical image of the mumbling, inarticulate, hood-wearing, happy-slapping, street-fighting youths who drink to excess and do burn-outs. Some experts explain this behaviour as "boys having new issues to face"; having thought they were superior, they now have to accept that girls outshine them at all educational levels. Their role models are male sports heroes who, in Australia, require basic training on how to treat females appropriately and drug-addicted stars whose examples will not help them to become good men. Smart or studious teenagers are labelled nerdy, geeky and definitely 'out'. Bright boys deliberately dumb themselves down in order to be considered socially acceptable.

Steve Biddulph, author of *Raising Boys,* confirms that boys are strongly influenced by male role models and need to meet men who excel in fields other than pop music and sport, neither of which provide realistic career goals. Men should teach positive values so that boys know exactly what they stand for and why. Biddulph accepts that it is hard for boys to find great male role models when fathers are physically absent from home through work or family breakdown or they are simply emotionally absent from their sons' lives. If the only way boys learn about masculinity is from the media — the Internet, computer and other games, TV and films — society is in big trouble. And if they encounter paedophiles skilled in making boys feel loved, important and special, they are at risk of even bigger trouble.

What has become clear is that the foundations for sound child development are laid at home. Good parenting involves getting the balance right between strong, protective parental instincts and helping children to learn responsibly. As they grow, parents must gradually step back and give them more responsibility and more independence, but the timing of this is absolutely crucial. Much will depend on children's confidence, their knowledge of and strategies on safety and the decisions they make.

BUILD STRONG FOUNDATIONS

The world is changing at such a fast pace that it is impossible to prepare children for every eventuality in an unknown future. For children to operate safely and independently, they need parental guidance to become confident, adaptable, knowledgeable individuals who are aware of both their rights and responsibilities. They need to be loved; however, love involves establishing predictable, safe routines, starting with regular mealtimes, baths and stories at bedtime. Children need to pick up and put away toys and clothes and know that they won't receive anything without saying "please" and "thank you". Rules and limits — and an understanding of why they are needed — are essential for sound emotional health. Children are encouraged to express their feelings and understand not only their rights but, most importantly, their responsibilities. Those individuals who are safe and secure are happier, learn more easily and make a greater effort to achieve than those who are not. They learn to trust people appropriately and make friends with similar values.

Kids need parents who listen to and support them. When they feel good about themselves and know the difference between appropriate and inappropriate behaviour, they are least likely to be targeted by bullies, sex offenders, drug peddlers and other criminals. Paedophiles are attracted to uninformed, sad, lonely, emotionally neglected, acquiescent children who lack self-esteem and need affection, approval and attention from an authority figure. Such children are the ones most likely to respond to the enticements, flattery, approval and feigned affection that paedophiles use successfully in what is referred to as the grooming process. This refers to the attractive inducements they use to manipulate and seduce victims so that they will tolerate abuse rather than risk losing the relationship. Paedophiles tend to avoid confident children, who are more likely to recognise and report criminal behaviour.

If children don't feel safe, secure and valued at home, they are more likely to become anxious and unhappy and will lack confidence at school and in their social circle. If we create strong children, we help them to succeed and protect them from a wide range of current and future hazards, including the risk of sexual abuse.

CHILDREN NEED LIMITS

Too many children suffer from living in homes where there are no predictable boundaries. Some parents aim to be their children's best friends, avoiding parenting. They are afraid that saying no might make them unpopular. As a result, they risk their children becoming insecure and developing serious behaviour problems. Kids can even end up parenting their parents and that, too, is psychologically harmful.

Young people may become emotionally disturbed if they lack confidence that their parents will protect them from themselves. For example, an American mother allowed her 12-year-old daughter to party with alcohol, experiment with drugs and sleep with older boys in their home, all three being criminal offences. Having allowed the child the freedom to behave as an adult, the mother hoped to receive love from her daughter in return. Instead, she encountered such serious hostile, antisocial behaviour that she sought help from a TV psychologist. The mother failed to understand that the girl needed the safety of limits and routines and would continue to misbehave until she found them. The psychologist forecast that the girl would end up hating her mother, especially if, being promiscuous, she became pregnant or contracted a sexually transmitted infection that could ruin her life.

Unhappy youngsters will kick, smash and throw things, hoping that someone will step in and help them to regain control. Limits must be clear and consistent.

The consequences for rule-breaking should be discussed with and understood by the child. Consequences must be:

- **Immediate**. Don't use the other parent as a threat and say, "Just wait until your mum/dad gets home," or "What will your dad think when he finds out that you...?"
- **Relevant** to the problem behaviour.
- **Safe**. The days of putting naughty children in dark cupboards are long gone, thankfully.
- **Respectful to the child.** Smacking demonstrates that adults are bigger and more powerful and it is OK to use violence if you are angry. Physical punishment has been banned in most European countries and New Zealand.
- **Consistent.** Children will feel insecure and "try you out" if behaviour that is allowed one day is punished the next.
- **Fair** and seen to be fair.

SUPPORT SERVICES FOR PARENTING

All parents need support and information at different times. Seeking and using support services is especially important for those who don't have family assistance. Government services publish easy-to-read tip sheets that are freely available and may be found in pharmacies and doctors' waiting rooms. There are some 150,000 entries for *Parent Tip Sheets* on the Internet.

Parenting styles change over time and some practices that were once widespread are now unacceptable. Not long ago, frustrated parents shook babies in the mistaken belief that this would stop their crying. Then it was found that shaking can cause brain damage and even death. Today, this is considered a criminal offence.

We often see film footage of babies being picked up by their arms. Today, we know that young children's arms are easily dislocated.

Health professionals once advised placing babies on their sides so that if they vomited they wouldn't choke. Then the advice was amended to placing the baby on his tummy to sleep. Now parents are instructed to lay babies on their backs because of the risk of Sudden Infant Death Syndrome (SIDS), a fear of which is common among new parents.

Confidence building begins at birth. From day one, children need to know that their basic needs will be met. They include:

- Love and attention (which must not be excessive or intrusive).
- Encouragement and approval for effort as well as achievement.
- Nutritious food when hungry.
- Consistent care and predictable routines with limits, to develop a sense of security.
- Safety and protection from potential dangers.
- Safe opportunities for play.

Your children need to know that you care and will help them when they are uncomfortable, afraid and upset. But also that you love them even when they are naughty ("I love you but not your behaviour"). They also need to know that there is a regular, reliable person looking after them, there are appropriate and immediate consequences for bad behaviour and that you will listen and will believe them and help to protect them from danger.

DEVELOP CHILDREN'S CONFIDENCE

Healthy self-esteem is your children's armour against the challenges of their world. A child with good self-esteem will have the confidence to try out new things, make new friends and succeed in life. A child with low self-esteem has a much tougher time and is likely to be plagued by negative thoughts, such as, "It's no good trying because I won't succeed anyway". Children with healthy self-esteem are less likely than others to be targets of abuse, drug pushers or bullies. To keep children safe, we must give them the knowledge and confidence to reject and report the sexual misbehaviour of those who are often bigger or better informed, more devious and more powerful. Self-esteem and confidence develop side by side. Confident children are better than insecure children at seeking help from safe adults and articulating and finding solutions to problems.

Developing a positive self-image lies at the root of confidence-building and self-protection. Because of society's high valuation of physical perfection, it is difficult for some youngsters to acquire a healthy level of self-esteem.

We judge ourselves by the way people react to us. When treated as helpless and hopeless, children are likely to view themselves as helpless and hopeless and become more vulnerable to the attractive grooming techniques employed by paedophiles. Devaluing attitudes leave some children with the notion that they have no control over what happens to them. This leads to a victim-oriented attitude to life which, in turn, leads to being vulnerable to abuse of all kinds. Teach children about their rights. Find out what your children think their rights are.

Don't let children blame others for their own behaviour. Don't accept, "He made me do it". With the child's help, reframe the sentence along the lines of, "I did it because I was scared he was going to hurt me". Then deal with the problem.

Along with their rights, kids need to know that they have responsibilities. They have the right to be safe with people but are responsible for their own behaviour and must not hurt or endanger others, their property or animals. These concepts require a great deal of exploration because, while we expect children to respect the feelings of others, it is the very fear of upsetting adults that makes them vulnerable to sex offenders.

ENCOURAGE APPROPRIATE ASSERTIVENESS

Children need to be able to consider safe options if a stronger person takes no notice when they try to stop unwanted or wrong behaviour. To be assertive means standing up for your rights without impeding on other people's rights. Assertiveness requires children to use the words "no" and "stop that," instead of weaker phrases such as "I don't really want to," or "I'm not sure that I should".

Teach assertive body language. Encourage your child to stand up tall, look a person straight in the eye and shake their head vigorously when saying no. Practice! Without practice, even the noisiest children will whisper unconvincingly. Practice is important for all children.

Teach children to resist arguing when someone wants them to engage in behaviour that is wrong. To stay safe, they need to provide a convincing "no" and get away from the situation as quickly as possible. Devious adults invariably use powers of persuasion that are difficult to resist. A Queensland boarding school housemaster told an 11-year-old student to meet him several times a week in a room for which he was the sole key holder. He said he was in love with her because she was so "very special". By the fourth week, he asked her remove her clothes. She said, "No". He then said, "Well, if I take my shirt off will you take yours off? That's fair." She was a child who lacked child protection education, but knew the importance of obedience to adults and reluctantly replied, "Oh, OK". She was then abused.[7]

Children who find themselves in potentially unsafe situations with older persons should never say, "If you don't stop now, I'll tell my mum/dad" because the other party will use threats or coercion. For example, the adult might say, "I wouldn't do that if I were you because...", threatening that terrible things will happen if the child discloses the behaviour. Alternatively they will use emotional blackmail, such as, "I thought you were my special friend," or "I thought you loved me". In New Zealand, children are taught to practice saying, "Yes I'm your friend but it's still not allowed". School programmes teach children to say, "Stop that! It isn't allowed!" then escape and tell a trusted adult.

Children need to understand that, although it can be difficult to say no to adults and people we like, a clear "no" is sometimes necessary. Furthermore, we can say no to other children without spoiling a friendship. We all have to accept being told no sometimes.

Children need opportunities to think through and provide solutions to different situations. Ask questions such as:

- Do you always have to do what adults tell you to do? Suppose that an adult said, "Go outside and play in traffic". Would you do it? Why? What could you say to refuse?
- Suppose that an adult said "Get lost". Would you get lost? Why? How can you say no instead?
- Suppose that an adult you like told you to put something yucky or stinky in your mouth. Would you have to do it? Why? What could you say or do to avoid doing it?
- Suppose that a big boy in a shop says, "See that video game? Put it in your pocket while I keep the shop assistant busy". Must you do it? Why? What could you say to avoid doing the wrong thing?
- Your grandma or other relative says, "Come here and give me a great big kiss". You don't want to be kissed.

Must you do it? Why? What could you do/say to avoid being kissed without upsetting grandma?

- The class bully says:
  - ▸ "Take the specs off that little kid and hide them just for fun."
  - ▸ "Let's skip school today and go somewhere really cool."
  - ▸ "Give me your lunch or I'll bash you."

Must you do it? Why? What can you say or do to avoid doing what you know to be wrong?

> Please bear in mind that when young children practice assertiveness, they will make mistakes by saying no to parents at the wrong time. When your child says no to going to bed, reply by saying, "It's important to say no if someone is giving you a wrong touch on the private parts of your body. You must say no when someone wants you to do something wrong. But is switching off the computer or TV or going to bed wrong? I don't think so."

USE PREVENTATIVE DISCIPLINE

Every child needs discipline to feel safe while testing the world.

So what is discipline?

Discipline is an old-fashioned word no longer in widespread use; professionals are more likely to talk about behaviour management. This is not being overly strict and doesn't involve smacking or frightening children with harsh words. It involves teaching them to gradually take responsibility for their actions and helping them to learn what is and is not appropriate behaviour in different situations. As they develop, they need to become *self-disciplined*, knowing how to behave safely in a variety of circumstances.

There are three types of behaviour management:

- **Preventive:** The adult discusses and establishes routines, clear rules, expectations and the relevant consequences for breaking them. Ensure these are understood and accepted by the child. Children as young as 5 years old like and remember school rules and will tell you what happens when kids break them.

- **Corrective:** The adult acts to correct anti-social or potentially dangerous behaviour. Think carefully about what to say and how you say it. It may be best initially to give simple directions, followed by warnings. For example: "If you continue doing that, the consequence will be _____. Is that what you really want?" Ask the child to repeat what you said so that you know s/he understood. Try to defuse situations, divert attention and redirect potential conflict between children. Give them simple choices and take them aside when they are losing control. If they understand the consequences of continuing, ensure that those consequences occur. "You knew what the consequence would be if you continued to _____. You chose to continue and now you must [go to your room, etc.]". Empty threats and inconsistent responses lead to far worse behaviour because children feel insecure and continue to test your limits.

- **Supportive:** Correction is achieved as fairly as possible and your relationship with the child is re-established. In supportive discipline we address disruptions later when the initial tension has subsided. We re-establish our relationship with the child and develop agreements about future behaviour and consequences. In other words, the child knows what s/he did wrong, why it is wrong and why s/he has been given a time-out. The message should be "I love you but not your behaviour. What you did was unacceptable because _____. Are you ready to come back now?" Agreements about future behaviour should be sealed with hugs.

If your children are driving you crazy, try to figure out why. Are they in need of your attention? Are your expectations unrealistic? Are your children bored? Are they unsure about your limits and are testing you out?

Smacking

Children become insecure, unhappy and badly behaved if limits are not consistently set and punishment is always negative. It usually focuses on hurting children or depriving them of something they value. It often reflects our own frustration and exhaustion rather than the seriousness of the behaviour. Children may learn to be afraid of you if you punish severely and they rarely learn acceptable behaviour by being struck.

To be effective, punishment must be consistent. Never make threats you won't or can't keep. Children will misbehave to test you out if you are inconsistent and ignore inappropriate behaviour one day and punish it the next. Try appealing for calm in a sad voice. "Look, I've got a headache. I've had a really bad day and don't feel well and would appreciate it if you played quietly," is more effective than shouting.

Smacking is not OK. It doesn't convey care or respect. Even young children recognise that it is unfair because it is an abuse of power; adults are bigger and stronger than they are. Smacking may stop unwanted behaviour momentarily because it hurts but it is a short-term solution that doesn't teach children what they should be doing. It results in humiliation and resentment. Successful discipline can be achieved without smacking or putting children down. Children who are smacked often become anxious, fearful, resentful or rebellious. Those who get into trouble for using violence in school are usually those who have been smacked indiscriminately. Physical punishment teaches children that violence is an appropriate way of handling frustration and that they can achieve their ends by inflicting pain on others. Children become so upset by violence that they forget why they were punished.

The good news is that research with Australian and New Zealand children in 2001[8] suggested that fewer parents resorted to smacking than did a decade earlier. Children who were not smacked proclaimed that they will never smack their own kids when they become parents because it is unfair, given the differences in size and strength. Those who were smacked said they will use physical punishment, not because it works but "because it hurts".

Alternatives to smacking involve:

- Distracting the young child. Naughty and mischievous behaviour often arises from boredom and frustration and it stops when kids are given something interesting to do.
- Giving children a choice: "If you continue to fight (etc), the consequence will be [that you will go to your room, etc.]. You have a choice. You can either behave or suffer the consequence. Which do you choose?"
- Ignoring minor misbehaviours if no one is being hurt. Children misbehave to gain attention. If they receive even negative attention, they will repeat the unwanted behaviour, despite the threat of punishment.
- Warning children that if the behaviour continues, they will have to go to a safe, quiet place for "time-out". This helps children over 3 years of age to stop inappropriate behaviour and manage their feelings while simultaneously providing you with the space to calm down. Never threaten children with scary places. Give them the opportunity to return when they are prepared to change their behaviour. At that time, sit close and talk briefly about what happened, why it happened and

what the child could do differently in the future. Ensure that time-outs are for learning. Cuddle your child for reassurance and provide another activity. For older children, design a plan together to ensure that it doesn't happen again.

- Counting to three. On the count of three, children know to expect a set consequence.

CHILDREN NEED AFFECTION, ATTENTION & APPROVAL

Modern parents are often too busy and too tired to give children the attention they need. The average dad spends only a few minutes a day in conversation with his kids. Young children can be at school and in care for most of the day. This makes it all the more important that, when children and parents are together, they enjoy quality time that enables them to know each other better.

Both boys and girls need safe, physical affection and approval from both parents. Switch off the TV and the computer and have fun with each child in turn.

Children now own more books than ever before but, in many families, only grandparents read to them. If you are not reading stories at bedtime, make a start now. It provides an opportunity for sharing confidences in a safe, cosy environment, not to mention its value for developing literacy.

Boys of 5 to 9 years of age say they love kicking balls and playing cricket with dads. Both boys and girls say they have more fun with dads than with mums, even if they see dads only once a month. They say that mums don't have time and that fun is materialistic, limited to shopping, buying ice creams and toys.

Boys and girls both say they have more fun with grandparents than with their parents. Unfortunately, some children are deprived of contact with one set of grandparents after their parents separate. Sometimes it is because children move to another area. Children are the big losers and often resent this when they are older.

Let each of your children or grandchildren know that you enjoy their company and are listening. Praise their strengths. Help them to make their own storybooks and illustrate them using photos. Put fun into their lives: play backyard cricket, push them on swings and kick a ball around. Play cards and other table games such as Snakes and Ladders, Ludo, jigsaw puzzles, Scrabble, Monopoly, draughts and chess, which provide opportunities to talk and laugh together. Children love it when you let them win. Invite them to help you make pizzas, biscuits and chocolate cakes; they love licking the spoon even if the mixture comes from a packet.

Children cite family conflict as the main cause of unhappiness

It is not surprising then that family conflict is the biggest factor in generating unhappiness among children, according to a survey by The Children's Society (2010 UK)[9] involving around 7,000 10 to 15-year-olds. The researchers asked children how different aspects of their lives affected their happiness. The survey found that 7 percent of children were significantly unhappy and that family arguments were the biggest factor. The structure of families made a negligible impact on children's sense of wellbeing.

Concerns about appearance were mentioned by 17.5 percent of respondents and 16 percent said they were unhappy because they lacked confidence.

One in 10 children surveyed said that the lack of freedom and choice in their lives made them unhappy. Schoolwork made 12 percent unhappy, while where they lived was a factor among 14 percent of respondents. Bob Reitemeier, chief executive of The Children's Society, said: "Family conflict emerges in this study as a major cause of childhood unhappiness. This report is a stark reminder that (a) our actions as adults can have a profound impact on our children's wellbeing and (b) the importance of listening to what children are telling us."

SEEK PROFESSIONAL HELP FOR DOMESTIC VIOLENCE

When we asked several hundred Australian and New Zealand multi-ethnic children of 5 to 9 years of age what scared them most, one-third said, "Mum and Dad fighting". If parents yell at or hit each other, they damage their children's sense of security and emotional development. Children know from an early age that some parents divorce. They are unable to distinguish between normal, adult arguments and serious fights and worry that their parents will separate and perhaps even abandon them. Children often want to protect their mothers from being injured and, in the process, may be physically hurt. Boys learn through domestic violence that it is OK for men to lose control and hurt women when they are angry and that this is the way males resolve conflict. They may fail to learn more appropriate responses needed to operate successfully in relationships. Girls, on the other hand, may withdraw and adopt a victim stance to life, choosing partners with characteristics similar to those of their abusive fathers.

If you are experiencing problems that involve adults throwing and smashing things, shouting, threatening, insulting or hitting each other, please seek help by phoning domestic violence services, a parent helpline or make an appointment to see a relationships counsellor. If the violence is serious and you are at risk of injury, you must contact police, domestic violence services or a women's shelter. If you are responsible for initiating the violence, please join an anger-management programme for your children's sake. Services can usually be found in the emergency section in the first few pages of your telephone book.

For children, witnessing domestic violence can have the same damaging effects as being abused: children can become anxious, fretful and lack concentration at school.

AFTER SEPARATION: WORKING TOGETHER FOR KIDS

More than a million Australian children live in separated families, said the Australian Institute of Family Studies in their evaluation of the 2006 Family Law that prioritised shared parenting. In Australia, about 13 percent of children show diagnosable emotional symptoms at any one time; separation and divorce double the risk, leaving children more likely to struggle with relationship difficulties, aggressive or anti-social behaviours, depression, anxiety and decreased chances of school achievement. When there is conflict in the separation, this risk rises to about 45 percent.

According to the Australian Psychological Society's 2009 position, the good news is that most children adjust well and don't suffer lasting behavioural problems. The other good news is that, if parents can work together, the risks to children decrease. Cooperation is, of course, sometimes difficult and not desirable if a parent or parent's partner is violent or abuses the child. The Australian Institute of Family Studies family law reforms showed that 60 percent of parents have friendly or cooperative relationships within 15 months of separation. About 20 percent had distant relationships and a little less than one-fifth had a high conflict and fear-based relationship.

Relationship breakdowns can bring out the worst in people. If a third partner is involved, there is often jealousy, anger, resentment and a desire for revenge. Both parties usually lose financially. A mother who was emotionally and financially dependent on her partner may feel totally inadequate as a sole parent. Life becomes harder if she and the children have to move to a less attractive area with a less attractive school. Fathers may find themselves paying rent for a small unit while their former wives and children live rent free in the family home that he paid for. If he loses his job, Centrelink may reject him because he is part owner of a house that he doesn't live in and, despite it being occupied by his children it is counted as a financial asset that he can sell. A large percentage of the father's untaxed salary may be deducted for child support regardless of the level of contact he has with his children. This is especially frustrating when mothers block contact.

On the other hand, some men find ways to avoid paying child support. For someone who is feeling helpless, hopeless, cheated and rejected, it is almost impossible to be mature and reasonable. Many parents in these situations suffer from depression. The 2006 Family Law reforms recognised that relationship problems made it difficult for parents to put children first, hence the creation of mediation centres to assist parents in reaching agreements. Educating parents about the harmful effects of parental conflict on children is a critical part of the mediation programme.

Children often blame themselves when parents separate: "If I'd been nicer to Dad, he wouldn't have left. He left because he didn't love me. He left because I'm not lovable". Alternatively, "If Mum loved me, she would have stopped Dad from leaving. He left, which means she doesn't love me. That must be because I'm not loveable".

Children hate it when parents criticise each other. A boy may think, "Everyone says I'm like my dad. But, if I'm like my dad, Mum won't love me". The child grows up lacking self-acceptance and, as a result, turns around and becomes highly critical of others. Children often have to develop dual lives; when their mum is there, they have to be indifferent to their dad, but when she's gone, the behaviour changes. The dilemma that children face is, "I want to be with Dad but I don't want to hurt Mum".

They have to accommodate the needs of adults and become peacemakers at a premature age. When Inter-relate's family mediator, Jonathan Toussaint,[10] asked a 13-year-old what messages he wanted to give to his parents, he replied that there were two: "When you speak to each other — or about each other — use each other's names, not insults; and don't use me as a message carrier. It's not my problem". Others say they hate being used to spy on what new purchases their dads have made since their last visit or whether there were signs of other women being involved in their lives.

Whether or not you are separated or together, parental conflict is bad for kids. Recognise that it is extremely hard to make the change from being an angry, jealous rejected ex to a caring parent, but counselling can help.

Dealing with the Most Challenging Parenting Moments

Parenting isn't what it is cracked up to be in the movies. In particular there are some specific instances where most parents are at the 'end of their tether'. These moments, and there are probably many others, that I deal with here are the crying baby, the temper tantrums, the rivalled siblings and the adolescent years.

The Crying Baby

The physical abuse of children most commonly occurs in their early years. Motherhood is glamorised in women's magazines. Movie stars say how wonderful it is but fail to mention the army of nannies and housekeepers helping them in the wings. You only hear the good stuff, never the nightmares. And if the reality fails to match the dream, then disappointment and a sense of failure are inevitable.

Parenting is rarely what we expect. Newborn babies cry; some cry more than others. Sometimes it is nothing more than a whimper but more often it is a loud, sustained scream. This is how they communicate. It is normal. And, as everyone soon realises, these screaming, pooping, vomiting, demanding bundles are wholly in control of their parents' sleep and lives and will be for months. This sudden loss of control is a new phenomenon to parents who were previously successful professionals.

Uneasy, anxious or depressed parents create anxious, unhappy babies. They sense anxiety and they fret and cry. At this point the parent becomes more stressed and the child cries even more. When your child screams for most of the night and leaves you exhausted, you feel more inadequate, resentful and guilty than ever. You do everything you can to provide comfort. You feed him (again), change him, give him a dummy, burp him, rock him, walk up and down with him over your shoulder and sing to him, all to no avail. You feel rejected and a failure. If sleepless nights persist, have your child checked out by your doctor, especially for ear and throat infections.

If you think that your baby's crying is a problem, then it is a problem. Depression among parents of crying babies is rife. A Finnish study (1996)[11] showed that, years later, these parents are more dissatisfied with parenting and have less empathy for these children than those who have not suffered.

The state of the parents' relationship is also important in determining the child's state of mind. Do you resent the fact that dad is working long hours and isn't providing enough support at home? Do you have help from grandparents or another experienced mother? It is often a chicken-and-egg situation where the parent is stressed because the baby is difficult and the baby is difficult because the parent is stressed.

Shaken baby syndrome — when the baby is shaken, brain damage occurs — and non-accidental infant deaths occur most often when there is a worn-out parent and a screaming child. We don't really know what makes one exhausted parent lash out and throw the screaming infant in the cot while another puts him down gently and walks away. Fatigue, stress, depression, anger, low tolerance and self-control, a history of abuse, money problems, personal and relationship problems, an unwanted pregnancy, disappointment with parenting, emotional immaturity, post-natal depression and lack of support can all contribute to children being seriously harmed. If you are losing your cool, take deep breaths and count to 20 before you react. Make sure your child is safe and go to another room. Call a friend, relative or a 24-hour parent help or crisis line (usually found in the emergency pages of your phone book). Stay on the phone until you are calm again.

Paediatricians recommend bathing fretful babies, wrapping them firmly and putting them to sleep on their side in a darkened room, while avoiding eye contact. If they cry for too long, massage the abdomen in a clockwise direction or pat gently until they fall asleep. The first few days can be hell but babies tend to respond to this routine.

> Remember, there are no perfect parents. Seeking help is not a sign of failure. The good parents are those who ask for help when they need it.

Get help quickly if any of the following occur:
- You have hurt or fear you may hurt your child.
- You or your partner, often lose control.
- Your child is afraid of you.
- Your partner physically fights with you or threatens your child.
- You feel you're not coping and things are getting you down.
- Someone in the home has a drug or alcohol problem.
- You feel you are a bad parent and get no satisfaction from parenting.

If you find yourself yelling and feel unable to cope, please seek help immediately. If you don't know of a parenting service, ring your child abuse report or crisis line (listed in the emergency section of your telephone book) and ask where you can get help to deal with a difficult child. There are parenting programmes and parent help lines available in most towns and cities. Most governments offer free advisory services.

> Seeking help demonstrates that you are a responsible parent, love your child, realise that there is a problem and want things to improve. You are not alone; there are thousands of exhausted parents just like you.

TEMPER TANTRUMS

Parental frustration is greatest when toddlers exhibit temper tantrums. These tantrums involve spectacular explosions of anger, frustration and violence (i.e., children "lose it"). Expect high-pitched shrieks, stiffening limbs, arching backs, falling down or flailing arms and legs. Some children hold their breath until they go blue. They may vomit, break things or kick and fight you. They throw tantrums when they find themselves in situations they can't handle.

American researchers asked over 1,200 parents about their children's tantrums and learned that:

- At 18 months to 2 years old, 87 percent of children threw tantrums on an average of eight times a week at the age of 1, lasting two minutes, to nine times a week lasting four minutes at 2 years of age.
- From 2 to 3 years old, 91 percent threw tantrums, reducing to 59 percent by aged 5. On average, tantrums occurred six times a week at age 3, lasting four minutes and five times a week, lasting five minutes, at 4 years of age.[12]

Boys often develop at a slower pace than girls and their tantrums may last longer.

Remember that children don't have tantrums just to annoy you. They happen when they are frustrated, stressed, insecure, tired, overstimulated or can't get what they want. You can probably change the events that trigger tantrums. If the first tantrum brings an increase in attention, it will be repeated and could become a habit.

> If your child is under age 2, be prepared. Plan ahead what you will do when s/he throws the first tantrum, bearing in mind that it could happen in a shopping centre, car park or other public place.

Preventing tantrums

Because tantrums are habit-forming, it is important that the first signs are handled well. Be aware of how children are feeling so that you can step in and distract them if you sense that a tantrum is imminent.

Once a tantrum occurs:

- Identify the triggers. Do they happen in the same situation repeatedly? Try to find ways of making the events easier for the child.
- Remain calm. Ignore the behaviour until it stops. Avoid eye contact, move away and, if necessary, leave the room. Once a tantrum is in full swing, it is too late for reasoning.
- Don't let your child sense that tantrums are rewarded with more attention. (This is obviously hard if the first tantrum involves holding breath or vomiting.) If tantrums occur because your child doesn't want to do something, calmly remove him. If the tantrum begins because your child wants something that he can't have, use distraction but don't give in or he will continue to throw tantrums when he sees something that he wants.

- Be consistent. If you give your child what he wants today and say no tomorrow, tantrums will become more frequent.
- Reward good behaviour and praise him when he manages frustration well.

If tantrums are severe, disruptive and cause stress or make you so angry that you feel like smacking your screaming child, the following steps might be useful:

- Keep a record of tantrums for 10 days. Create a chart with four columns recording the day, the time, where it happened and what happened before and immediately after it.
- Note patterns in events and triggers that make tantrums more likely (for example, tiredness, shopping, washing hair, mealtimes). Work out how you can make situations less stressful for your child.
- Identify the consequences of tantrums. Is the behaviour inadvertently rewarded by your actions or the actions of others?
- Establish an appropriate reward system for encouraging your child to stay calm.
- Help older children who lose their tempers to practice coping skills for situations where they could have a tantrum. For example, "In five minutes time, I am going to ask you to turn off the TV. This is a chance for you to show how calm and grown up you can be. OK?" If necessary show what five minutes will look like on the clock. Or, before saying no to a demand, say "Emma, take deep breaths. I want you to stay calm after I give you my answer. Can you do that?" If that doesn't work, try using a time-out. This is effective if tantrums are severe or you find it impossible to ignore them.

Tantrums can be enormously draining, embarrassing and stressful, especially if they happen in public. At a time when there was no child-care or helpful grandma available, my two-year-old son, who didn't like shopping, specialised in holding his breath until he turned purple and collapsed spectacularly on shop floors, attracting everyone's attention and sympathy.

Remember that you can't control a child's emotions. You can only keep them safe and respond in such a way that tantrums become less likely to occur.

Accept that it will take time for changes to take place. Remember he isn't having tantrums just to annoy you. He is stuck in a bad habit or lacks the skills to cope with the situation. Also, try to keep your sense of humour. Try to see the funny side of your child holding his breath and turning blue on the supermarket floor.

Train yourself to ignore onlookers who sympathise with your child and criticise you. They have either never had children or it was so long ago that they don't remember what it is like. But, most important, don't judge yourself as a parent based on your child's tantrums. Gauge yourself instead on how you respond. Even then, allow plenty of leeway to be human and make mistakes.

There is no sense in suffering high levels of stress on your own. Don't hesitate to ask for professional help if you find it hard to keep tantrums in perspective, if they become more than just an annoyance or you have trouble keeping your temper and want to strike your child. Also, seek help if you restrict your own activities because of tantrums.

AVOIDING SIBLING RIVALRY

Parents lose their tempers most frequently when siblings fight. Brothers and sisters can act as worst enemies. Arguments, jealousy, competitiveness and aggression are common and normal but they can be especially annoying when everyone is tired. Siblings fight to gain your attention. They are often jealous when they feel, rightly or wrongly, that their brother or sister is being treated preferentially. Gifts have to be shared equally because children associate material goods with being loved and valued. If you don't want them to fight over chocolate cake, ask one to cut the cake while the other takes the first piece. That guarantees equal portions. Children of different ages should be allocated times for one-on-one attention.

To reduce sibling fights:

- Sit down together with a snack when children return home and encourage them to talk about their day, especially if they are squabbling to get your attention.
- Give plenty of warning that mealtimes and bedtime are approaching.
- Identify problem times and defuse the emotionally charged situations by providing individual attention and stories. Refer to it as their special time.
- Share everything equally to avoid children perceiving that they are valued less than their sibling(s).
- Ban teasing and bullying and establish and maintain clear, consistent rules.
- Hold family meetings to air grievances and discuss feelings, fairness and how problems can be resolved. Ask "Did you have the right to take it from your sister without permission? How do you think she felt? What should you have said/done?" and "How did you feel when he said/did that? What would you like to happen to put things right?" This dispenses with arguments about who started it first.
- Be fair and be seen to be fair; use rosters for the distribution of tasks.
- Go on family outings and identify jobs that you can all do together.
- Help children to resist unwanted behaviour. For example, teach them to say, "I didn't like it when you did that. Please don't do it again."

- Teach children to say, "You didn't have the right to take my pen (or other possession) without my permission. I will lend it to you if you ask me properly". Early childhood teachers find that children are capable of sorting out problems in this way, requiring little or no adult intervention. Avoid arguments about who started it.
- Time the use of popular, shared equipment, such as the computer, taking the volume of homework into account. Boys tend to demand more computer time than girls and older children expect to have more time than younger ones, arguing that they have more homework. Ensure that extra time is used for homework, not games. Also, ensure that agreements are kept.
- When children fight over the possession of a toy, remove it and say you will return it only after they have reached an agreement on ways to share fairly.

PARENTING ADOLESCENTS

Adolescence is the time when your children begin to see themselves as separate, self-governing individuals. They need to gain autonomy gradually to develop a sense of identity. Autonomy means developing the capacity to regulate one's own behaviour in the absence of parental monitoring. Relying on oneself has both vital emotional and behavioural components. Making decisions involves weighing up experiences (which are usually limited) alongside the advice of others to form a judgment. Problems arise when the desire to be one of an 'in' group takes precedence and group values conflict with family values. Adolescents who successfully adopt meaningful values and goals are autonomous. Over time, autonomy gained in a warm, supportive parent-child relationship is the most reliable. It predicts a high level of self-reliance, work orientation, academic competence and self-esteem during the adolescent years. Teenagers in conflict-ridden families are at a distinct disadvantage.

The task for parents is about when and how to relax control, when the young person is ready for a greater level of freedom, without threatening the parent-child bond. The successful parent is one who sets limits in early childhood and now provides flexible guidelines that are open to discussion and implemented in an atmosphere of concern and fairness. In a sound relationship, it is comparatively easy to explain the reasons for decisions, seek and consider the adolescent's viewpoint and gradually modify the rules as the adolescent moves towards adulthood. This blend of independence and connection promotes the development of the young person's identity.[13] Again it is a matter of getting the right balance.

Adolescents want more quality time with parents

You may be surprised to know that, whereas earlier generations craved more freedom, today's teenagers actually crave more time with and attention from parents. A survey of Australian teens (Australia SCAN 2008) showed that, for the first time ever, teens would rather hang out with parents than have more freedom. They are saying they have too much freedom and not enough time with family members. What may also be surprising to learn is that most 10 to 17-year-olds think their parents understand them "a lot" even if they habitually keep secrets and limit what information they share. Two-thirds of 10 and 11-year-olds said they told parents everything and 78 percent thought their parents knew them extremely well. At 16 to 17 years of age, only one-third confided in parents, yet 67 percent still felt their parents understood what made them tick. Nevertheless, two-thirds of parents wished they had sources of parenting advice and 23 percent felt that child rearing was very stressful.

A 2010 study by the University of Southern Queensland was another eye-opener. This asked Australian kids what made them happy. If your kids are hanging around right now, unplug their headphones and ask them. Their answers might surprise you. If you thought it was the latest technological gimmick, you would be wrong. Their answers exploded the common belief that today's kids just want trashy music, iPods and becoming famous or infamous. Fewer than one in five listed possessions. The remainder answered on the lines of, 'a family that loves me' or 'someone who cares about me'. Just over half registered family issues as their biggest concern, such as someone dying, mum and dad breaking up or having to choose between mum and dad. Kids just want stable, happy homes and we have to do what we can to provide them.

TEENS AND SCHOOLIES WEEK

An estimated 20 percent or 55,000 Australian school leavers participate in Schoolies Week each year. This can be a parents' nightmare. Not only do they go to coastal towns but they now head for Bali and the South Pacific islands to party with friends on beaches. Safety precautions are essential. Drug Arm's Centre for Addiction shows that 90 percent of participants consume alcohol and should be advised to drink in the hotel and consume water in-between. Drink spiking is a risk and young people should be warned never to leave a drink unattended or accept drinks from strangers. If they feel sick and dizzy they should tell a trusted friend or bar staff. Reinforce messages such as, "Don't drink and swim, or drink and drive, and don't accept lifts from others who have been drinking". Drugs are also a risk and about one quarter of schoolies week participants admit to using marijuana. Drugs and alcohol are a potentially lethal combination. Ensure that your teenager is aware that 'toolies' (older predatory men) hang around in the hope of having sex with young girls and boys.

La Trobe University's research centre in Sex, Health and Society reported in October 2010 that in a sample of 5000 students in Years 10–12, 38.2% of boys and slightly fewer girls admitted having sex with three or more partners in the previous twelve months; the number had doubled in ten years. Alarmingly fewer were using contraceptives than a decade ago. Given that casual, unsafe sex is associated with alcohol and drug use, discuss the dangers and ensure that your kids carry condoms 'just in case'. If someone is persistent in giving unwanted sexual attention, threatening that you are about to vomit often works.

The National Schoolies Week website www.schoolies.org.au provides information and hints on how to enjoy what is available and stay safe. A list could be provided as follows:

- Stay with friends but remain alert because even friends have been known to spike drinks 'for fun'.
- Always carry enough money to get a taxi back to the hotel/apartment.
- Carry coins for the phone, just in case you lose your mobile.
- Carry a personal alarm.
- Lock your hotel room.
- Never give your hotel room number to people you don't know.
- Check the whereabouts of emergency points at events and use them as meeting points.
- Seek help from police if you feel unsafe.
- Text mum daily.
- Avoid communicating with 'toolies'.

SUMMARY OF POSITIVE PARENTING TIPS TO CREATE STRONG FOUNDATIONS

- Notice and comment on the things children do well, not the things you don't like. Make children aware that you notice and appreciate the good things. They are then less likely to misbehave.
- Praise children for effort as well as achievement.
- Praise good behaviour and ignore marginally unacceptable behaviour unless safety is at risk or there is damage to property. Discuss the issues and the impact of the behaviour.
- Negotiate rules and limits using respect and safety as guidelines.
- Ensure that children understand the consequences of unacceptable behaviour and that they know they have choices and those choices have consequences. Don't use humiliation, as this merely causes resentment.
- Listen respectfully to what your children say without interrupting. Acknowledge what they have said before expressing a differing opinion.
- When there is conflict, try to offer a calm, low-key response rather than argue. Shouting only inflames the situation.
- Remember that you are modelling the behaviour that children will learn.
- Provide opportunities for children to learn new skills and help them to learn from their mistakes.
- Learn about the norms of development; problems often arise because parents' expectations are unrealistic.

- Show your kids that you love them by spending time with them, talking, listening, praising, hugging, cuddling, offering help when they need it and treating them with the same respect that you expect from them.
- Take note of children's feelings.
- Teach appropriate assertiveness skills.
- Remember that the safest kids are confident and knowledgeable.
- Use positive, preventative, child management techniques.
- Seek professional help when help is needed.

Chapter 2

Choosing Safe Services For Your Child

This chapter provides hints for assessing safety in children's services, including childcare centres, schools and church groups, out-of-school care, family day care and care provided by relatives.

CHILD PROTECTION STARTS AT BIRTH

Child protection starts at birth because, unfortunately, some infants and toddlers are assaulted and injured by carers who can't cope when they cry. Other children are used for sexual purposes or to make pornography, which is sold on the Internet worldwide.

Child protection begins in the family and should involve friends, relatives and the employment of child-minders. It should also include early childhood services, such as family day care, childcare centres and kindergartens, play groups, schools, out-of-hours care, camps, sports clubs and sports training, Scouts and Girl Guides, Sunday schools, church and other crèches and should also extend to the use of mobile phones and computers. This may seem to be a mammoth task but, unfortunately, it is necessary because sexual predators go wherever children congregate, especially on the Internet.

Mothers often say, "I know my children are safe because we drive them everywhere and know where they are". Thinking that only strangers are dangerous, they trust everyone in the centre, church, school, club, etc., including unknown visitors and volunteers. Child protection is not simply about transporting children to a venue or protecting them from persons they don't know. Strangers are the ones least likely to molest your kids. They account for only about 10 percent of reports and the true figure is probably even less, given that they are more likely to be reported than family members.

You need to be alert to what is happening around your home, extended family and neighbourhood. Sadly, mums and dads are often the ones who trustingly and unwittingly place their children directly into the hands of abusers, leaving parents guilt-ridden and angry for the rest of their lives.

Without child protection knowledge, parents seldom dare question professionals although, if they did, they would find that few have been adequately trained in matters relating to child abuse and child protection. With knowledge, you can identify and challenge unsafe practices and insist on the adoption of safer practices in schools, centres, camps, childcare facilities and occasions when your child travels for student exchanges or sports activities that involve home-stays. With knowledge, you can be alert to potentially unsafe situations and the risk of accidents. With knowledge, you can ask to see a copy of the child protection policy in your child's club, school or centre. If there isn't one readily available, ask why that is so. With knowledge, you can warn a complacent management board that it can be sued for negligence if problems arise. This chapter is designed to help you to acquire the knowledge you need.

CHECK SERVICES BEFORE USING THEM

Before enrolling your child at any early childhood centre, school, sports or other club:

- Ask to see a copy of the child protection policy and procedures (protocols) and read them carefully. If the organisation doesn't have them, don't hesitate to ask why not. This could be an indication that children's safety is not a priority.
- When you read the policy, note whether child abuse by school personnel has to be reported to police/child protection services or to senior staff, school principals, committees or bishops. Despite the massive compensation claims resulting from keeping abuse in-house to protect the institution rather than the child, some independent schools still require reports of abuse to be passed through the diocesan hierarchy instead of informing police. School principals should not be expected to interrogate accused staff. Apart from this breach of the confidentiality of the victim, these unqualified people decide whether the offender is guilty. As no one wants to admit they might have a paedophile on their staff, offences tend to be minimised or dismissed and the offenders escape punishment and continue to abuse other children. Child sex abuse is a crime that should be reported immediately to the police. Look closely at the school's child protection policy and if the police are not the first port of call for reporting, point out that the policy may be ordering staff to commit an offence which can incur a hefty fine.
- If there is no policy, ask to see any written rules relating to staff and visitor behaviour with children. For example, are members of staff banned from being alone with children in bathrooms and storerooms? Are they banned

from acting as childminders for students? Where are rules displayed? If there are none, why not?

- Is there a child protection curriculum? If not, why not? This is provided for all early childhood centres and schools in New Zealand, South Australia and New South Wales.
- Ask questions if you have concerns or are unclear about the contents of a document.
- Do not accept excuses such as, "We trust all our staff" or "We trust all our parents". As one childcare centre director said, "There are 22 staff here, plus students on work experience. How can you possibly know that we are all trustworthy?"

Safe practices are used to protect children from the risks of abuse by strangers, other children, volunteers, visitors (especially workers' own family members, college and university students, researchers and secondary students on work experience), as well as staff. The child protection policy should include identified, safe practices that show the organisation is seriously concerned about child safety and contain the following requirements:

- All staff and visitors (including professionals, student teachers and those on work experience) read and agree to meet its requirements. In some Australian states, all voluntary organisations involving children must produce a policy of which all adults must sign. Risk assessments are undertaken annually. There are heavy penalties for groups that ignore these laws. Check out the requirements for your state or country.
- Staff members and possibly volunteers, depending on local laws, have police checks conducted on them before being permitted to have contact with children and at regular intervals thereafter.

- Staff members are trained in child protection practices, which include what to do and say to a child if abuse is suspected or revealed.
- A public commitment by the organisation to protect children from harm and the risk of sexual abuse.
- Staff members teach personal safety skills to children in partnership with families. Unfortunately, these days, children must be equipped to identify and report criminal behaviour, given that staffing ratios make it impossible for supervisors to be everywhere.
- The organisation will develop and maintain knowledge of current child protection and family support agencies that provide services to support families and/or children.
- A designated person will disseminate information relating to domestic violence services, treatment facilities for both abuse victims and offenders (including juvenile sex offenders) and counselling for the non-offending parents of sexually abused children who need help for dealing with emotional and practical factors associated with the disclosure.
- Special attention is given to children's safety in toilet blocks; ideally classrooms should have individual, adjacent toilets, as at home.
- No one is permitted to be alone with a child.
- The centre has an open door policy for parents.

In 2007, the policy of one childcare empire required staff to ignore state mandatory reporting laws and report child abuse to their directors, then line managers who, in turn, reported to their Queensland-based staff, who then reported to the company's own investigatory team. Such a policy could lead to staff being prosecuted for failing to report abuse.

By emphasising child safety, child protection policies protect staff from the risk of wrongful accusations as well as children from ill-treatment. Although such occurrences are extremely rare, when owners of private childcare centres removed children to make pornography, they chose victims whose mothers were in full-time employment and were not likely to return unannounced.

Without being paranoid, we recommend that parents or close family members drop into centres without warning from time to time. Staff should encourage such visits. Concerns about children's safety have led some childcare centres in the USA and Western Australia to offer video access so that mothers at work can observe their children while they play.

Before enrolment

Before children are enrolled in a service, parents should:

- Enquire whether all staff and volunteers have undertaken police checks. This does not guarantee children's safety but it should preclude *convicted* sex offenders from gaining employment with children.
- Observe whether children's rights and safety are being respected in relation to toileting and nappy-changing. If they are old enough to understand, are they asked permission for nappies to be changed or are they simply lined up and changed routinely? If they say no to being changed, are they asked to return to staff when they are ready? This is viewed by some centres as important because it teaches children that they are in charge of their own bodies and can say no to unwanted touching. In a respectful setting, children will be given the opportunity to use the toilet or undress in privacy. Children who want to clean themselves after using the toilet should have their wishes respected, with staff talking them through the process if they have difficulties.
- Ensure that the child protection policy is implemented in daily practice. If this is not obvious, parents should

ask for specific examples of how the service caters for children's safety. Watch out for evidence that children's bodies, opinions, relationships and feelings are respected. Listen to how staff members communicate with children. Are they calm, patient and respectful? Or do they ignore children's feelings? Watch out for any adults left alone with a child in a room with a closed door.

- Check that information about child protection and services for parents are displayed. Does the centre advertise what the children are taught about safety, why and how you can help? Are library books and resources available for parents to reinforce safety skills at home?

- Observe staff reactions to children when they fall or need help. Do they respond sympathetically or impatiently?

- Look around to see whether fences and gates are secure. How easy would it be for a child to escape or be snatched?

- Rely on your gut feelings relating to the atmosphere in the centre, especially in regard to the warmth of the welcome.

- Note if there is evidence that staff members fail to observe good standards of hygiene.

- Do the adults handle bullying effectively?

- Note whether toys are readily accessible or on shelves out of reach when you drop in unexpectedly.

- Observe whether outdoor play is well supervised.

Child protection agencies, such as Child Wise (www.childwise. net), can help with further advice on what to look for.

FAMILY DAY CARE

Family day care involves people who take children into their homes for payment. The carer usually has to be minimally trained and registered, the home inspected periodically and there are regulations relating to how many children can be cared for at any one time.

Very occasionally, the registered carer's male partner or adolescent son has sexually abused children in family day care settings. It is obviously harder to protect your child in someone else's home than in a centre, given that most carers work in isolation and visits from supervisors are rare and usually pre-arranged.

If you are planning to use family day care, see if you can visit several carers with your child to see which home s/he prefers. Talk to children about their day with the carer. How do they feel about the carer and family? Be alert to signs of distress and investigate if your child regresses, returns to bedwetting, has nightmares or suddenly resists going to the home.

USING CRÈCHES AND PLAY ROOMS

Parents were horrified when, in 2004, a young Australian child was used to provide oral sex for a man while in a crèche at a prestigious hotel in Bali. There have also been isolated cases where children were abused after being left in play areas adjoining family restaurants, hotels, on cruise ships and at fitness centres. Ideally, parents should be able to leave children safely in crèches (and most do) but, as in other settings, it is advisable to check provisions made for children's safety. Spend time observing how easy it would be for a stranger to take your child to a toilet or remove your child from the room. Given that the client population changes constantly in crèches, investigate what checks are made on adults who come in to collect children.

Parents should be aware that crèches are often subjected to different, less stringent regulations than nursery schools, kindergartens and childcare centres and, therefore, caution is imperative. Crèches should be used only as a last resort and when parents are satisfied with the precautions taken and children are comfortable about being left in new situations with strangers and children they don't know.

It is important that parents are aware that overseas resorts are not expected to adopt our standards of child care. They can be very different. Parents planning to place their children in schools or childcare facilities overseas are encouraged to research carefully and satisfy themselves regarding the standards of security and staff training of those establishments.

CHILD-MINDERS

Before employing a child-minder, references should be sought and checked. Even if you know the minder, ask past employers if they had any reason to distrust this person. Did their children like her? Was there any suspicion that the minder may have behaved inappropriately?

Be aware that most child sex offenders, both male and female, start offending in early adolescence, many when they are employed as babysitters. Researching with 16,000 subjects, American psychiatrist Dr. Gene Abel[14] found that one in every 20 adolescent males was sexually attracted to and fantasised about sex with children rather than with same-age kids, pop stars or sex symbols. Our Australian research with offenders[15] also showed that some started offending at a relatively young age, while babysitting. This was also confirmed by 5 to 8-year-old New Zealand children who revealed (accidentally, when asked about their play with babysitters) that 10 percent had been sexually abused by minders,[16] most of whom were adolescent relatives. Abuse was presented as a secret game. None of the children had reported it.

Never give minders responsibility for undressing or bathing children and putting them to bed. This provides opportunities for sexual crimes. Single mothers also need to know that child sex offenders deliberately target them to gain access to their children. They develop the mother's trust and create an emotional bond with the children, acting as ideal father replacement figures before introducing sex.

In 2007, a Canberra man was charged with sex offences against several children. The court heard that he had advertised babysitting services on the Internet using three false names.

Too often, parents choose child-minders for convenience, without making the necessary checks or taking precautions. They miss or ignore the clues and hints that children give.

Summary of hints for employing child-minders

- Don't ask or allow a minder to bath, change, undress or put children to bed.
- Never give the minder permission to punish your child; sex offenders use this as an opportunity to commit sexual crimes.
- Ask your children whether they like their babysitter. If not, why not? Involve them in choosing a sitter and rely on their gut feelings which are often more reliable than yours.
- Tactfully inform the babysitter that your family has a no secrets policy. Put a notice on the fridge that says, "This is a no secrets home".
- Ask your child what games s/he plays with the babysitter. Tell the minder that boisterous play and tickling are banned as it makes your child excitable. Evidence of tickling should be a signal for you to discuss safety strategies.
- Teach children how to contact you if they are worried when left with a minder. If they call you and it isn't an emergency, don't be critical. If you show displeasure, they may not contact you again if a real emergency arises.

- Children are made vulnerable to sexual abuse when parents give the message that, to be good, they have to obey older people. Children think they can't say no to minders because the minder will get mad.[17] Teach children that they not only can but MUST say no to adults if they feel uncomfortable about what the adults want them to do; for example, if adults give a wrong touch, show dirty/rude/sex pictures, engage in dirty/rude/sex talk or sexual misbehaviour. Young children must say no if someone wants to touch, play with, kiss or tickle their breasts (both boys and girls) or genitals or if they ask children to touch, kiss or play with their private body parts. Give children the opportunity to practice saying no in a big, loud voice. Louder still! Practice holding arms outstretched, creating personal space. Say, "No! Stop that! It isn't allowed!"

This boy shows us how to practice saying, "No! Stop that! It isn't allowed!"

CHECK SAFETY AT THE CHILDCARE CENTRE BEFORE YOU ENROL YOUR CHILD

Bearing in mind that most centres employ untrained staff, it is a good idea to ask about staff qualifications before you enrol your child in a centre. How many unqualified staff are employed? In 2010, the Australian Government's National Childcare Accreditation Council found that 243 child care centres failed to meet minimum standards. There was nothing new about this. Their 2007 survey of 1,972 childcare centres found that one-quarter failed to meet acceptable safety standards.[18] More than 23 percent left dangerous items (e.g., harmful gardening products, plants and objects) accessible to children; 377 centres failed to "ensure that buildings and equipment were safe"; 323 centres were unsatisfactory in acting to control the spread of infections. Some staff left medication and detergents accessible to children. Containers for soiled nappies were left uncovered.

In South Australia, 41 centres were investigated in July 2008 as a result of complaints. These involved the number of unqualified staff employed, the inappropriate use of force, language and restraint, unexplained injuries, inappropriate behaviour management, nappy-changing routines, infection control and hygiene. One worker was charged with assault.

In Victoria, some children were abused, battered and abandoned by childcare workers. More than 53 children and babies were said to have been mistreated or lost over a three-year period. Some were subjected to shocking, illegal punishments. Toddlers at two centres had their mouths taped. A 5-year-old was put in a nappy and left in a cot as a punishment for incontinence. The lives of five toddlers were put at risk by medication mix-ups. One was hospitalised after receiving 15 times more medication than prescribed; 25 children, including one of 17 months, walked away from centres.

Forty-five incidents led to cautions against 24 centres between 2004 and 2006, but the state government refused to reveal their whereabouts, claiming it would be a breach of confidence and inhibit their own capacity to collect information. There was a reluctance to prosecute anyone because bad publicity would place further strain on overstretched services! "If parents heard what happened at some centres there would be a stampede to get their kids out," a department spokesperson told the press. Through Freedom of Information, the *Herald Sun* newspaper found that only four deficient centres were prosecuted, all for allowing children to wander away. Some parents were not told that their children had been placed at risk. A worker was accused of smacking three children, pushing one off a swing, pinching another and pulling a child's hair. She was not dismissed. A worker who dropped babies on the ground and force-fed them was sacked. There were claims that the same worker hit a baby with a laminated sheet. A father found his son crying in a small, locked cupboard when he went to collect him. Children were left unattended in fenced areas. Members of staff were instructed not to comfort crying children.

Despite previous publicity, the National Childcare Accreditation Council's report, published in 2009, showed no improvement. Childcare centres were routinely breaching health and safety rules with one in 20 caught failing to protect and properly supervise children. Unsafe buildings or equipment were found in five centres and a similar number failed basic hygiene and food safety standards. Eleven percent failed inspections by the National Childcare Accreditation Council. Twenty-six percent of 1,530 long-day care centres breached rules by failing to keep potentially dangerous products, plants and substances away from children. More than five percent ignored basic safety concerning electricity. The same number failed to store food safely.

Furthermore, workers in 20 centres did not wash their hands after changing nappies, wiping noses or before serving food. The State of Victoria was said to have the worst ratio of qualified staff to children in Australia. Centres should have one qualified carer for every five infants up to two years of age and one carer for every 15 children aged 3 to 5 years. Union representatives claimed that staff members were 'burnt out', not just because of the number of children involved but because of other chores that they were required to do. Workers were also in short supply, with the award wage being one of the lowest in the workforce. Early Childhood Australia has demanded that governments lift the quality of childcare nationally and enforce standards.

Most children are happy in their childcare centres but it pays to be observant and choose your centre with great care.

What to look for

Regulations vary from state to state but children's safety should be paramount. Check the Internet for regulations that apply to your region before looking for a centre. If you are taken on a prearranged tour, you may find children playing with an array of toys. This may be window dressing and those toys are put away when visitors leave.

Drop in unannounced and note what items children are playing with and what is being served for lunch.
Observe children in the outdoor play area. Physical exercise is important for their development. The area should present challenge, variety and adventure while being suited to the child's age and ability. It should also furnish protection from the sun, using sails or other shade equipment. Look around to see if sunscreen is readily available and used. Equipment must be constructed safely. Close supervision is essential.

Be alarmed if you see children alone or unsupervised out of doors, especially if they are on large equipment.
The outdoor play area must be easily visible, easily supervised and hygienic. Outdoor equipment and the surfaces under and around that equipment must comply with and be maintained to meet national standards. Look to see if a child would potentially fall on a soft versus hard surface.

In Australia, all outdoor play equipment must be appropriate to the age and ability level of children in care, maintained in a good state of repair and positioned and stored safely.

Outdoor equipment must be supervised when in use. Watch out for carers casually chatting to each other, with their backs turned to children.

Bikes and other mobile equipment must be used in supervised areas away from potential hazards, such as swings and slides. Children using bikes with two wheels must wear well-fitting safety helmets that meet the national standard.

Injuries associated with playground equipment are significant; the most serious involving falls from heights of more than one metre and falls onto hard surfaces, such as concrete or bitumen. Young children can be badly injured when they walk in front of others on swings. You need to report unsafe practices to the government department responsible.

Daily check of the play area
Each day, a responsible person must check that there is no loose rubbish in the play area. The sandpit and soft-fall area must be raked. In instances where the public has access to playgrounds when centres and schools are closed, fixed equipment and sandpits must be checked daily to ensure that vandals have not caused damage that could harm children and that dangerous objects have not been left there overnight, such as needles used by drug addicts or condoms children may mistake for balloons and try to inflate, risking a child's exposure to HIV and other

sexually transmitted infections. Centres should have a roster with a list for staff to check all equipment for hazards. Sandpits must be securely covered when not used.

What steps can be taken to reduce the chance of injuries?

Kidsafe Australia reports that 100,000 children are injured in playground accidents every year and 7,000 need hospital treatment. Play areas should be designed for adventure *and* safety, incorporating the four main play elements: active, passive, creative and social. Where there are quiet places for a child to be alone, such as a cubby house, supervision is still important. Knowledge of the requirements of playground standards is useful. More information is available from Standards Australia (www.standards.com.au).

Extra care should be taken when examining the outdoor play area of family day care homes.

Children at a rural primary school told me that they'd complained for three years to two successive principals that the old tractor in the playground was rusty and unsafe and should be removed. They were ignored. This was a state school that boasted having a committee that included class representatives who supposedly had a voice.

It is important that you know how to contact the chairperson of the school council or body responsible for the school, if your or your child's voice isn't heard.

Unsafe trampolines:

Given evidence of risks of injury to a child's spine, internal injuries and complicated fractures, trampolines are not recommended. If they are provided, they must be closely supervised, preferably built into the ground with underground metal treated with anti-rust. Only one child at a time should jump and they should be taught to jump in the centre. There should be a soft surface around it. Ensure that there are no loose springs or bent frames.

Sandpits:

A sandpit provides for creative, imaginative and constructive play. It needs to be well constructed and have good drainage. The sand must be cleaned regularly.

Other potential hazards:

Dogs are attracted to children's playgrounds. They must be removed before children use them and the play area should be checked for faeces. Children under 12 years old are at highest risk of attack by dogs. Bites tend to occur when children are patting, feeding or playing with a dog.

Teach children never to:

- Approach an unfamiliar dog.
- Run from a dog, screaming.
- Look or stare a dog in the eye.
- Disturb a dog that is sleeping, eating or caring for puppies.
- Pat a dog without supervision and before allowing it to see and sniff them first.
- Play with a dog unless supervised by an adult.
- Attempt to remove food or other items from a dog's mouth.

Tell them to stay still when an unfamiliar dog approaches ("stand still like a tree").

If knocked over by a dog, children should roll into a ball, tuck their face and neck out of reach and lie still. Parents are advised to wait until children reach school age before owning a dog.

Safe nursery equipment and toys

One in five injuries to children younger than 5 years old is associated with nursery furniture. Ten nursery furniture-related child deaths occur in Australia each year. Babies have been strangled or smothered in cots or prams. An Adelaide baby suffocated after being left by her carer on a triangular pillow.

Injuries requiring hospital emergency treatment are over-whelmingly the result of falls (65 percent). Australian and New Zealand parents should check that the equipment they buy and the equipment in centres complies with national standards. (This information may be found easily on the Internet.)

Since toy production has moved offshore to developing countries, some with lax regulations, costly problems have emerged for the most reputable companies. Over 10 million toys were recalled in the USA in 2006 alone. Mattel recalled 1.5 million of their Chinese-manufactured Sesame Street and Nickelodeon plastic toys after discovering that the smiling faces of Elmo and the gang contained high levels of toxic lead paint.

Then the Consumer Product Safety Commission struck again: 18.2 million Polly Pocket and related dolls worldwide were recalled because their tiny magnets could cause intestinal blockage or perforation if swallowed. Aqua Dots from the Spin Master Corporation, deemed appropriate for children 4 years or older, were recalled because the balls could render kids comatosed if swallowed. The beads were part of a kit intended to let children create 'multidimensional designs' but when water was added to the plastic balls, the outside coating became toxic. The result: curious kids who licked the balls experienced the effects of the date rape drug, GHB. They could fall into a coma, develop respiratory depression or have seizures. In 2006, the State of Victoria's annual inspection of toy sales resulted in the seizure of a total of 31,128 toys already on sale, which contravened bans and prescribed safety standards. Details of toys (including images) and the hazards they present are published on the Consumer Affairs Victoria website.

Regulations specify that toys for children younger than 3 years old must not have parts that can pose an ingestion or inhalation hazard. Generally speaking, any object smaller than a table tennis ball or one that fits in a 35mm film canister is deemed to be an ingestion or inhalation hazard. Small toys or parts of toys that detach easily or toys that break easily are all potentially dangerous and must be kept away from children under 3 years old.

Parents and carers are advised to check toys thoroughly before purchasing. For children less than 3 years of age, avoid toys with small parts completely.

Harmful plants

Although harmful plants are most likely to be found in gardens, the Australian National Childcare Accreditation Council (NCAC 2007)[19] reported that more than 23 percent of childcare centres failed to keep dangerous products, including gardening products and dangerous plants and objects away from children. Similar concerns were reported in 2009. This was despite the NCAC Quality Practices Guide Principle 5.3, which says, "Staff will ensure that potentially dangerous products, plants and objects are inaccessible to children". This principle specifically states that "poisonous or hazardous plants will not be accessible to children" and stipulates that the service must provide current safety information to families. The Quality Practices Guide is published by the Australian Government and is available to the public. The requirement applies to childcare centres, family day care and out-of-school care programs, but relative carers may not be aware of the dangers. Pictures of poisonous flowers and photographs for identification purposes can be accessed on the Internet.

Police checks and the Paedophile Register

In most Western countries, police checks are required for people whose work and volunteering brings them into contact with children. Police checks are not reliable, however and should not lead to complacency.

Be aware of the following:

- Unless fingerprints are taken (as by the FBI in the USA), child sex offenders can change their names and adopt new identities.
- The majority of sex offenders are not prosecuted and convicted if children are the only witnesses. Only convicted offenders appear on paedophile registers.
- Even when offenders are convicted, there is a good chance that they will win an appeal, based on a technicality that has nothing to do with their offences.
- Reportedly, a number of convicted teachers have been allowed to return to the classroom and convicted priests have been welcomed back into their churches, with continuing unfettered access to children.

In 2006, the Premier of the State of South Australia admitted to Parliament that only 1.8 percent of reported sex offenders were convicted and punished. That means that a frightening 98.2 percent of reported offenders do not appear on any register and they can be employed with unrestricted access to children. Paedophiles will try to beat the system.

In a single year in Queensland, 204 applications for police clearance were received from convicted sex offenders. A further 500 applicants withdrew applications when they were questioned about their past records. Thus 704 convicted people could have gained access to children, had it not been for these checks[20]. In the meantime, almost 200 reported and 80 convicted Australian paedophiles applied for employment in teaching and childcare in New South Wales. In 2008, there was uproar when Victorian parents learned that 4,000 teachers had been employed without police checks. Some convicted teachers have been allowed to return to New South Wales schools, while in Victoria a man convicted of five counts of sexual abuse involving young girls and who failed to disclose this when applying for police clearance, obtained voluntary work with children and then successfully appealed to the Victorian Civil and Administrative Appeals Tribunal. The judge excused the man's offending on the grounds that he had been a trade union leader and was stressed at the time. It should also be noted that some convicted child sex offenders have been 'reintegrated' into churches.

What becomes clear is that no one can be trusted on the basis of their professional status and we have to be vigilant and careful; however, we also have to bear in mind that most child sex offences occur in and around the home and that the abusers are known and trusted by the children and their parents.

Chapter 3

Protecting Your Child From Bullies

BULLYING: A COMMON PROBLEM

Canadian researcher Deborah Peppler claims that one in 12 school children experiences regular harassment, one in five is bullied occasionally and more than one in seven children admits to bullying others. In a medium-sized school, bullying happens once every seven minutes.

Childhood bullying is also widespread in the UK. Surveys reported by Britain's Royal College of Psychiatrists show that in one in four primary schools and one in 10 secondary schools, pupils are bullied.

In the US, 15 to 25 percent of children are bullied frequently and the same number of children admitted bullying others frequently. Some schools experience more problems than others.

Bullying makes everyone feel unsafe. The chosen children are often those who are not socially well integrated with peers. It follows that your children will have a better chance of avoiding the attention of bullies if you can help them to acquire the social skills needed to form lasting friendships. When children have close friends to whom they can turn for help, bullying episodes may end more quickly because their friends intervene. Friends can also assist with the emotional fallout.

Bullying occurs in all situations where children congregate: schools, clubs, sports groups and local neighbourhoods. It affects children of all races and socio-economic backgrounds. Bullying should concern everyone, not just the bully and the victim. We need to implement relationship solutions.

Schools, education and health authorities have long been aware of the ill effects of bullying and there are many Internet websites to help parents, teachers and children deal effectively with the problem. Anti-bullying programmes and policies are widely used in schools, some more successfully than others. For further information on programmes and their effectiveness, see P.K. Smith, et al.'s *Bullying in School: How successful can interventions be?* and www.education.unisa.edu.au/bullying, written by Dr. Ken Rigby.

WHAT CONSTITUTES BULLYING?

Bullying involves an individual or group deliberately hurting or controlling others. The behaviour is usually repetitive and designed to generate maximum distress and fear in its victims. Bullying differs from conflict insomuch as there is always an imbalance of power. It can be physical or verbal, but psychological abuse is always involved.

Bullies can be members of the same class, group or school, who are bigger, stronger, or more physically or verbally aggressive than others. Victims are predominantly those who are perceived as different by appearance, dress, speech or even the types of food they carry in their lunch boxes. They are especially vulnerable when they are overweight, a member of a minority ethnic group, religion or culture or speak a different native language. Children with disabilities can also be vulnerable.

In Australian and New Zealand schools, young people have even admitted being bullied because their mothers were perceived as different, by virtue of their age, weight, makeup, accent, clothing or other aspect of their appearance.

Bullying is different from conflict in that it involves an individual or group using power inappropriately to cause distress. Young children who travel without adult supervision on a school bus or public transport often complain of bullying by bigger or older students who gang up on, taunt and intimidate them. Surveys show, however, that most bullying happens on school premises. It can be persistent and extremely harmful, making victims feel socially isolated and lonely, embarrassed, inferior, ashamed, fearful, unsafe and different in a very unhealthy way. Some victims dread and refuse to go to school and develop a physical illness, complaining of headaches, stomach pains and nausea. Some experience nightmares, refuse to get out of bed, lose concentration, appear visibly unhappy or play truant.

American surveys suggest that only 25 to 50 percent of victims confide in an adult. Some are afraid to say anything because they fear the bullies will find out, resulting in more serious retaliation if parents lodge complaints. They also fear that parents will disbelieve, ridicule or blame them. Boys are least likely to disclose what is happening because of the cultural expectation that males should be brave and able to defend themselves. Victims often experience a sense of isolation and loss of confidence. In serious cases, it can lead to depression and, in extreme situations, suicide. Bullying can also have a negative effect on the children who simply witness it.

Bullies have their own negative outcomes to deal with, too. They risk rejection because peer loyalty and admiration are short-lived, based unhealthily on the fear of being the next victims. International research shows that typical bullies are unhappy kids who have a diminished capacity to learn, concentrate or analyse. They fail in school and have higher than average dropout rates. The antisocial behavior of persistent bullies can continue well into adulthood. They are at higher risk than others of perpetuating violent behaviour, abusing alcohol and drugs, carrying weapons, stealing and being convicted of offences when they become adults. They tend to have problems holding down jobs, maintaining relationships and commanding respect and bullying may become inter-generational when they bully their own offspring.[21]

Just as we wouldn't expect child victims of other forms of abuse to resolve it all by themselves, we shouldn't expect children to be able to handle bullies without adult help. Don't say, "You should hit him back". Victims who retaliate with violence don't feel better about themselves. They are also likely to get into trouble and risk suspension from school. Don't say, "Ignore them", because ignoring doesn't work and the child victim shouldn't have to bear the responsibility. Victims are better advised to keep talking to school staff until they find someone who doesn't accept the old saying, "Sticks and stones may break my bones, but harsh words cannot hurt me". Harsh words *can* hurt and often do!

Adults have a responsibiliy to stop bullying. The problem requires a whole school/centre approach involving staff, children and parents. There has to be a change of climate and a change in the norms of behaviour so that bullying is no longer perceived as 'cool'.

Physical bullying includes:

- Hitting, jabbing, poking and punching, kicking, pinching, pulling hair, restricting movement.
- Fighting and enlisting others to fight the child.
- Standover tactics, extortion.
- Blocking the victim's path.
- Stealing, damaging, destroying or hiding the victim's work, possessions, school uniform or sports gear to get them into trouble or cause distress.
- Chasing, cornering and tripping.
- Unwanted touching (note that this constitutes sexual abuse, not bullying).

Psychological abuse is involved in all forms of bullying and includes:

- Belittling, mocking, embarrassing, making fun of others, constant teasing.
- Name calling.
- Threatening, stalking.
- Offensive racial or religious comments.
- Saying or publishing false, malicious (including sex-related) gossip about the child or members of the family (e.g., the child has AIDS; the mother is promiscuous) to cause distress and make the child unpopular.
- Writing graffiti about others.
- Getting others to gang up on another.
- Shunning, ignoring or excluding another child from a group.
- Ostracising victims, persuading others to reject them.
- Threatening children directly or anonymously, e.g., sending unsigned notes, emails or sending text messages on mobile phones to instil fear.
- Stealing, hiding or damaging a child's school uniform, spectacles or possessions to get the child into trouble and/or cause distress.
- Forcing victims to do wrong things against their will.
- Stopping victims from joining activities or games.
- Distressing children by insulting their parents who are perceived as different.
- Cyber-bullying, which mostly includes posting malicious information on websites.

A comparatively new problem is that of unprovoked violence which is filmed on mobile phones and subsequently posted on the Internet. This involves both girls and boys and seems to be driven by a desire for celebrity status. It involves both the physical and psychological abuse of victims. In addition, sexually explicit images are widely distributed in schools. Some girls have taken photographs of their genitals and breasts for boyfriends who then circulated them throughout the school to humiliate the girls and raise their own status. The resultant embarrassment led to one American girl committing suicide.

Girls have traditionally used more psychological bullying than boys to isolate others and gain power over social groups. However, this is changing; boys are now also using psychological methods, while girls are becoming more physically violent.

Age-old techniques include:

- "I won't invite you to my party" (when children want and expect to be invited).
- "Don't play with her because she stinks."
- "I won't be your friend anymore."
- More recent additions include sexual insults, such as:
- "Don't play with her. She has AIDS."
- "She's a lesbian/dyke/leso."
- "She's a slut. She has sex with everybody."
- Similarly boys are taunted with:
- "He's a poofter/homo/gay/faggot."
- "Stay away from him. He has AIDS."

Some children as young as six engage in sexual insults. Although they may not fully understand what is meant, they know the comments are insulting and victims become upset, which, of course, is the bully's aim.

All children, including thin ones, may be called "fatso". Boys with fat breasts are often prodded and taunted that they are girls. Intelligent children are referred to as "dummy", along with those who have disabilities. For decades, children who wear glasses have been called 'spec-four-eyes'. Some victims stop wearing their thick-lens spectacles in school to avoid bullying; bullies of both sexes have stolen them and thrown them into school toilets. While most victims become extremely distressed, some shrug and allege they are not concerned. Discounting is a coping method that enables others to perceive them as strong. Many say they are sad and angry, however and some become depressed. Others will retaliate subversively or openly, often getting into trouble as a result.

Children with disabilities are targeted more frequently in mainstream schools than in special education settings. On the other hand, children who attend special schools are often ridiculed and stigmatised by students from other schools when they meet them in the street or on public transport.

Some parents and teachers regard bullying as nothing more than an uncomfortable aspect of growing up that we must endure. This enables adults to turn a blind eye. Some are unsympathetic and instruct victims to walk away. That does not work.

Bullying generally takes place out of the sight and hearing of adults. The majority of peer group observers do nothing to stop it because they are afraid of being the next victims. About 20 to 30 percent of onlookers encourage bullies and may join in. This provides power, protection and a sense of security that they would not otherwise have. There are three distinct roles in the bullying group: defenders and assistants of the bully; defenders of the victim; and observers who won't get involved. That is why it is important to mobilise the peer group against the bully, by emphasising the relationship issue rather than the bully/victim problem.

Cyber-bullying

Cyber-bullying is when the bully uses emails, chat rooms, Facebook or other social networking sites, a discussion group, instant messaging services on mobile phones (texting) or other cyber-technology on the Internet to denigrate or cause fear in recipients. Cyber-bullying is usually anonymous. It is now the most common and insidious form of bullying, used specifically to intimidate young people. In a recent study quoted by

Australia's NetAlert, one in five 13 to 17-year-olds said they had witnessed someone abusing other young people online.

Typical cyber-bullying tactics include:

- Sending mean, threatening or insulting texts, emails or instant messages. Both boys and girls receive text threats to the effect that they must provide sex or they will be hurt in some way.
- Posting nasty images or untrue, derogatory messages about others in blogs, websites or social networking pages such as Facebook, MySpace or Bebo.
- Removing peers from friends lists on social networking websites as a form of social exclusion.
- Using another person's user name to spread rumours or lies about someone.
- Tampering with or otherwise altering another person's online profile/blog/email and circulating it with the specific intent to damage their reputation.
- Harassing or threatening people in the network.
- Putting pressure on someone to give out personal and private information, with the intention of disseminating it to others.
- Posting images or videos (doctored or otherwise) with the purpose of degrading others.
- Publishing victims' photographs superimposed onto pornographic images.
- Filming or photographing people without their knowledge or consent, with the intent to publish the images to humiliate those involved.

Although cyber-bullies often have similar motives to traditional bullies, victims claim they have a greater impact, particularly when the threats are anonymous. An MSN study[22] and another carried out by NetSafe (New Zealand's national cyber-safety service), showed that young people will not turn to parents for help, because they perceive adults as technologically ignorant. The mobile phone is essential for their social lives and their greatest fear is that parents will confiscate it.

It is much easier to participate in cyber-bullying than in traditional bullying because the bully can remain anonymous and doesn't have to confront the victim. Text-bullying is difficult to avoid because of the relationship young people have with mobile phones. Most are never turned off; hence, a victim can be harassed at anytime, anywhere, even at home in bed. Home is no longer the sanctuary that it used to be. A recent phenomenon is the cyber-bully who demands sex from both boys and girls with threats that terrible things will happen if they don't comply the next day.

Do not allow children to leave their mobile phones on when they are in bed because the receipt of these messages can cause great fear.

Cyber-bullying is not only wrong; it is a crime, which comes with very real consequences.

Parents can help to stop it by talking about the size and nature of the problem:

- Discuss with your children how they behave online.
- Teach your children that taking a stand is the first step in making cyber-bullies stop. There's no such thing as an innocent bystander. If kids see cyber-bullying, they should report it. If they are doing it themselves, they should stop. Hurtful comments and nasty rumours spread via text messages can be more threatening and hurtful than face-to-face bullying.
- When cyber-bullying occurs, the first step is to save the message for future evidence. The second is to turn off the technology. Tell your child never to reply to a bully because replies make the bullies feel very important.
- The second step is to contact the service provider to find out if and how emails and texts from that person can be intercepted and stopped. If this can't be done,

temporarily open a new email address and pre-paid mobile phone number, ensuring that the new details are only given to closest friends. Of course, close friends could be the bullies, in which case the calls will continue and they can be tackled head-on.

- Keep a printout or record of any worrying emails or online messages (including date and time) to help you or police locate the sender, if that becomes necessary.
- Check the terms of use policies on websites. In many cases, reporting bullying or threatening behaviour can result in the offender's account being deleted.

If messages are threatening or serious, contact police as well as your phone or Internet provider and report what is happening, with a view to blocking some calls.

To reduce the risk of cyber-bullying you should:

- Supervise and stay in touch with what your kids are doing online, discuss Internet issues and experiences and watch for behaviour changes around online activity.
- Educate your child and yourself — reinforce safety messages and cyber-rules and keep in touch with latest developments, using the websites of NetAlert (Australia), Netsafe (NZ) and other government-sponsored initiatives.

WHY KIDS BULLY OTHERS

Children give many different reasons for why they bully others. These include:

- Others did it and got away with it.
- It happened to them.
- They like showing off to attract an admiring audience.
- It is what you have to do if you want to hang out with the right crowd.

- They feel stronger, smarter or better than the person they are bullying.
- They enjoy the power associated with controlling and upsetting others.
- They think their victims deserve it.
- They want something the victim has.
- "It wasn't my fault — s/he made me do it."
- "It's fun — it was only a joke!"

Some may be under pressure to bully. Quiet, scared kids can become bullies in the company of persuasive others. They target victims who look as if they can't stand up for themselves and are easily distressed. The bully is deprived of satisfaction when victims fail to react.

Whatever the reasons for bullying, we need to recognise that it can have a terrible effect on others, leading to depression and even suicide. It may not be happening to your children today, but it could be their turn tomorrow. Working with both your child and the school should enable you to improve your child's life.

HOW YOU CAN HELP

Be open to the possibility that your child may be bullied. Parents sometimes don't think of bullying as a possible reason for their child's distress or their reluctance to attend school. Given that only 25 to 50 percent of children tell an adult about bullying, your child could be a victim, a witness or even the bully, without your knowledge.

Be alert to symptoms and changes in mood and behaviour. Victims may cry more than usual, have night terrors, nightmares, become withdrawn, complain of headaches, stomachache or feeling sick, and make excuses to avoid school. Young children may find it difficult to explain what is wrong.

Discuss bullying with your child, whether it is happening right now or not. Explain what bullying is and why it has to be stopped in the early stages. Books and Internet sites are widely available, offering tips on how to respond to bullies.

Encourage and listen to your child talk. Calm listening without blaming is one of the most important things you can do when bullying is a problem. Bear in mind that victims are often too embarrassed or fearful to talk about what is happening. They fear you will be disappointed in them and are risking rejection and blame. They fear that bullies will find out that they've told and bullying will increase, making life even more intolerable. Some victims believe that it is their own fault that they are bullied and they deserve what happens. Victims of cyberbullying fear they will have their phones confiscated or Internet access removed if parents discover what is happening.

It takes great courage to tell an adult and sympathetic listening helps. Never tell children to stand up for themselves. This is particularly unrealistic if a group is involved. Similarly, it doesn't help if parents are over-protective and say, "I'm not sending you back to that terrible school. You can stay at home and I'll take care of you myself."

Take your child seriously. Many children suffer in silence for a long time before they tell anyone.

Try to find out exactly what happened without holding an inquisition. What preceded the bullying? Did your child say or do something that might have provoked or caused irritation? Bear in mind that bullies and victims are not homogenous groups; there are different types. There are also passive victims and provocative victims, and they require different approaches.

What happened after the bullying? Who else was involved? Was the teacher informed? If not, why not? If yes, what was the response? How did the child feel? Listen, empathise and assure your child that bullying is not acceptable. Ask how long this has been happening and how your child has dealt with it to date.

Discuss strategies for dealing with bullying.

Always include your children in making decisions about how to tackle the problem. It is best if children (with a background of sound advice) can decide to do things for themselves.

What strategies did your child use at the time? What worked (if anything)? What didn't? Make a realistic assessment of the bullying.

Bullying is serious if the child is assaulted, experiences serious, wilful damage or is afraid to return. In such circumstances, responsible staff must always be contacted. Resist tackling the bully directly. Instead, record details of the event and report it to the school.

Strategies to use with children include asking:

- What they say or could say to bullies who call them names.
- Is your child comfortable being assertive? If not, practice how to be assertive.
- Is s/he overreacting/provoking the bully? How can the response be changed?
- If school or public transport is used, what form of bullying is involved and how might it be handled?
- Where is the safest place to go at lunchtime or at other times when the bullying might occur? Where are the places to avoid? (A South Australian primary school found it necessary to fence off an area of the playground close to the staff room, to provide a safe space for girls and reduce intimidation by boys.)
- What happens if the victim ignores the bully and walks away?
- What can a victim do if ignoring the bully doesn't work?
- What if others are involved? (Tell the child to report to you, the teacher on duty at the time, the school counsellor or a senior member of staff.)

- How might your child create opportunities to make new friends, given that bullies don't pick on groups? Can s/he find a more robust ally for protection in the schoolyard until the bullying stops?

Does the school have a buddy system to provide support for newly enrolled and isolated children? If not, suggest how such a system could be adopted.

If your child is often bullied, would s/he be interested in joining judo, kick-boxing or other self-defence instructional groups to develop confidence? A confident child who can brush insults aside with the contempt they deserve is much less likely to be bullied than a frightened, anxious child.

Ask your child to name people who listen and can help.

Enquire whether others are targeted by the same bully. What happens and what are the circumstances?

Don't blame victims, even if you can see that their response may have aggravated the situation. Discuss other forms of response.

Praise your child for telling you.

Do not promise to keep the bullying secret. Something must be done about it. Reassure your child that you and school staff will try to make things better. Point out that teachers don't always know when a child is being bullied unless the child tells them. Police must be informed if violence is involved.

Enquire whether the school or centre has an anti-bullying policy and programme.

Irrespective of whether your child is being bullied, investigate your school's anti-bullying policy and the processes for reporting. If there is no programme or policy, ask why not. Try to persuade the principal, school council and parent-teacher body that there is a need for both, as well as a whole school approach to reduce bullying. *P.E.A.C.E. Pack, A Program for*

Reducing Bullying in Our Schools by Phillip T. Slee, is a useful approach to bringing the community together.

A programme called *Friendly Schools* is promoted in Australia. See http://wachpr.curtin.edu.au/html/projects/project_detail_FSBIP.html for more details.

If there is a programme, check its rate of effectiveness in P.K. Smith, et al.'s *Bullying in School.*

Bullying expert Dr. Ken Rigby reports that some programmes have not demonstrated much success despite considerable publicity. He recommends 'The Method of Shared Concern', which has a non-punitive, problem-solving approach to tackle moderately severe cases, affecting upper primary and secondary students. This was pioneered by Swedish psychologist Anatol Pikas and has been used successfully in a number of countries, including England, Scotland, Australia, Sweden, Finland and Canada.

Recently, a version of this approach was created by Dr. Rigby and formed the basis for a DVD. It is described on www. readymade.com.au/productions.html, where video clips may be viewed and purchase information is located. You can also download papers on *Shared Concern* by Pikas: *New Developments of the Shared Concern Method* (PDF) and by Rigby: *The Method of Shared Concern as an Intervention Technique to Address Bullying in Schools: An Overview and Appraisal.*

If your child has been bullied, establish the facts and report what happened to the school or centre's senior staff or group leader. Ask what is being done to stop bullying. How do they deal with bullies after they have been reported? Parents of victims have the right to seek help from the organisation where bullying occurs. Teachers and group leaders have a responsibility to help.

Regardless of the response, please stay calm! It is a common and understandable mistake for victims' parents to become angry and accuse the school of negligence. This can result in defensiveness and a reduction of cooperation, when the opposite is what you need.

Explain to your child the difference between reporting bullying and telling tales. Emphasise the importance of children reporting to responsible adults when someone takes or trashes belongings, threatens them, or hurts them physically or with words. Reporting can prevent the bully from hurting and distressing others. Reporting is done to help a victim, whereas tittle-tattling is designed merely to get someone else into trouble.

In some countries, a school has a legal obligation to protect children from the effects of bullying, even if the bullying is occurring outside school time (provided that both victim and perpetrator attend the same school).

All schools should have a clear anti-bullying policy that teachers, parents and children understand. A policy should state that bullying or aggressive behaviour will not be tolerated. The Royal College of Psychiatrists confirms that those schools with the fewest problems are those with policies where every incident of bullying is taken seriously. The best way to address bullying is for everyone in the school community to take a strong, proactive stance.

WHAT IF YOUR CHILD IS THE BULLY?

Never deny that your child has bullied others when faced with evidence to the contrary. Most children bully someone at some time in their lives. Instead, ask your child why they behaved in this way. To create change and reduce the risk of repetition, you need to find out what those reasons are.

You need to discuss this with your child, but without putting words into your child's mouth. Be calm instead of accusing. Encourage explanations rather than excuses:

- What led up to it?
- Why was that particular child chosen?
- Who else was involved and how?
- Was your child a leader or a follower? Why and who did they follow? Children who wouldn't dream of bullying alone may participate in a bullying group out of fear of the leader or to gain peer approval.
- Ask your child to place himself or herself in the victim's shoes. How would they feel to be in that situation?
- In some circumstances, a restorative justice approach may be possible. This can involve victims being given the opportunity to tell the bully just how the behaviour made them feel, provided that it is done in a safe way, so that the victim is not made to feel intimidated. It can help bullies to understand that their actions have real consequences, because bullies generally don't care. Talk about what can be done to make the victim feel better. Can your child phone or write to apologise for their part in what happened?
- Discuss what can be done to stop bullying in the peer group.
- Ask your children why bullying is wrong and fill the gaps in their knowledge. Bullies often lack a conscience about the effects of their behaviour. They may think it is fun. They are unaware of the hurt they cause because they are part of the group dynamic.

Some kids resort to bullying when they are worried about something that has happened to them. Some feel powerless and gain temporary satisfaction from taking it out on someone else. Some bully to even the score for a perceived injustice while others are prejudiced against groups or types and think those groups deserve to be treated badly. Some do it in the belief that their capacity to boss people around gives them status. There are also impulsive, unhappy children who have short fuses and simply find it hard to control their anger.

Consider whether your bullying child feels neglected, frustrated, insecure or jealous at home or school and wants to hurt others as a consequence. Knowing why a child resorts to bullying is helpful for creating plans for change, but explanations should not be regarded as excuses. Emphasise that we are all responsible for the choices we make.

While you should not automatically assume that you are to blame for your children's misbehaviour, it might be useful to look closely at the models that children see at home and consider whether they are copying the behaviour of other family members. Calmly share your concerns about the well-being of the victim and firmly insist that the behaviour must never happen again. Some schools require children to make plans for changing their behaviour and share them with the class.

RESOURCES FOR PARENTS

There are many resources freely available for parents using the Internet and parenting services.

In Australia, children can receive professional counselling on bullying from Kids Helpline (free call: 1800 551 800). Free parent help lines are available in all states (see the emergency page in your telephone book).

The Australian Government published a booklet and distributed it to all homes in 2007. *NetAlert Protecting Australian Families Online* has a section on cyber-bullying (www.australia.gov.au/netalert, Tel: 1800 880 176).

Dr. Ken Rigby also wrote booklets for the Australian Federal Attorney General's Department for parents and teachers of young children, available on www.education.unisa.edu.au/bullying.

In Canada, The Alberta Teachers' Association (ATA) provides anti-bullying resources for parents and students. The ATA's *Safe and Caring Schools Project* (SACS) was established in 1996 to address issues of safety and social responsibility in schools. Its goal is to encourage school practices that model and reinforce socially responsible and respectful behaviours so that learning and teaching can take place in a safe and caring environment. The SACS programme is offered at all grade levels, though early intervention is key. SACS spokesperson Sue Sheffield, says that, "when correcting aggressive behaviour, the earlier, the better".

Researchers and professionals have devised the *Canadian Initiative for the Prevention of Bullying,* www.bullying.org, a project for children and adults in which government leaders, national organisations, community groups and schools are collaborating in the creation of nationwide safe, respectful environments for children and adolescents. The ATA released a parent guide entitled *Bullying — Everyone's Problem.* The association knew that, with the cooperation of parents and counsellors, teachers can help children deal with bullying in ways that discourage this harmful behavior. The Association has bullying information on its website.

For kids, also see : www.cyberbullying.org or www.cyberbullying. ca (Canada).

The U.S. Department of Health and Human Services has launched a nationwide media campaign, *Stop Bullying Now* (www.stopbullyingnow.hrsa.gov) which is a comprehensive prevention website for adults and children. It also raises awareness of the harm caused by bullying, through TV and radio announcements.

In New Zealand, Telecom has a toll-free helpline: 0800 NO BULLY (0800 66 28 55) or visit their website, www.nobully.org. nz. A leaflet, *Stop Bullying: Advice for Parents and Caregivers* is published by New Zealand police. The Police Youth Education Service also promotes and supports the use of an anti-bullying programme, *Kia Kaha,* in schools. NetSafe runs a toll-free helpline for victims of cyber-bullying, 0508 NETSAFE (0508 638

72.33). Free pamphlets about text-bullying are available from the NetSafe website www.netsafe.org.nz.

In the UK, a useful website is the Royal College of Psychiatrists' www.rcpsych.ac.uk/mentalhealthinformation/mentalhealthan dgrowingup/18bullyingandemotion.aspx.

RCP recommends:

- ChildLine, which provides a free and confidential telephone service for children. Helpline 0800 1111, www. childline.org.uk.
- Department for Education Northern Ireland's information on bullying. www.deni.gov.uk.
- Kidscape, for advice, training courses and helpful booklets and information about bullying. 2 Grosvenor Gardens, London SW1W ODH; Tel: 020 7730 3300; www. kidscape.org.uk.
- www.antibully.org.uk
- www.bullying.co.uk
- www.bbc.co.uk/education/archive/bully
- The *Mental Health and Growing Up* series, containing fact sheets on a range of common mental health problems, including bullying. Obtainable from Book Sales at the Royal College of Psychiatrists, 17 Belgrave Square, London SW1X 8PG; Tel: 020 7235 2351, ext. 146; fax: 020 7245 1231; email: booksales@rcpsych.ac.uk or you can download them from their website.

Other useful websites include:

- www.bullyingnoway.com.au
- www.curriculum.edu.au/mctyapdf/netsafeschools
- www.bullying.org/help
- www.kidshelp.com.au/INFO7/linksforparents
- www.nobully.org.nz/advicep.htm
- www.parenting.sa.gov.au/pegs/29.pdf
- www.dfes.gov.uk/bullying

Useful books and articles

Berne, S. (1996) *Bully-proof your child.* Melbourne. Lothian.

Bernstein, J. Y. & Watson, N. W. (1997) Children who are targets of bullying: a victim pattern. *Journal of Interpersonal Violence,* 12, 483 to 497.

Chesson, R. (1999) Bullying: the need for an interagency response. *BMJ,* 319, 330 (www.bmjpg.com)

Field, E.M (1999) *Bully Busting.* Finch, Lane Cove, Sydney

Griffiths, C (1997) *What can you do about bullying? A guide for parents.* Meerlinga Young Children's Foundation, East Perth.

Leff, S. (1999) Bullied children are picked on for their vulnerability. *BMJ,* 318, 1076 (www.bmjpg.com).

Rigby, K (2007) *Children and bullying: How parents and educators can reduce bullying in schools.* Blackwell.

Rigby, K (1996) *Bullying in schools and what to do about it.* Melbourne: ACER.

Rigby. K (2002) *Stop the Bullying.* Melbourne: ACER. (NB: This is used in all South Australian schools)

Rigby, K. (2004). *Bullying in childhood.* In P. K. Smith & C. H. Hart (Eds.), *Blackwell handbook of childhood social development* (pp. 549 to 568). Malden, MA: Blackwell.

Sullivan, K (2000) *The anti-bullying handbook.* New York. Oxford University Press.

Zarzour, K. (1999) *The schoolyard bully.* Toronto. Harper Collins.

Chapter 4

Promoting Healthy Sexual Development In Children

FROM BIRTH TO AGE FIVE

C hildren have a natural curiosity about their bodies. Babies enjoy touching and having their bodies touched. Boys are fascinated by their genitals because they protrude, have elasticity, make interesting playthings and touching may produce pleasurable sensations.

Observing our reactions and attitudes, children gradually learn what is expected of them as males or females. By the age of 3, they show an interest in other people's genitals and how the other sex uses the toilet. Before they start school, girls may try to urinate while standing up, like their dads or brothers. There are books to use with the youngest of children going through this stage of development. For example, *My Potty Book for Boys*, by Andrea Pinnington, is geared towards young boys about to embark on this new venture. Sensitive photographs show boys following the potty-training process. In hatumorous, step-by-step sequences, toddlers teach their teddy bears what to do. Narrated by young children in lively, rhyming text, this book places the emphasis on praise for success.

With increased language, 3 to 5-year-old children ask questions, including how they came into their mummies' tummies. If girls see dads or brothers naked, they wonder why they haven't a penis. School children as young as 5 are aware of the existence of naughty children who engage in indecent behaviour (often referred to as 'rude' or 'dirty', but use the language that your child would be familiar with) but they don't expect adults to behave in that way. They say that adults "tell children off for being rude."

USE CORRECT VOCABULARY FOR GENITALS

We give children the correct words for other body parts but often avoid using correct vocabulary for genitals. Adults refer to 'ninny', 'down there', 'between your legs' or even 'front bottom' and 'back bottom' for girls, while boys are given silly names for their penis, including names that no one else will understand. By doing this we give children the message that we can talk about other body parts, but that genitals are invisible and unmentionable.

Children recognise our hypocrisy when we say, "You can tell me if something is worrying you" when, by our very avoidance of the subject, we indicate that we can't handle anything that involves discussing the lower half of the body.

Why?

The only logical explanation for this behaviour is that we want to avoid being embarrassed by young children referring to their genitals in public. A little girl who had just learned that she had a vagina, accompanied her mother to a Mothers Union event and in a very loud voice said, "Mummy, have all the ladies in this room got vaginas?"

Let's face it, children will inadvertently embarrass us from time to time. My 4-year-old waited until she was walking down the aisle of London's St. Paul's Cathedral to pipe up in a very loud voice, "Mummy, what does 'f___ off' mean?" Her words echoed audibly through the building.

Teachers using child protection programmes occasionally hear a mother complain, "My son is too young to know the word 'penis'." In 2009, ABC radio journalists in Queensland criticised South Australia's education department for introducing a child protection curriculum to schools that used the correct vocabulary for genitals. Teaching boys that they have a penis would spoil their innocence, they claimed.

Similarly, Australian Family Association spokesperson Jerome Appleby told the *Sunday Mail*[23] that teaching the correct anatomical names for genitals would "destroy the innocence of children," adding that, "They aren't ready for those sorts of adult concepts and it is a sad indictment on society". So we teach children that a nose is a nose and an eye is an eye and an ear is an ear, but we have to give them silly names for genitals!

> It is important to realise that the use of correct vocabulary is not what spoils a child's innocence — it is child sex abuse.

The adult's discomfort with body part names is not a good enough reason for avoiding them. Just as other words are introduced casually, the words penis, testicles, scrotum and vagina or vulva can be introduced when young children are having a bath or shower.

In a class of 6-year-olds, the author found 20 different names used for penis. They included cock, dick, prick, thing, tossy, wee-wee, pee-pee, winky, winkle, tinkle, sausage, noodle, worm, crown jewels and even grub, as well as names such as John Henry, Willy and John Thomas, in addition to ethnic names that others wouldn't understand. The most unusual was "golf set", explained as a stick and two balls in a bag. Parents thought this highly amusing until it was pointed out that a teacher on playground duty would be unlikely to help their son if he said, "someone touched my golf set".

If you have used pet words for genitals, find the opportunity to say, "Now that you're growing up, I think it is time we used the adult words for these special parts of your body. What you have is called a _____ . Can you say that? Let's use the grownup words from now on."

INTRODUCE BODY PRIVACY

Introduce the word 'private'. Make sure that your child understands what 'private' means.

It means 'Keep out,' 'Don't touch,' 'It belongs to me,' 'It's my body' and 'I'm the boss of my body'.

When children are capable of washing and drying themselves, tell them that, now that they are growing up, they can take responsibility for looking after the private parts of their bodies, which include all the parts from their mouths down to their knees. This includes breasts/nipples, penis, testicles/scrotum, vagina and buttocks. 'Private' means other people are not allowed to touch, tickle, look or play around with them. Mum or Dad might take a look if a child has a problem and a doctor may need to look, too, but Mum or a nurse will always be there.

Tell children that genitals are important places that we have to take good care of, acknowledging simultaneously that touching them can be pleasurable. Tell children they can touch their own private body parts in the privacy of their bedrooms or bathroom but we don't do it in the lounge, the shops, the street or places where there are other people. Why? Because we have to look after them. When we grow up, we might want to share our bodies with someone special and it takes a long time to choose that special person. We have to choose very carefully if that person is going to be the mummy or daddy of our children.

Proceed as slowly and repetitiously as necessary.

Mouths are private places, too

Because of the widespread use of children for oral sex by both juvenile and adult sex offenders, the mouth must be included among the private places that require special care. Discuss how we look after our mouths. For example, we wash hands that touch food, clean our teeth and avoid germs. Emphasise that, "No one is allowed to put anything yucky or stinky in your mouth. No one is allowed to put any part of their body in your mouth. Your mouth belongs to you and it is private. Yes, a dentist might put something in your mouth but he wears special gloves to protect you and keep the germs out".

"If someone tries to put something you don't want in your mouth, step back, hold out your arms and say 'Stop that! It isn't allowed!' Get away as fast as you can and tell me about it. Practice saying, 'Stop that! It isn't allowed!' and 'It's my body' in a big, loud voice."

Working with your child to make the mouth private

These are some statements and questions to work through with your child to make the mouth a private place:

- Your mouth is a very special, private place because it has an important job to do.
- Why do you think it is important?
- How do you look after your mouth?
- What could happen if we didn't look after our mouths?
- We have to take special care of mouths because we don't want germs to go inside and make us sick. That's why we must wash our hands before we eat.
- Nobody is allowed to put anything yucky in your mouth.
- Nobody is allowed to put anything stinky in your mouth.
- No one is allowed to play around or mess around with your mouth.

- No one is allowed to kiss you if you don't want to be kissed (and grownups should never kiss you on your mouth).
- Just as important, you mustn't kiss other kids if they don't want to be kissed.
- No one is allowed to put anything in your mouth unless you have to take doctor's medicine and you can't pour it out by yourself.
- No one is allowed to put any part of their body in your mouth — not fingers, not toes, not their tongue, not anything. Keep germs away.
- We always have to take good care of our mouths and keep germs away.

Questions
- Is it OK for mum or dad to put medicine in your mouth if you can't manage to do it yourself?
- Is it OK for someone to put a piece of chocolate in your mouth if you say you'd like a piece?
- What if you said you didn't want it and they put it in just the same?
- Is it OK to suck your own fingers? What if they are dirty?
- Suppose that someone bigger than you told you to kiss his body?
- Suppose that someone gives sloppy, wet, mouth kisses that are really yucky?
- Suppose it was your favourite aunt and you didn't want to hurt her feelings?
- What could you do? What could you say? Let's practice!

Breasts are private places, too

Sex offenders frequently start out by fondling a child's breasts (both boys and girls). If the child doesn't object and stop it, the abuse increases.

Here are some suggested phrases to help you to discuss with your child keeping their breasts private: Say

- You know that mouths are private but did you know that breasts are private, too? Some people call them silly names, like boobs or tits, but we're going to use the adult word.
- Everybody has breasts. When girls grow up, their breasts change shape, to prepare for when they're older and ready to feed their babies.
- When boys grow up, their breasts don't change because they don't feed babies. Whether you're a boy or a girl, breasts are private parts of your body.
- Nobody is allowed to touch, kiss or play around with your breasts.
- They're yours and you're the boss.
- If you have a bad cough your doctor might listen to your chest with a stethoscope but your mum or dad or a nurse will be there, so it's okay.
- Those are the rules.

And more private places

When children can wash and dry themselves tell them that it is time for them to take care of the special, private parts of their bodies. *Emphasise that their breasts, genitals and buttocks are private parts that belong only to them.* They are tucked away and covered up with pants "because we have to take good care of them".

Here are some suggested phrases to use to discuss keeping other parts private:

- A boy has a penis and testicles. They are very special and private things to have if you're a boy. Bottoms are private places, too. We have to keep them clean.
- Nobody is allowed to play around or touch or tickle those private places if you are a boy. If someone tries to put a hand in your pants, stand back, hold out your

arms and, in a big, strong voice shout, "Stop that! It isn't allowed!" Run away and tell.

- Nobody is allowed to touch or tickle or play around with your breasts, your bottom or vagina if you are a girl.
- Our private parts are so special that we keep them covered up most of the time.
- We don't show them to the neighbours.
- We don't show them to people in the supermarket.
- We don't let people touch them on the bus.
- We don't even share them with friends and relatives.
- Your private parts are yours and nobody else's.
- It is OK for *you* to touch them, but nobody else is allowed to put a hand or anything else inside your pants. Private means keep out. It isn't allowed.
- Some kids might want to take a look to see if your special private places are the same as theirs. Remember that you are the boss of your body.
- Those are the rules. You can say, "Stop that! It isn't allowed!" to whoever it is. Hold out your arms and walk away. Then tell someone who can help you to make sure it doesn't happen again.
- Everyone has to take care of their private places.
- If you have a sore bottom, your doctor may need to look at it but he will use gloves to keep the germs away and your mum or dad or a nurse will be there. That's the rule.

For young children, this is a good time to read Family Planning Queensland's *Everybody's Got a Bottom,* by Tess Rowley, obtainable online. It is beautifully illustrated and comprehensive in its coverage. It takes the hard work out of teaching children to stay safe. Children enjoy it from age 2 to 3 and up. For slightly older children, also use *What's Wrong with Bottoms?* by Jenny Hessell. Published in 1984, it is still available online and in libraries and can be found in many early childhood centres.

Young children like rules

Confirm rules for private places. These rules should be:

- No one is allowed to touch or tickle or play around with your private places.
- No one is allowed to look at your private places just for fun.
- We don't show our private places to other people.
- We don't touch other people's private places.
- Your private places are yours and no one else's.
- If someone breaks the rule, it is OK to scream, it is OK to yell, it is OK to shout and it is definitely all right to tell.
- Practice standing back, maintaining eye contact and yelling, "Stop that! It isn't allowed".

If children ask why we have these rules, explain that when they are little it is OK to run along the beach or play in the garden without clothes "but I don't think you'd want to go to the shops without any clothes on now, would you? There are some special beaches where people are allowed to go in the sea without clothes but if they walked naked along the street or at a cricket match, police would take them to the police station and they'd pay a lot of money as punishment for breaking the rule".

In the book, *What's Wrong with Bottoms?*, the boy has been touched inappropriately by a favourite uncle and is asked to keep it secret. Mum explains that the uncle knew that it was wrong because he made it a secret. She points out that the uncle didn't expose his bottom (meaning penis) while they were all sitting around watching TV but waited until he and the boy were on their own.

Teach children what to do if someone tries to touch the private parts of their bodies.

Tell your child that, "If someone tries to touch the private parts of your body, step away, hold out your arms" (to create a personal space), "and shout, 'Stop that! It isn't allowed!... It's my body" using a big, loud voice. Get away and tell me or a teacher" (if it is at school), "as soon as possible". Emphasise that you need to know what happens because older kids and grownups know they are not allowed to play around with children's private body parts. Also say that kids can't always stop bigger people from misbehaving and "it is never a child's fault if someone does something that makes you uncomfortable or gives a wrong touch". Find out what experiences your school-age children have had involving sexual (rude) behaviour and point out that some rude kids grow up to become rude adults if they are not stopped.

Masturbation

It is normal for young children to touch and play with their genitals. They may do this out of curiosity, because it gives a pleasant 'tickly' feeling or they do it to relax. It is most likely to happen when they are tired, bored, anxious or upset. Disturbed young children may masturbate for comfort. Children generally understand if you tell them that it is okay to do this in the bedroom or bathroom with the door closed but we don't do it in public places (and grownups and older kids are not allowed to do it at all when children are around). Say, "You don't see Mummy doing that when we're watching TV".

Masturbation is normal when it is occasional. Usually children can be easily distracted and they learn to follow the rules regarding privacy. However, be concerned if masturbation becomes obsessive. Children may masturbate habitually when they are emotionally disturbed or have been sexually abused and are obsessed with sex. Accept that it feels nice. Ask who showed them how to do that. If that person is an adult or older child, report this to police or your child abuse report line found in the emergency section of the phone book.

Never interrogate or challenge sex offenders or the parents of juvenile offenders (regardless of whether they are members of your family). Parents of offenders invariably deny the behaviour or blame the child.

Scolding or punishing will not stop masturbation but it will cause shame and send the behaviour 'underground'. With toddlers, it is best to ignore it and use distraction. If it is still happening when a child starts school, say:

"I know it feels nice when you touch that part of your body but people usually do it when they are on their own in a private place. Why do you think that is?"

If the problem persists, seek professional help from child and youth health services.

DEVELOPING A POSITIVE BODY IMAGE

To develop a positive body image in your child, aim to develop the child's body awareness by reinforcing the fact that we own our bodies. Also, develop a positive self-image by emphasising that we are all different, have different abilities, can do different things and are valued.

Activities for young and disabled children to develop a positive body image include:

- Making fingerprints with paint or ink to demonstrate how all bodies are different.
- Using a large mirror, asking children to look at and describe their bodies in a positive way — including rear and side views. Focus them on how they use those limbs and other body parts to demonstrate how amazing the body is.

103

- Encouraging children to identify the things they can do with their bodies without help, the things they can do with help and what they would like to be able to do next. Make a record so that things they want to do can be ticked off as they achieve them.
- Creating and displaying a checklist to let children tick off the things they can do for the first time. For example, fastening buttons, putting on shoes, dressing with some assistance, dressing without assistance, cleaning teeth without help, washing hands and face well without help, bathing or showering without assistance, drying off all over without help, eating without help, throwing a ball, catching a ball, using a knife and fork, using a computer, remembering their name, remembering the house number and street where they live, remembering their suburb or town, using the toilet without help, wiping their bottom clean without help, choosing what clothes to wear, telling people how to help them, making a phone call without help, remembering emergency numbers, getting ready for bed and telling mum or dad that something is wrong.

The list can be extended to match the child's stage of development. Other related activities could be to:

- Draw the child's silhouette or body outline on a large sheet of paper and ask the child to label all the body parts, including genitals, using the correct names.
- Compare hand sizes and look at them with a magnifying glass.
- Use cut-out body shapes which provide opportunities to dress and undress males and females. These can be made or bought.
- Show which body parts the child likes to be touched and indicate the body parts that other people are not

allowed to touch, tickle and play around with, including the mouth.

- Use the opportunity to confirm that your child is the boss of his or her body.
  A useful little book that confirms this message is, *It's My Body* by Lory Freeman, published by Parenting Press. Published in the 1980s, it is available online.
- Engage in activities that draw attention to body parts such as, 'The Hokey Pokey,' 'Hands and knees,' 'Simon Says,' 'Heads, shoulders, knees and toes,' 'One finger, one thumb, keep moving,' and 'Hands, Knees and Bumps-a-daisy'.
- Draw attention to the fact that we are all different. Some people have brown eyes, some have blue. Some have brown hair, grey hair, blonde hair and some dye their hair different colours. Some are tall, some are short. No two people are exactly the same. Our bodies are all different. Your body starts at the top of your head and goes down to the end of your toes. Some of us look a bit like our mums and some look like our dads. Compare photographs. Some look like our brother or sister but no two people are exactly the same, not even identical twins. We are all different and special. And we have to take good care of our bodies. "Tell me how you take good care of yours?" Discuss *why* we do it. What would happen if we didn't wash our hair, our feet, etc.?
- Help your child to make a book called, *How We Take Care of Our Bodies,* using pictures, drawings and, if the children can't write, let them dictate to you so that you act as the recorder. Use the book for reading purposes.
- Make a book about the progress of your child. If s/he can't write, use dictation and photos for illustrations.
- Identify the different jobs that different body parts can do.
- Introduce the concept of body ownership using the song, *My Body,* by Peter Alsop.

My Body

Omit verses that are not appropriate for children with disabilities.
The chorus is repeated after each verse.

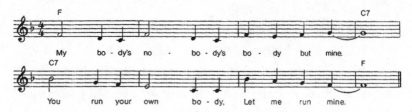

Chorus: My body's nobody's body but mine!
You run your own body
Let me run mine

My legs were made just to dance me around,
To walk and to run and to jump up and down.

My nose was made to sniff and to sneeze,
To smell what I want and to blow when I please!

My lungs were made to hold air when I breathe,
I am in charge of just how much I need!

My mouth was made to blow up a balloon,
I can eat, kiss and sing, I can whistle a tune!

My body loves me to pedal a bike,
Our bodies do just whatever we like.
Don't hit or kick me; please don't push or shove,
Don't hug me too hard when you show me your love.
When I am touched, I know how I feel,
My feelings are mine and my feelings are real.
Sometimes it is hard to say, "No," and be strong,
When a "No" or creepy feeling comes, then I know
something's wrong

My body's mine from my head to my toe,
Please leave it alone when you hear me say, "No!"
My body's mine to be used as I choose,
It is not to be threatened or forced or abused.
Secrets are fun when they are filled with surprise,
But not when they hurt us with tricks, threats and lies.

This is my body. It's one of a kind.
I've got to take care of this body of mine.

This is a very lively, popular song with words written by Peter Alsop ©1983, Moose School Music (BMI), additional lyrics by Green Thumb Theatre and reproduced by kind permission of the National Film Board of Canada on behalf of the Green Thumb Theatre People. The music has been published in the *ABC Song Book* and featured in the Rolf Harris child protection video, *Kids Can Say No.* Both are available in most libraries as well as online.

FROM FIVE TO EIGHT YEARS OF AGE

Normal sexual play around the age of 5 consists of "You show me yours and I'll show you mine", to see whether our bodies are the same as others.

Children in this age group may repeat swear words they've heard or talk about toileting using vulgar language to gauge your reaction. As they start school, they develop a sense of what is acceptable behaviour. Because they have no memory of events, most children like to hear stories about their birth and what happened when they were small.

From 5 to 8 years of age, children may continue to engage in play, driven by sexual curiosity. Boys in particular repeat off-colour jokes without necessarily understanding them. The fact that they generate a reaction is what makes this exciting.

We draw attention to sexual differences by separating boys' and girls' toilets at school. Typically, boys chase girls into their toilets to see what's happening that is different.

Sexual exploration usually involves friends of the same age. Normal sexual curiosity involves equal sharing and no coercion or threat involved.

Children aged 5 plus are aware of 'rude' behaviour and rude children. They think that:

- Rude (indecent) behaviour and rude (or dirty) talk are naughty.
- Naughty means you're bad.
- Naughty means no one will love you.
- Naughty means it is your fault and you are to blame.
- Naughty means you'll get into trouble and be punished.
- Naughty means you're unlovable.
- Naughty means you have to keep it secret.

Without information to the contrary, children think they can't tell you about sexual misbehaviour because it involves 'rude talk' and they'll get into trouble for that. And if someone tells them to keep sexual misbehaviour a secret, they have to comply. They think that if they tell their mum that someone behaved sexually, she will tell their abuser. They believe they will then be punished twice over: first by their mum for the rude talk and then by the abuser for telling the secret. Therapists have long wondered why victims of child sexual abuse blame themselves. Self-blame for other people's sexual misbehaviour is well established from early childhood. This inhibits the reporting of sex offences.

It is not enough to ask children to tell you if someone touches them inappropriately. They need to know what constitutes inappropriate touching and know **from experience** that you can cope with information without getting upset.

OVER EIGHT YEARS OF AGE

Puberty has arrived when your child's body develops adult sexual characteristics, such as underarm and pubic hair, body odour, breasts and menstruation in girls and enlargement of the testes and penis, followed by erections, sexual fantasies and 'wet dreams' in boys. Puberty is when young people become *physically* capable of having children of their own, which, thankfully, most delay until they are older and more mature.

In your parents' youth, puberty was more likely to happen between the ages of 15 to 18 years. Now, it begins between age 8 and 12 years in girls and 9 and 14 years in boys. Child sex abuse victims sometimes experience premature puberty. When it begins before 7 to 8 years in girls and 9 in boys, it is referred to as precocious puberty. If it becomes a problem, doctors can provide hormones to delay its onset so that children's emotional and social development can catch up with their physical development.

There are some valuable, well-illustrated and amusing books available online at www.secretgb.com for both boys and girls, explaining body changes. The books, written by Fay Angelo, Heather Pritchard and Rose Stewart are:

- *Secret Girls' Business*
- *More Secret Girls' Business*
- *Special Girls' Business*
- *Puberty and Special Girls*
- *Secret Boys' Business*
- *Special Boys' Business*

The books for girls talk about menstruation and how to use sanitary protection. They emphasise that it is OK to have either large breasts or flat chests. It is important for girls to receive reassuring information about the changes that occur, as well as information relating to sexual behaviour, privacy, contraception and personal safety. Girls are helped to make the transition with dignity. There is a section for parents and another has handy hints for schools and teachers.

Special Girls' Business is about girls managing puberty when they have intellectual and physical disabilities, autism and communication disorders. The book offers a step-by-step approach with handy hints for carers and school staff. *Special Girls' Business* comes in a large format and uses engaging illustrations and clear text. Family Planning Queensland also has brochures and fact sheets available via their Internet site.

For boys, there is *Secret Boys Business,* by the same authors. This helps boys aged 10 and above to understand the changes that occur at puberty and it dispels myths and fears. It covers important issues such as erections, wet dreams and masturbation and is cleverly and amusingly illustrated. It tells boys what few dads care to discuss, but paedophiles routinely introduce. Boys need this information before puberty because their curiosity about male bodies makes them vulnerable to sex offenders. We also want them to be happy about their bodies and who they are. In addition, there is *The Big Book of Boy Stuff,* by Bart King, published by Gibbs M. Smith and Kaz Cooke's *Girl Stuff — Your Full-On Guide to the Teen Years.*

Maintain parent-child communication

Unfortunately, parent-child communications usually deteriorate when children reach adolescence. Australian research has shown that parents are both complacent and unrealistic about their contributions to their children's sex education. A study involving 98 parents and their 16-year-old children found that, while 88 percent of parents claimed to have had open discussions on sexual matters and 89 percent said they discussed safe sex and sexually transmitted diseases, their children said they were lying. When challenged, the parents said they would have answered questions if their children had initiated them.

It is important to remember that young people will never ask questions if you have avoided a sensitive subject.

A second survey of 1,800 adolescents and their parents confirmed that 81 percent of the teens had never discussed sexual matters with their fathers and 69 percent had no discussions with their mothers. La Trobe University's Professor Doreen Rosenthal confirmed that, while parents had a rosy glow about their role as sex educators, they deluded themselves about their contributions. Although we know that adolescents are likely to be sexually active, parents are hiding their heads in the sand.[24] For their own comfort, "most choose to avoid acknowledging their children's sexuality, irrespective of their age. They are too embarrassed to deal with it."

Parents deserve sympathy. They are faced with situations they've never encountered before. Most parents know nothing of sexually transmitted infections and how to discuss homosexuality with sensitivity, how to share a son's fears about being gay when they have no experience of what being gay is like. Parents clearly need help to deal with the issues that adolescents face.

Avoidance harms children and child protection efforts by sending a mystical and confusing message. On the one hand, we want open communication and encourage reporting sexual abuse. Simultaneously, by avoiding the mention of genitals, we demonstrate our inability to talk about even the simplest aspects of sexuality. The confusing message given is that, while we regard these body parts as invisible and unmentionable, our children must come to tell us immediately if someone touches them inappropriately.

Paedophiles take advantage of parents' avoidance of sexuality education. They incite victims' curiosity with sex talk and pornography. They tell children that they are providing essential information that their own parents neglected to provide, implying that the child's parents don't care enough to keep them informed. An insidious aspect of child sex abuse is that the offender systematically alienates victims from their protective parents, ensuring that children don't turn to them for help.

Differentiating between sexual curiosity and signs that the juvenile initiator has been abused

When dealing with children who initiate sexual misbehaviour that causes concern, parents and teachers often don't know the difference between normal curiosity and signs that a child is re-enacting sexual abuse and needs professional help. Sexual curiosity is when there is equal power between participants along the lines of, "You show me yours and I'll show you mine". Interest is short-lasting, participants giggle and, when caught, they are likely to be embarrassed but are easily distracted. Juvenile sex offenders are more likely to be angry and in denial, blaming the victim when caught.

Normal sexual curiosity versus indicators that a child is replicating abuse

When children exhibit sexual behaviours that are *inappropriate* for their stage of development, there are three possible reasons: they have been traumatised and are re-enacting what they experienced as victims of sexual abuse; they witnessed disturbing adult sex or sexual violence; and/or were exposed to and are re-enacting disturbing pornography.

All of the above constitute child abuse and should be reported to the child abuse report line, investigated and the perpetrator offered therapy as necessary.

It is NOT normal curiosity when a child's sexual behaviour involves:

- Demands for or offers to provide oral sex.
- The insertion of fingers, objects or a penis into anal or vaginal openings.
- Negative effects on a child's social, emotional or cognitive development.
- Coercion, intimidation, tricks, threats, secrecy, blackmail, bribes or force.
- Emotional distress.
- Targeting vulnerable children, such as children of different ages, developmental and intellectual levels (by two or more years).
- Repetition in secret, after intervention by adults.
- Obsessive behaviour at a high frequency.
- The use of adult, sexual language.
- Aggression.
- Angry, vindictive, punishing behaviour.
- Sadness and loneliness, often paired with aggressive behaviour.
- Incidents over several days or weeks.
- Sharing sexual knowledge and experiences for kudos.
- Denial when caught, with the initiator becoming abusive, angry or withdrawn.

Children who exhibit inappropriate sexual behaviours or who abuse others often live in chaotic families with histories of sexual and/or drug abuse or absent, non-functioning or violent father-figures, resulting in the children's lack of understanding of boundaries.

Normal curiosity involves:

- A limited number of behaviours, such as looking, peeking and possibly touching.
- Young participants who are easily distracted.

- Intermittent activity at age 4 to 6 years and again at 8 years.
- No age difference in participants; they are usually of a similar size and at the same stage of development.
- No coercion.
- Silliness, giggling and the activities are usually spontaneous.
- Motivation that is exploratory and sensual; they want to know how others are constructed.
- Children from any family.

Developmentally appropriate sexual behaviours to be ignored when children are younger than 5 years old include:
- Occasional masturbation for comfort, that isn't obsessive.
- Exploratory self-touching, especially in the bath.
- Uninhibited looking at or touching other children's private body parts out of curiosity.
- Intense interest in the toileting activities of others.

Problem behaviours exhibited by children younger than 5 years old may include:
- Demands for or offers to provide oral sex.
- An obsessive interest in genitals per se.
- Obsessive masturbation.
- An obsession with sex talk and sexual behaviour; the child is not easily distracted and may be angry and in denial when caught.
- Re-enactment of specific adult sexual behaviour the child has physically experienced or witnessed, using dolls, other children or animals.
- Describing sexual acts in such a way that suggests experience.
- Coercion, threats, tricks, force, secrecy, violence, aggression, blackmail.

- Targeting a younger, less informed, powerless and/or disabled child for sex.
- Threatening the targeted child to keep the behaviour secret.
- Developmentally inappropriate acts.
- Asking the target if s/he likes what s/he is doing.
- Producing sexually explicit drawings.

Developmentally appropriate sexual behaviours exhibited by children aged 6 to 10 years include:

- Genital or reproduction conversations with peers or similar age siblings.
- Telling dirty jokes.
- Isolated incidents of peeping, genital exposure.
- Continuing to fondle and touch own genitals and masturbate (but not excessively).
- Playing at doctors and nurses, involving undressing.
- Becoming more secretive about self-touching.
- The interest in other children's bodies becomes more game playing than exploratory curiosity (e.g., "I'll show you mine if you show me yours.").
- Lifting a dress and tugging at pants to pull them down.
- Comparing penis size with other boys.
- An extreme interest in toilet activities, sex, sex words and dirty jokes.
- By the age of 10, the child is seeking information about bodily functions.

Problematic sexual behaviour by children of 6 to 10 years may include:

- Re-enactment of specific adult sexual behaviour the child has physically experienced or witnessed, replicated with dolls, other children or animals or teaching others how to do it.

- Exposing a precocious sexual knowledge beyond what is normal for their stage of development.
- Simulating intercourse or foreplay with dolls or peers under or over clothing.
- Sexual graffiti — often deliberately brought to the adult's attention.
- The frequent use of sexual innuendo.
- Interest in pornography.
- Demands for sexual activity involving coercion, force, threats, tricks, secrecy, violence, aggression and blackmail, to gain compliance.
- The child targeting a younger, less informed, powerless and/or disabled child to provide sex.
- Bullying others into committing sexual acts while watching.
- The child threatening the targeted child to keep the behaviour secret.
- Producing sexually explicit or other significant drawings.
- Obsessive preoccupation with genitals, masturbation, sex talk or other sexual behaviour; is not easily distracted and may be angry and in denial when caught.
- Sexual penetration of a child using fingers, objects or a penis.
- Genital or open mouth/tongue kissing.
- Demanding, offering or forcing a child to provide oral sex.
- Asking or forcing another child to masturbate him.
- Simulated or attempted intercourse.
- Demonstrating to other children how to have sex.
- Asking the target child if s/he likes it (i.e., being touched sexually).
- Using adult, sexual language.
- Sexually explicit conversations among others of significant age differences.

- Sexually explicit proposals or threats, including the use of written notes or text messages.
- Inducing fear with threats of force to commit sexual acts on another child.
- Using tricks, bribes or blackmail.
- Evidence of genital or anal bleeding not attributable to accidental causes.

Children who have learned that they have to behave sexually to please adults may also behave in a sexually provocative manner with adults who are the same sex as their abusers; most notably, abused girls may touch a male teacher's crotch.

Developmentally normal sexual behaviours for children aged 10 to 12 years of age include:

- Sexual conversations with peers and/or dirty jokes within age-related norms.
- Solitary masturbation.
- A focus on establishing relationships with peers.
- Sexual behaviour with peers, e.g., kissing, holding hands, sexual innuendo and flirting.
- Identifying someone as a boyfriend or girlfriend.
- Primarily heterosexual activity but not exclusively; boys may compare genitals and erections and demonstrate ejaculation with friends.
- An interest in bodies, particularly those of the opposite sex.
- Interest in sexual graffiti.
- Seeking sexual information from the Internet.

Problematic sexual behaviour for the 10 to 12-year age group primarily includes:

- Any sexual activity with children who are younger, disabled or less informed.

- Violating the personal space of others, e.g., touching breasts, lifting skirts or pulling pants down or exposing themselves ('flashing') to others.
- A chronic preoccupation with sexual matters and sex talk.
- Downloading or making pornography using mobile phones.
- "Mooning" and making obscene gestures.
- Injury to the genitals of others.
- Sexual activity with children of any age that involves anal or vaginal penetration, coercion, tricks, force, bribery, aggression, animals or secrecy or involves a substantial peer or age difference, which should be considered highly problematic and warrants serious attention. Perpetrators usually lack empathy for victims and lack an understanding of sexual boundaries.

TABLE 1:
THE SEXUAL BEHAVIOURS OF ADOLESCENTS

Normal behaviour	Problematic behaviour
Masturbation in private	Obsessive masturbation, exhibitionism, masturbation in public
Sexual arousal	Voyeurism
Sexual attraction to others	Stalking and/or sadism, sexual aggression
Consensual touching of genitals	Groping/forced touching of genitals
Consensual sexual intercourse	Sexual assault, rape, coercion used
Consensual oral sex	Coercive oral sex

Normal behaviour	Problematic behaviour
Behaviour that contributes to positive relationships	Behaviour that isolates the adolescent and is destructive to relationships
	Sex with animals (bestiality).
	Obscene phone calls, sexual harassment
	Any sexual behaviour with younger or less informed (e.g., disabled) children
	Touching, pinching, grabbing or rubbing against someone in a sexual way
	Creating or distributing pornography, e.g., using mobile phones
	Persistent sexual behaviour after being rejected

It should be noted that most of the problematic behaviours of adolescents listed here are, in fact, reportable crimes.

The assessment and treatment of sexual misbehaviours calls for careful attention to a number of considerations, including the nature of the behaviour; the methods used to gain the victim's compliance; evidence of premeditation and planning; the perpetrator's history of inappropriate behaviours or obsession with sexual matters; age and developmental differences between victims and their perpetrators; the nature of the relationship with the two, if any; the level of coercion or aggression used; the power differential between perpetrator and target child; and the effects or likely effects on the victim in relation to where the incident(s) occurred. For example, if at home or on school premises, this may suggest that the perpetrator is re-enacting his or her own experiences of abuse and other incidents, involving the same or different children/young people.

Responding to sexual play

Adults typically react emotionally when they see children engaging in sexual activities. Angry responses create feelings of shame, guilt and confusion. Try not to be dramatically reactive. Stay calm and casually enquire, "Who showed you how to play that game? Where did you play it (or see it played)? Who else plays with you? Are you pretending you're grown up now?" Instead of showing disapproval, this is the ideal opportunity to gather information.

If you discover that an older person has engaged or tried to engage your child or another in sexual activity or that someone has shown your child pornography, avoid upsetting the victim; however, this should be reported immediately to the police child sex abuse unit or paedophile task force.

When raising children, you need to discuss issues of personal safety and privacy with them and set limits as to what is and isn't acceptable.

When you find children pretending to be nurses and doctors, stay calm and say, "I see you're examining your friend just like a doctor does, but your penis (or vagina) is private and pants must be kept on when you're playing at hospitals. If you want to know what a boy/girl's body looks like, we can find some pictures and look together." (See Briggs and McVeity's *Teaching children to protect themselves,* published by Allen and Unwin, Sydney or Briggs' *Developing personal safety skills in children with disabilities,* published by Jessica Kingsley, London.)

Note: Never confront a juvenile abuser's parents because they will typically defend their child. It is also possible that the abuser was abused by a family member, including a parent. If you suspect that the other child is being sexually molested, report it to your local police paedophile unit or child abuse report line. You are guaranteed confidentiality. If unreported and the matter is ignored, there is a possibility that the perpetrator will continue to abuse children.

Responding to swearing and sex jokes

Young children repeat what they hear. They show off to friends or deliberately shock you to test your reactions; it's a natural part of learning by testing boundaries. Unless it happens often, it is best ignored. If it continues, calmly discuss with them what the words mean and why they are considered offensive. Dirty jokes lose their appeal when you say, "Oh, I heard that when I was at school."

When children approach puberty, swearing may be an expression of frustration or a way of demonstrating their newfound "maturity" to peers. A sense of belonging is important but, if swearing is excessive or distressing, you may need to negotiate guidelines, such as confining this language to when they are with like-minded friends. It is important that children don't associate anger with sex. Help them to identify what is making them angry and discuss healthy ways of responding. Encourage the expression of emotions.

If you don't want children to swear in school or their early childhood centre, don't swear in their hearing. When children are reprimanded for swearing at school, they often say, "Well, my Dad says it." In 2007, New Zealand's child protection services distributed a t-shirt, which said, "If you want your children to behave — behave yourself."

When boys dress up in girls' clothes

Young children enjoy dressing up to act out roles. Young boys and girls will dress up in women's clothes, teeter around in high heels and carry handbags in an effort to understand what it feels like to be their mother. This is harmless and rarely indicates sexual identity issues. It is good to have play clothes available for both boys and girls so that they can have fun and practice make-believe. When they dress up as cops or Indian chiefs, they gain a sense of power that isn't available to them in real life.

Communicating about sexuality

Sexuality education is not about reproduction; it is about our bodies. It can be uncomfortable to talk to kids about sexual matters and how they were conceived. After all, we remember being shocked when we first learned that our own parents did *that* at least once to conceive us. Adolescents view sex as the purview of their own generation and are repulsed by the thought of older people "doing it."

Talking about sexuality includes talking about bodies and body privacy, growing up, being a boy or girl, relationships and being a family, as well as being safe. It is about showing children that we are happy and willing to talk to them because they are important to us. With adolescents, we need to talk not only about relationships but, even more important, the intense feelings that accompany them.

Some parents hand their children books to read when they reach puberty, but by that time, it is much too late. We want kids to be positive about their bodies as they grow. We must remember that our children live in a new world of commercialised sex, where inappropriate messages are picked up daily from an early age via TV, the Internet, magazines, music, advertising, mobile phones and friends. It is important that children receive positive messages to counteract these potentially negative ones.

Kids recognise the benefits of communicating openly about sexual matters and will do this with someone else if they can't do it with you. This makes them vulnerable to predators, as well as receiving faulty information.

Children who receive comprehensive, positive, sexuality education from an early age are most likely to understand and confidently accept their physical and emotional changes, feel positive about their bodies, appreciate and accept individual differences and make informed, responsible sexual decisions later in life. They are also more likely to feel good about themselves as males or females, communicate about sex matters, differentiate between appropriate and inappropriate behaviour and be less vulnerable to exploitation, sexual abuse, STIs and unwanted pregnancies, especially those children with learning disabilities.

Won't information spoil a child's innocence?

This question is often asked and stems from the belief that information about our bodies is dirty, wrong and somehow spoils childhood. We confuse ignorance with innocence.

Children who are well informed about their bodies are more confident and more likely to resist abusers who try to tap into their curiosity. This is especially so when children have intellectual disabilities. Well-informed youngsters are also the least likely to view their bodies as shameful.

The second most frequent question is, "Won't they experiment if I talk to them about sexual matters?" No. In fact, the opposite is true. International research has shown consistently that those countries and states, which banned sex education in schools, had the highest number of unwanted teenage pregnancies (e.g., New York City). Young people who received effective sexuality education were the ones most likely to delay sexual intercourse and subsequently use contraception. Information can protect innocence.

WHEN DO I START SEXUALITY AND CHILD PROTECTION EDUCATION?

Now!

Children learn from the ways in which we relate to our partners, whether they're affectionate, respectful, thoughtful or otherwise. They learn from how we touch, speak and play with them. With preschool children, it is easy to start at bath and bedtimes. These are intimate times when you have the opportunity to talk about privacy and they can learn to dry the special private parts of their bodies that bigger people are not allowed to touch or play with. It is much harder to start discussing sexual matters when children are older. If you feel embarrassed, admit that to them, pointing out that no one ever talked to you about such things when you were young but that you wish they had. Instead, you had to find out from your friends and they often gave you wrong information. Your children will respect your honesty.

Answering questions

If your child asks questions, consider yourself lucky. If you don't have the answers, to gain more time say, "That's an excellent question. What made you think of that? Let's look up the answers together". Give just enough information to satisfy their curiosity. Seek clarification from them when their questions are unclear. Take the cues from your child. Don't overload and give them more information than they can handle or want.

Susan was a mother discussing basic sex education with her 7-year-old son, Peter. He yawned and said, "Mum can I ask you a question?"

Susan assumed he wanted to know how he'd been conceived. Instead, he asked, "What makes my eyelids flutter up and down?"

On another occasion, in order to dispel the myth that Peter had been purchased from a hospital — he had been born at home — Susan turned on the TV. The BBC was broadcasting an excellent TV sex education series for children.

"Not that boring sex stuff again," groaned Peter. "Will I ever have to get pregnant?" Susan smiled.

"No, but your wife might."

"Then I don't need to know about it," he grumbled and changed the programme. Peter now has four children.

Kids will only take in as much as they can understand and want to know. They switch off when they reach information overload. Listen and ask questions. Don't talk *at* them.

Giving factual information is important but children also benefit from discussions about feelings, values and attitudes. Say what you believe and why, without dictating what they should do or think. As children mature, let them know that there is a range of beliefs about sexual issues and when they are older they will have choices. Say that many people choose to wait until they are married to have sex because they want to share their bodies with someone they love and with whom they want to have children. Others wait until they feel sufficiently mature and have found someone they feel safe and happy with. Point out that girls and boys who engage in sex with lots of people, especially when they don't use contraception, not only lose everyone's respect but they risk sexually transmitted diseases. Girls also risk unwanted pregnancies, while boys find themselves saddled with paying child support for the next 18 years.

As children approach puberty, encourage them to compare different options, opinions, benefits, advantages versus disadvantages and consequences. Some girls (and boys) think they have to offer oral sex to boys to be 'hot' and accepted by their peer group. It can happen at parties, under desks at lunchtime and at recess. Given that girls are merely being used and there is no pleasure in it for them (and there are hygiene and emotional factors involved), the topic of peer group pressure should be discussed. As indicated in Chapter 3 oral sex also features in the bullying of both boys and girls, often via text messages.

Some youngsters worry that they will be viewed as unattractive because they are still virgins at the age of 15; some girls brag that they are pregnant when they are not because they think this gives them status. Some who feel unloved get pregnant because they naïvely think that the child will love them and government handouts will make them rich. Others

125

who are not succeeding at school have motherhood as their only goal because it will provide an income and government housing. Quite frequently, girls assume their mothers will take care of any unwanted children they conceive. It is important to open up conversations with your teens to find out what is happening in their world and understand the pressures young people face.

At 12-plus years, some girls engage in unprotected sex because boys say they don't like condoms and girls lack the confidence to assert themselves. They do whatever the boys demand because they want to be popular. Our research has shown consistently that boys don't relate sex to pregnancy and they don't understand the possible long-term consequences of being adolescent fathers. Girls on the other hand frequently proclaim that if they become pregnant, it is their mother's responsibility to care for the child. If your sons or daughters are sexually active, it is imperative that they use contraception for their own protection. This is especially important if the girls drink alcohol because of the risk that a child could be born with foetal alcohol syndrome that severely damages development.

Many parents avoid discussing sex, convinced that schools will take responsibility. Whether we like it or not, we are our children's primary sexuality educators. Furthermore, school sex education is often inadequate; it needs to be part of a cooperative effort with families. Studies show there is a mismatch between school curriculum and the experiences of young people and that many schools lack comprehensive programmes at all. Lessons seldom address relationships and how to negotiate and make decisions about whether or not to have sexual intercourse.

Some parents emphasise abstinence or, at the opposite extreme, encourage sexual freedom, allowing youngsters to sleep together without first discussing with them all the possible ramifications. In adolescence, friends influence most decisions for good or ill and they fill the gaps left by schools and parents. Unfortunately, friends are unreliable informants and can be a dangerous influence. It is important for parents to press for comprehensive sexuality and relationships education in schools so that teachers, families and communities can work together to help address children's fundamental needs. Our children need to know that we care about them, want them to be safe and make healthy life decisions. The issues of sexuality will not go away no matter how long we ignore them.

Whether we like it or not, adolescents are sexually active

Ninety percent of participants in a 2006 Australian study were sexually active by the age of 18, with half of the boys and a third of the girls having had sex by the age of 16. A staggering 32 percent of these girls experienced sexual assault. Experiences of first-time sex were characterised by disappointment and regret. Casual sex, one night stands or 'hooking up' were common among 64 percent of participants. In these encounters, alcohol was a key factor, there was little discussion between the parties, going home with someone implied consent to sex, sex always meant intercourse and establishing boundaries rarely involved saying no.

Casual sex was mostly about the act, not the person. For boys, the self-described "going wild" and sexual gratification were the keys. For girls, not knowing their sexual partner inhibited their ability to define what was happening. There was no negotiating about what was or wasn't okay. Few could recall anything in their school sex education that was relevant to complexity of their lives. Lessons were biological and didn't deal with violence in relationships. At best, they mentioned contraceptives. Mixed classes prevented participants from freely discussing issues of sexual intimacy.

Young people said they wanted to know about:

- *Communication:* how to communicate effectively with potential sexual partners.
- *Consent*: how to handle the grey area between yes and no. ("No means no" is not enough.)
- *Gender and relationships:* how they impact on sexual intimacy; male violence. Girls need to know that the male sex drive doesn't necessarily imply romance or that they are even attracted to the partner. Girls need to understand the possible dangers of flirting and behaving sexually in unsafe environments. Boys need to know how to resist aggressive girls seeking sex while maintaining their own and the girls' self respect, i.e., when their bodies are interested but their minds give a different message.
- *Ethical intimacy*: maintaining self respect in sexual relationships — reflecting on expectations before situations arise, increasing awareness about choices; values involved in boundary setting, the effects of alcohol and drugs on decisions, resisting pressures to "go the whole way" when sexual intimacy has begun and issues relating to male sexuality.
- *Challenging violence*: addressing sexual assault in an informed way. Girls, even university students, naïvely think they can change their boyfriends' violent behaviour. They dismiss it as "he's just frustrated and it will stop when we're married," when violence is actually more likely to increase after the wedding.
- *Education:* on sex, intimacy and sexual violence, which should start in school at Year 7. Education on bodies, growing up and being safe should start much sooner.

Sexologist Bettina Arndt (2008)[25] confirms that current youth culture makes it easy for adolescents to behave sexually irresponsibly. She says that oral sex is 'common-place' and widely expected by young males. She describes it as the young generation's equivalent to the goodnight kiss of their grandparents. Boys demand it and girls are pushed into providing it because they think, mistakenly, that it will increase their power and popularity in the peer-group. Younger boys are also pressured into cooperating because they are afraid of violent retribution if they resist.

Despite more than 30 years of feminist lobbying and demands for equal opportunity, double standards and expectations about male sexual entitlement and female acquiescence persist, preventing young people from negotiating sexual encounters. They continue to report gender inequality. Girls need to know that labelling has not changed. While promiscuous boys are identified as 'studs', girls are still labelled as 'sluts', 'slags' or 'whores' when they engage in casual sex. Furthermore, young people often participate because they want to be viewed as popular, *not* because they enjoy it. This is especially true among girls who offer sex to boys they scarcely know.

Julie Richters, author of *Doing It Down Under* says that we have a generation of young people who have grown up thinking they have the right to do whatever they like. They don't have a mother's voice in their heads telling girls about physical safety with males. She said, "They (girls) get drunk and randy and do silly things, like going into the toilet with males. It's like accepting a lift with someone you don't know; once you are in their car, they are in control. They've got all the power." Richters said that the greatest danger for girls is not 'catching the clap' but being sexually assaulted. There is a point where girls think 'they'd better go through with this' because if they try to stop it they will be in big trouble. There is an abuse of power that is rarely reported [26].

If you help your children to develop confidence in their own values, they will be more likely to stand up for their rights and beliefs and be assertive when necessary. Help children to develop decision-making skills by encouraging them to identify and consider their choices. They won't always make the right decisions but we all learn by our mistakes. Most important is to tell your children that you love them and credit them with their efforts, talents and accomplishments. If you believe in them, you help them to believe in themselves. They are then less likely to engage in meaningless sex in a vain search for love and approval.

Discussing homosexuality

Some sex education programmes promote the normality of homosexuality, bi-sexuality and anal sex. They aim to reduce homophobia, which is rife in boys' groups. Programme writers argue that this is necessary because gay boys are vulnerable to bullying, ostracism, self-destructive behaviours and suicide.

There is a downside to this, however. They don't take into account the common ploy used by paedophiles to convince boys that they are being sexually abused because they are gay and, therefore, the abuse is their own fault. Boys are easily convinced of this when their bodies respond to sexual touching, as can happen even when the incident is unwelcome. Confusion about their sexuality then silences them and causes even greater psychological problems, including the risk of suicide in adolescence.

A second factor is that a young person may develop a crush on someone of the same sex as part of their normal development before they take an interest in the opposite sex. That doesn't make them gay or lesbian. It is important that young people know that if they are attracted to someone of the same sex, opposite sex or both, it is OK and that you care and will talk to them and help them to feel safe and valued.

While some boys may be born gay, far more will be confused about their sexuality because they were abused. They need to know that boys are not chosen for abuse because they are gay but because they are young, uninformed and powerless.

Furthermore, it is normal for boys' bodies to respond to being touched, regardless of the circumstances.

Sexual response needs to be addressed in education programmes to help relieve the stress that many victims feel. In adolescence, confused, male abuse victims may experiment with gay men, often disastrously because they place themselves back in the victim role. As adults, they are likely to become angry as they realise that they are not gay but were simply tricked.

The effects of commercialised sex on children and young people

In recent years, children and young adolescents have been presented as mini-adults in sexually provocative poses, wearing sexually provocative clothing in advertisements, girls' magazines, most forms of media including TV programmes, music, lyrics, movies, video games and the Internet. From an early age, girls receive messages about how they should look and behave. They learn that what matters is how hot or sexily they behave and dress. They are also surrounded by powerful, indirect messages, through the widespread use of sex in movies, TV programmes and advertising targeted at adults.

Sex is being inappropriately and prematurely imposed on children. The messages are encouraging the sexualisation of girls long before they are emotionally and physically ready for sexual relationships.

Leading department stores sell mini-bras for preschoolers and skirts for young adolescent girls that scarcely cover their buttocks. Girls as young as age 10 dress provocatively to parade along the main streets of major towns and cities late at night, seemingly oblivious of the risks they take.

Six-year-old girls are said to be demanding birthday 'pamper parties' with manicures, pedicures and facial masks. A beauty technician told Adelaide media that she was overwhelmed by the number of bookings. Services include temporary tattoos, manicures and pedicures, chocolate facials, strawberry honey facials, hair braiding, hair styling 'for the evening' and flat-ironing hair, assuming that nothing looks less sexy on a kid than wavy hair. Some children's toys have a sexualising effect too; for example, some dolls and makeup kits promote an adult, sexy appearance.

The values implicit in these images are that physical appearance and being sexy are intrinsic to self-esteem and success and they are the values to aspire from a very early age, to the exclusion of other qualities.

The American Psychological Association's Task Force on the sexualisation of girls (2007)[27] showed that the cumulative exposure of children to sexualised images has the following negative effects:

Cognitive issues

Girls learn to view themselves and their bodies as sex objects. This reduces their ability to concentrate, whereby schooling can be adversely affected.

Mental health problems

Depression, low self-esteem and eating disorders, especially in girls, can occur when sexual objectification destroys confidence in and comfort with their bodies, leading to a range of negative, emotional consequences. They feel despondent and rejected because they don't fulfil the expectations of sexiness of their peer group. Young people in Australia need to know that they can call Beyond Blue (1300 224 636), Kids Helpline (1800 551 800) and Lifeline (13 1114) if they feel depressed. Specialising in suicide prevention, The Samaritans is a world-wide organisation that offers a telephone and email service and operates from Tasmania, Western Australia and throughout New Zealand and the UK.

Identity development, attitudes and beliefs

The message that young people are receiving is that it doesn't matter what they do; it is only their appearance that counts and if they don't look and behave as sex objects, they will be neither popular nor successful. This possibly accounts for girls offering oral sex indiscriminately to boys at parties and even at school; there is no sexual pleasure in it for them but they mistakenly feel they must do this to be accepted.

Generally, societal effects include an increase in sexism and disrespect for women as a whole, fewer girls pursuing careers, increased rates of sexual harassment, unwanted pregnancies, sexually transmitted infections and sexual violence (as youths and young men, through pornography and the media, are led to believe that this is what girls want). In various media, sexual aggression in males is often presented as manliness and females are presented as responding with instant orgasms. Research now shows that viewing sexual aggression adversely affects male attitudes, producing little, if any, self-censure for their own sexually aggressive acts.

The Australian Psychological Society (2008)[28] suggested that a number of strategies were needed to counter the insidious and gradual effects of child sexualisation. First, the media can play a pro-social role in promoting positive role models. Second, parents should lodge formal complaints about advertisements, billboards and programmes that present inappropriate role models. Third, parents can help girls to develop a positive self-image to counter less desirable influences.

While boys can sometimes be the target of sexualised messages, worry about their bodies and suffer from eating disorders, girls are portrayed in a sexual manner far more frequently.

Parents can teach girls to value themselves for who they are, rather than how they look. If you have sons, you can teach them to value girls as friends and sisters rather than as sex objects. And you can advocate for change with manufacturers, politicians and media producers. The Australian Psychological Society provides the following tips:

Tune in and talk. Watch TV and movies with your children. Read their magazines. Look at the websites they are viewing and at their social networking pages. Ask questions to make them think about why there is so much pressure on girls to look like sexy adults. What do they like most about the girls they want to spend time with? Do these qualities matter more than how they look? What do they think of the different roles that are usually assigned to boys and girls? Are they portrayed fairly? Discuss current peer group influences. Really listen to what your kids are saying.

Question their choices. Girls who are overly concerned about their appearance often have difficulty focusing on other things. If your daughter wants to wear something that is inappropriately sexy, ask what she likes about it. What doesn't she like about it? Is she dressing to please herself, the boys or her girlfriends? What messages are girls giving when their skirts reveal their panties as well as their midriff? If it's a consideration, talk about being sun-smart, given that there's nothing sexy about getting skin cancer.

Speak up. If you think a TV show, CD, DVD or clothing is inappropriate, explain why. A conversation with children about the issue will be more effective than simply switching off or banning the product. Don't put your old TV in your child's bedroom because that prevents you from monitoring what is watched. Support campaigns, companies and products that promote positive images of girls. Complain to manufacturers, advertisers, television and movie producers and retail stores when products sexualise children. Encourage children to complain, too.

Try to see it their way. Young people often feel pressured to watch popular TV shows, play the same games, listen to the music their friends like and conform to certain styles of dress. Help your daughter make wise choices among the trendy alternatives. Remind her that what she can accomplish is far more important than how she looks. Highlight successful women who don't look like pop stars and point out the pop stars who quickly faded from the screen. But keep in mind that dress can be an important social code for girls. Girls really care about their looks because they can provide a more obvious and tangible way to compare, contrast and belong. Other personal qualities are less reliable as a way to evaluate self and others. After all, young people change so much at this time that their personalities and values can fluctuate and be unpredictable. Looks are more predictable, so it is not surprising that they consume so much time and attention.

Find out why your daughter wishes to look a certain way. Instead of making judgments, ask whether her choice of clothes and accessories sexualise her and give a wrong message. Understand that looking different and reacting against a parent's generation is a part of growing up. You might not like what she wears, but she may not stand out when with friends at a time when most kids don't want to be seen as different.

Encourage. Sports, music and other extracurricular activities emphasise talents, skills and abilities over physical appearance and help develop self-confidence. Encourage your daughter to discover and pursue her interests. Find ways to celebrate being female — a special lunch, a girls' day out or flowers can mark when a girl gets her first period.

Educate. You may feel uncomfortable discussing sexuality with your kids, but it is important. Talk about when you think sex is OK as part of a healthy, intimate, mature relationship. Ask why girls often try so hard to look and act sexy. What is in it for them? What are the risks? Effective sex education involves discussion of media, peers and cultural influences on sexual behaviours and decisions, how to make safe choices and what makes healthy relationships. Find out what your school teaches so that you can follow up on what she is learning about at school. Let the school know if you think there are gaps in what they are teaching.

One way to open a discussion about sex without lecturing (which a lot of youngsters hate) is to say something along the lines of, "I've realised I don't really know what your values are about sex, etc. and I'm really interested in what you think". It is easier to discuss your values if you have listened to their's first; and easier for them to hear what you have to say when they know you are willing to listen. It is often surprising how conservative they really are!

Provide healthy role models. Marketing and the media also influence adults. Parents need to be careful before talking about diets or passing comments on their own weight and body image (e.g., "Do I look fat in this?"). It can be more helpful to talk about healthy eating and to show children that health is related to more than just weight. Try not to criticise your children about how they look; this can create an unhealthy attitude towards their appearance.

Male carers and fathers can be important in the development of a girl's self-image and in their son's attitudes towards females. The way men treat and talk about both women in the family and women in general is a powerful model for how sons will behave with their own children and how girls expect males to behave towards them.

Encouraging children to find healthy heroes is also important. People who are perceived as heroes today are often viewed as such for shallow, superficial reasons, because they are rich, handsome or thin, rather than because they have demonstrated positive values. Who does your child admire and why? Draw attention to positive role models. This helps your child to understand how people demonstrate real worth in the world.

Be real. Without nagging, help your kids to focus on what's really important: what they think, feel and value. Help them build strengths that will allow them to achieve their goals and develop into healthy adults. Remind your children that everyone is unique and that it is unfair to judge people solely by their appearance.

Maintain a balance. Try to take advantage of opportunities that arise in conversations, but do not become too preoccupied with all the experimentation your child tries through dress or mannerisms. Sometimes adults see sexual references that mean nothing to young children. Remember that it is your example and values that your children will likely imitate. Remember, too, that, despite differences, maintaining a good relationship with your children is paramount.[29]

Discuss program contents and advertisements; encourage children to think about the messages that advertisers or scriptwriters are trying to give. Ask them why they think these subliminal messages are being given. What might be the effect on kids? You can help to make sexualisation messages more visible by pointing them out and discussing them. You can counteract these in many ways by teaching children to value themselves for their qualities rather than how they look and by pointing out people who have succeeded without being sex symbols. Boys can be taught to respect and value girls, including sisters, as friends and not sex objects.

Useful information on the promotion of sound, sexual health is readily available on the Internet and from government health and parenting services. Ideally, this should be read by both parents and children and discussed freely.

Chapter 5

What You Need To Know About Child Sexual Abuse

INTRODUCTION

C hild sexual abuse is a secret epidemic that should concern all parents and adults who care about children and the future of society. A staggering number are affected by sexual crimes every day in every community; all children are vulnerable by virtue of their innocence.

Western governments accept that at least one in every three to four children are sexually abused before they leave school. A 2007 study[30] found that almost half of all Australian girls experienced some form of sexual abuse in childhood. University of Melbourne psychiatrist Dr. William Glaser[31] who works with both child sex abuse victims and offenders leaves us in no doubt that child sex crimes have reached plague proportions — a plague that has been largely ignored. It presents a serious health and social issue because victims are 16 times more likely than others to experience mental illness, self-destructive behaviour and suicide, as well as drug dependency and alcoholism. The majority of prisoners have been victims of abuse. The majority of drug abusers use drugs to hide the pain left by childhood experiences; drugs relate to further child abuse and other crimes. Dr. Glaser suggests that the effects of child sexual abuse are more devastating and more widespread than any other health problems that take up community resources: road accidents, heart disease and AIDS, for example.

A massive Australian survey of the medical records of those over 60 years of age demonstrated that childhood victims suffered more physical and mental illnesses than patients who had not been abused in childhood; and the negative effects are long-lasting.

Child sexual abuse is the most secret, prevalent, underreported, least acted upon and least punished crime, despite the horrendous damage it causes in the lives of its victims. When you become involved in child protection, you are helping to make the entire community a safer and healthier place.

Yes, you can make a difference

Knowledge is power and knowledge is crucial to the protection of children. Learn to recognise the signs and symptoms of abuse and the signals that children give.

Learn how sex offenders operate and how they gain the trust of everyone who has responsibility for the safety of children, especially their parents. Trust your gut feelings and what you see and hear. Have the courage to report suspicions as well as evidence that offences have been committed.

Bear in mind that it takes a massive amount of courage for a child to report abuse to an adult. It is said that, on average, children will disclose what's happening to up to 12 different people before anyone believes them and takes action. Make sure that you listen to children so that you don't miss the signals that they are victims. Adults have to give children a voice to help them to break the silence and escape from abuse. Few parents or professionals are adequately informed, largely because abuse makes us feel uncomfortable and we'd rather not know about it. Abusers use that to their advantage. To protect children adequately we have to put our own feelings aside. You can help by knowing the facts and by giving children the information they need to stay safe and by lobbying the politicians who make the laws and allocate funding to services.

UNDERSTANDING WHAT CONSTITUTES CHILD SEXUAL ABUSE

Children can be sexually abused by adults or other children in schools, early childhood centres, churches, Scouts and other social venues, in public toilets, sports changing rooms, clubs, in groups and, most frequently, around the home by someone in the family circle.

The United Nations Convention on the Rights of the Child defines *child* as someone below 18 years.

Abuse can include:

- *Voyeurism.* The teacher who hides a camera in the toilets, the carer who undresses a child unnecessarily and offenders who persuade boys to masturbate for payment, using webcams and the Internet, are just some examples.
- *Exhibitionism.* An example would be the youth or adult who exposes himself outside a school or in the park. Internet offenders frequently send images of their erect penises by email to children they meet in chat rooms.
- *Sexual harassment.* This includes sexual comments and suggestive behaviours. This is especially common when children enter Internet chat rooms unsupervised. Some secondary school students have complained of teachers engaging in this behaviour. Harassment usually precedes abuse, especially when young people are on campouts, home-stays and overseas exchanges. If the child is unable to put a halt to sexual harassment at the outset, it can escalate to abuse.
- *Showing pornography to a child.* Using the Internet, photos, videos, films or magazines, child molesters use pornography to stimulate the curiosity of targeted

victims (especially boys), to desensitise them to deviant sex and to present it as normal. "Look, they make videos/publish magazines. Everyone does it. It's fun. Why don't we do it?"

- *Deliberately exposing a child to adults engaged in sexual acts.* This often happens in homes where drugs and alcohol are involved.
- *Contact abuse.* This includes, for example, stroking or kissing breasts of both boys and girls and genital or anal touching.
- *Masturbating.* Doing this in the presence of a child or getting the child to masturbate.
- *Penetration of vagina or anus.* Using an object, finger or penis.
- *Providing or demanding oral sex.*
- *Involving children in the production of pornography.*
- *Involving children in prostitution.*
- *Requiring children to perform sex acts.* Offenders have children perform sexual acts on each other, either for pornography purposes or for the sexual gratification of the controlling adult.
- *Torture and terrorism.* Sexually-related acts designed to terrorise, torture and degrade children, sometimes involving bondage, urination, defecation or Satanism.
- *Bestiality.* This involves having children engage in sexual acts with animals.

In Western countries, a child's willingness to participate in sexual activity with an adult or older youth is not acceptable as an abuser's defence in a criminal court. This is because children lack the maturity and knowledge needed to make *informed* decisions about participation and it is the adult's responsibility to provide protection.

INCEST

Incest is defined as sexual activity between persons who are related by blood and may not legally marry. When adults use their own children, grandchildren or other close relatives and when siblings use younger brothers and sisters for sex, it constitutes a serious crime, not just from a legal standpoint but because family members possess a unique position of authority and trust, which is breached by the commission of these acts. Incestuous parents engage in role reversal whereby the child must remain silent to protect both the parent from prosecution and the family from breaking up. That responsibility is psychologically damaging. Incest is also banned because of the very high risk that children conceived in these relationships will be born with genetic defects and disabilities.

Sibling incest usually involves an adolescent who uses innocent siblings, male or female, for sex. Children with intellectual disabilities are especially vulnerable. When they are abused by older brothers or sisters, they are also likely to be victimised by the sibling's friends.

Sibling incest is substantially underreported and its prevalence and seriousness underestimated, although it is potentially just as violent and damaging as adult abuse, especially when the offender is defended and the crime minimised by the victim's parents. If, as a parent, you find your child or know of another victim of this traumatic situation, it is critical that:

- The victim is believed and supported.
- The offender is neither protected nor defended.
- There is recognition that both victim and offender have problems that require specialist assessment and treatment as soon as possible.
- Counselling is sought for both the victim and the parents.

Typically, mothers defend their sons and dismiss serious abuse as normal curiosity. The assessor should find out whether the abuser has also been abused. Failure to believe the victim and/ or take action against the abuser is likely to damage the victim's relationship with the parent forever.

Sex abuse by teachers

Australian teachers may commit a crime if they engage in sex with students under 18 years old who are enrolled in their own schools, irrespective of whether they have them as students. This is older than the legal age of consent. Just as it is professionally unethical for a doctor or psychologist to have a sexual relationship with a patient, it is professionally unethical and a breach of trust for a teacher to have sexual contact with a student. The relationship of lecturer/teacher to student is always unequal and involves a power dynamic.

Internet offences

Most Western countries now have laws that make it a criminal offence to use cyberspace for the sexual exploitation of children. This includes sending sexual material by text, email and chat rooms or downloading child pornography.

CHILD SEX ABUSE IS A GLOBAL PROBLEM

In addition to abuse by family members and trusted adults, millions of children around the world are exploited sexually through prostitution, pornography and child sex tourism. UNICEF confirmed that, in 2005, 150 million girls and 73 million boys were known to have been forced to provide sexual intercourse or suffer other forms of sexual violence involving physical penetration at the hands of adults.[32] Although the number increases each year, most cases remain unreported. The UN attributes the increase to the Internet, which enables offenders to:

- Contact each other to reinforce their sexual attraction to children.
- Share information.
- Download, create and sell child pornography. People who download child pornography are sexually stimulated by images of babies, toddlers and children being raped and used for oral sex. Desensitised to children's feelings and needs, it is a short step to progress to offending with real children.[33]
- Find new victims easily through chat rooms, etc. In August 2005, a visiting American FBI consultant, Laura Chappell, gave journalists in Sydney a demonstration of dangers to children by signing into a chat room pretending to be a 12-year-old girl seeking a new, same age friend. Within minutes, she received six replies, every one of them from an adult male pretending to be a child. They all asked her to disclose her email address, which she did. In the privacy of email, the men quickly introduced sex. Four out of the six men were local Sydney residents. Some sent obscene images of their genitals. A 50-year-old man bragged about the advantages of sex with older men and asked if he could phone her, the next step being to arrange a meeting. "Parents are shocked when we show how easy it is for predators to access their children," Ms. Chappell said. "These men spend hours working on child victims to gain their confidence once they have established contact."[34]
- Use child pornography to convince new victims that sex with children is normal, widespread and fun.
- Randomly sending text messages, such as, "You look cute". While an adult might ignore it, a child will respond, "Who are you?" and communication begins. Once a victim is hooked, the writer typically suggests a meeting, pretending to be a same-age male or female.

LAWS RELATING TO REPORTING CHILD ABUSE

All Australian states have laws requiring certain professionals and volunteers in child-related institutions to report suspected child abuse and neglect. These usually include doctors, dentists, social workers, police, clergy, physical and mental healthcare providers, teachers and other school personnel and childcare providers. Many American states also require film developers to report suspected child sexual abuse photos. In 2008, New Zealand and the UK still lacked similar legislation. Eighteen American states, Australia's Northern Territory and Tasmania have laws requiring *any* person to report signs or suspicions of child abuse. *You would be wise to educate yourself as to the reporting laws in your state.*

You can make a report anonymously to a child abuse report line or police and confidentiality is guaranteed. The caller will be asked for the name, address, age of the child, the school attended and what caused the suspicion.

Failure to report suspected child abuse can result in you being taken to court and fined several thousand dollars, depending on in which state you live. Failure to report abuse can also result in civil liability, possibly years later, i.e., the victims can sue you for vast amounts of money if you failed to report signs or disclosures of abuse and said abuse continued as a result of your inaction. A person who reports suspected child abuse in good faith is immune from both criminal and civil liability if the report isn't substantiated.

If you make a report to a child abuse report line, keep a record of what you reported, to whom and when you reported it. If nothing happens to stop the abuse, report it again. If you are still dissatisfied, ask to speak to the duty officer or manager. If nothing happens, contact the chief executive officer of the state's child protection or child safety department and the state government minister responsible for child protection.

WHY ALL CHILDREN ARE VULNERABLE TO SEXUAL ABUSE

So, you think you don't need to concern yourself with child protection because the kids in your family aren't likely to be victims? Maybe you think you don't know anyone who would do such a thing.

That's what most parents say!

Unfortunately, all children are at risk, regardless of whether they attend elite, expensive schools or a state primary school in a deprived area. Sexual abuse can affect children of all nationalities, religions and social backgrounds.

All are vulnerable because:

- *They are powerless; they trust and depend on adults.* Sexual abuse is about power. It's about the strong controlling and manipulating the weak.
- *Young children can't assess adults' motives.* Children take people innocently at face value; they judge people as good or bad based on appearances. If they look and seem kind, they are assumed to be kind and trustworthy. Predators are often viewed as kindly when they provide treats and convince a child that they understand them and love them more than the child's own parents do.
- *Children will tolerate the most painful abuse to maintain emotionally rewarding relationships.* As adults, male victims in particular may continue to think of their paedophile/pederast abusers with affection. They say, "He was the only one who said he loved me". Until they have therapy, they don't comprehend that they were manipulated to gain their compliance for sex. It is painful to admit having been tricked and used.

147

- *We teach children that goodness involves obedience to adults.* Never say, "Be good and do as you're told" when you leave children with other people. Children will obey an abusive child-minder even when they know that what is happening is wrong. They fear that disobedience will result in the minder and parents being angry and they risk losing their parents' affection.[35]

- *Boys are especially vulnerable because of their curiosity about male bodies.* Boys' genitals are less private than girls', given that they handle them daily in school toilets and touching can be pleasurable. They are sexually aroused by the sight of other boys' erections and sexual interaction may result. Sexual peer groups have the exciting quality of belonging to a secret club. This increases opportunities for encounters with boys who have been abused, share their knowledge and persuade others to meet their abusers, who offer them money for what they are already doing. Boys think they are smart when they go along with this. They are trapped when they receive payment, cigarettes, alcohol, marijuana, pornography or other products, which are banned at home. Although current thinking is that it is OK for children to explore each other's bodies, if your pre-pubertal son is spending a lot of time quietly out of sight with others, check out what they are doing. Sexual activity should be discouraged because of the risks.

- *Sexual abuse by adults is confusing.* Children freeze when an adult introduces sex. The sight of sexually aroused male genitals and what follows shocks them. School-age children know about poorly behaved kids but don't expect adults to misbehave, given that they reprimand children for being rude. They don't know what to do and, on the first occasion, may wish to believe they were mistaken. They feel dirty and guilty for thinking that they saw what they saw. The problem is that, if the first sexual act isn't forcefully rejected, the abuser regards the child as a willing participant and the abuse escalates.

- *Sexual abuse can occur anywhere, including school toilets, changing rooms and early childhood centres.* Offenders can be adults or children.

RECOGNISING AND ADDRESSING THE SEXUAL ABUSE OF BOYS HAS BEEN NEGLECTED

We don't really know how many children are sexually abused each year, given that most crimes go unreported and statistics rely on reports. We do know that the abuse of boys is substantially underestimated because they don't recognise sexual misbehaviour as reportable or they are too embarrassed to do so. Boys are vulnerable, both as individuals and in groups and this fact has been largely ignored. This is unfortunate, considering that, when victims, boys are more likely than girls to re-enact their abuse and become victimisers.

In our Australian survey of 198 male victims of childhood abuse, 36 percent said females first introduced them to sexual activity. These were often older sisters and their friends; others were babysitters, teachers, aunts and even a grandmother. Although they didn't regard this as abuse (because it didn't hurt), their premature introduction to sex was damaging, described by some as "letting the tiger out of the cage". They became obsessed with genitals, couldn't concentrate at school and were punished for sexual misbehaviour with other children. Their sexual experience was reflected in their body language, which male predators recognised; they were then abused again and again. The 198 boys were each abused by an average of 8.6 different offenders! Only 26 boys attempted to report one offender. Twenty-five were rejected and even punished. Only one was successful and his abuser wasn't prosecuted. Thus, 1,702 child sex offenders got away with committing their crimes and, without a doubt, continued to damage other young lives.

Our research for New Zealand Police from 1990-2006 consistently demonstrated that boys do not understand what child abuse is. They regard child protection messages as only relevant to girls and say, "Only girls get raped, unless you're a poof and then you ask for it/deserve it". Boys confuse paedophiles with homosexuals and readily accept the message that being victimised means they must be gay. Offenders promote this belief because they know that it silences boy victims. Regardless of the level of violence involved, boys think that abuse is what happens to other people. Even when victims realise that it is wrong, they keep offences secret, whether asked to do so or not. They tend to reveal what happened only when they are adults, secure in their sexuality and relationships and are well supported.

Why sexually abused boys didn't disclose their abuse

Abused boys did not report what happened because:

- Providing masturbation ('wanking') and oral sex ('blow jobs') for older boys is so prevalent that they accept it as normal.
- Victims do not report abuse because they fear disbelief and rejection, violence and being given derogatory labels, such as 'poofter'.
- Sex (other than anal rape) is a secret, 'private matter,' according to some.
- They don't want to upset their parents.
- Most victims thought it was normal. One said, "I was a good Catholic and knew sex was wrong but I thought sex was about men and women making babies. It had nothing to do with what was happening to me".

- They didn't think they were being abused if money or gifts were involved or if they enjoyed any part of the relationship with their abuser.
- They were emotionally dependent on the abuser and feared that reporting would result in the loss of the relationship and treats.
- Genital fondling and receiving oral sex were pleasurable and, when their bodies responded to sexual touching, abusers blamed them (and they blamed themselves) for their abuse.
- They struggled with issues relating to their sexuality when abused by males.
- Victimisation is the antithesis of masculinity, associated with being weak, feminine and gay; boys are taught that 'real' boys must fight back and be strong.
- To report sexual abuse, they would have to speak of sex related things for which children are typically reprimanded or punished.
- Cultural pressure encourages participation in sex with older females, causing them to suppress and deny anxious feelings.
- They fear parents will get upset with or blame them and say things like, "Why didn't you stop him? You knew it was wrong" or "Why didn't you tell me before?"
- They fear they will lose their independence if parents find out about the abuse.
- Abusers typically encourage affectionate feelings and loyalty or fear.
- Abusers manipulate parents into providing opportunities for abuse.

- The abuser says it only happened to the boy because he was bad and it was his own fault. "You should have said no at the beginning but you didn't."
- They feel they can't report it if they accepted alcohol, cigarettes, cannabis or looked at pornography, because they'll get into trouble.
- They were threatened with violence or removal from home if they reported it.
- It was happening to other kids so they assumed they couldn't do anything about it, (e.g., in boarding schools, at camps and in paedophile groups).

Many of these explanations may also account for girl victims remaining silent but, when older males abuse boys, the boys are likely to bear the additional burden of confusion about their sexuality and masculinity.

We know from the research that, when boys are abused in early childhood, the abuse is likely to continue into adolescence. When boys' emotions become sexualised, they may look for sex, mistaking it for love and approval. Abusers then have no conscience about using them. It should be noted that men who abuse boys commit far more offences and choose much younger victims than those who abuse girls.

When boys have been victimised, early intervention is crucial to disrupt and prevent deviant and unhealthy behaviour patterns, providing healthy alternatives. For further reading on the abuse of boys, see *Don't Tell: The Sexual Abuse of Boys,* by Michel Dorais.

CHILDREN WITH DISABILITIES ARE THE MOST VULNERABLE TO ABUSE

There are many reasons why children with developmental delays and learning and communication disabilities are the most vulnerable to all forms of abuse. First, society in general does not value the disabled as highly as non-disabled children. They are more isolated, less able to communicate, less informed about their rights and less able to distinguish appropriate from inappropriate behaviour, especially when they need assistance for personal care. Most offenders function in a caring role, are bus or taxi drivers or members of the extended family.

Children with disabilities are vulnerable because:

- They are often eager to please. Internet paedophile clubs have suggested that members should select children with Down's syndrome because they are easily identified and police are unlikely to prosecute if they are the only witnesses.
- They often have restricted social environments. They may require special transport and lack the opportunities to develop friendships and normal peer relationships. Their lives often conform to strict routines dictated by professionals and carers. They can become adult-orientated and desensitised to the norms of adult behaviour outside institutional settings. It is then more difficult for them to discriminate between appropriate and inappropriate touching. With restricted opportunities for independence, they miss out on the daily problem-solving, decision-making and confidence-building experiences that are available to other children.
- Some carers permit differing standards of behaviour and adopt different expectations, unwittingly increasing children's vulnerability to predators. Children with intellectual disabilities are often permitted to be

indiscriminately affectionate to strangers who visit their homes or schools and even social workers have turned a blind eye to under-age sexual relationships with adults.

- Sex-offenders regard those with disabilities as safe targets because, even if they report abuse, police are unlikely to act if the only witness possesses a communication disability.

- They are powerless. The ability to exercise power relates to the child's need for approval and acceptance. The greater the need, the greater the risk of victimisation and the less able the child is to exercise any power. Children with disabilities are the ones most likely to suffer from feelings of low self-worth, social isolation and helplessness. Compliance and powerlessness increase with a reduction in communication skills.

- In residential settings, they are further disadvantaged if their lives are ordered in such a way that they have no control over what they do. They don't learn to make choices or question their environment when most things are done for them.

- They are disadvantaged by the volume of touch and the nature and frequency of touch contacts. Fewer people touch non-disabled children as they grow older, but the opposite is true for children with serious disabilities. Some must depend on others for personal hygiene and basic care. Strong emotional attachments are often formed with carers. This is generally a good thing, but vulnerability to abuse increases with prolonged dependency and the number of carers involved. The children's lack of choice in who performs the most intimate tasks increases powerlessness. The more they are touched, the greater the risks.

- Some are abused by older students. In 2005, 44 percent of a sample of boys with learning disabilities attending a residential secondary special education centre said they had to provide oral sex for older youths.[36] By comparison, 44 percent of girls in special education said they'd been raped in and around the home. A few years earlier, 81 percent of girls with intellectual disabilities and emotional problems in special education said they'd been sexually abused by more than one person before the age of 14.[37]

- Some children with disabilities are deprived of any form of sexuality education. Information about their bodies should be taught alongside personal safety programmes. Information is essential for recognising sexual misbehaviour and that, in turn, is essential for controlling risks.

- Adolescents with disabilities may have no outlet for their sexual urges. This increases the potential for victimisation because, when they don't understand what's happening, they are unlikely to say no to inappropriate behaviour. Kept in ignorance, children are vulnerable to offenders' attractive incentives.

- Disclosures of abuse are often ignored. Children with learning disabilities are less likely to be believed and helped than non-disabled children and offenders are more likely to be given the benefit of the doubt. This can be attributed to the myth that children with disabilities are immune from abuse because they are not sexually attractive by popular media standards; few people realise that abuse is about power and control, not about sex appeal. Inadequate training is a problem, as are staff shortages and high turnover in services for children with special needs, which lead to the increased use of volunteers in services for children with disabilities and group solidarity in support of the accused staff member or volunteer. Unfortunately, in the past, police disinterest has made some staff think, "What's the use of reporting if they do nothing?" In particular, girls are less likely to be believed than boys because of the prevalent assumption that girls with intellectual disabilities act promiscuously or make up stories to get attention.

- Children with disabilities are especially disadvantaged by communication barriers. Those with severe speech and hearing impediments are vulnerable because they either may use different communication systems or have inferior skills to adults. They may lack the means to discuss sensitive issues and, in sex and personal safety education, they may miss or misinterpret essential detail. In addition, offenders have been known to learn sign language specifically to target children with hearing impediments. Neither prosecutors nor lawyers nor courts have shown any willingness to accept evidence from children with cerebral palsy who use electronic communications or computer keyboards. Until courts accept all forms of communication, these children will remain severely disadvantaged.

- Children with intellectual disabilities are disadvantaged by the myth that sexual abuse does no harm because they don't understand what's happening. This belief has enabled adults to turn a blind eye to the abuse of these children. The reality is that those with disabilities typically suffer the most violent, severe, chronic forms of sexual abuse, involving multiple perpetrators. Victims lose the capacity to trust and they develop and exhibit multiple problems that were not previously present. About two-thirds suffer from extraordinary fears and experience difficulties at school. One-third of victims experience sleep problems and exhibit regressive behaviours. More than one-third begin behaving promiscuously and more than two-thirds re-enact the abuse. Irrespective of the level of disability, victims feel betrayed, stigmatised and powerless, especially when the offender is a trusted carer. This can increase problems in all their interpersonal relationships.

In her work with deaf victims, Margaret Kennedy concluded that abuse compounds the emotional problems associated with children's disabilities. Both abuse and the child's disability produce a sense of isolation and withdrawal, low self-esteem, feelings of rejection, confusion, depression, anxiety, self-blame, powerlessness, frustration, anger, fear, embarrassment and stigmatisation.[38]

The abuse adds an extra dimension to children's existing problems; for example, hatred of sexuality, their bodies and their abusers. Confusion leads to questioning: "Why did this happen to me? Why didn't it happen to other kids? Life isn't fair." Powerlessness resulting from the disability is duplicated by sexual abuse. Stigmatisation can result from the negative reactions of others to both the child's disability and the disclosure of abuse.

Some parents ignore disclosures or suspicions of abuse, if reporting will necessitate changing the school or residence and there are no convenient alternatives. Mothers may also minimise or reject complaints if they are financially dependent on the abuser. It is easier to believe that a disabled child is lying, mistaken, at fault or unharmed than to accept that someone you rely on is a child molester who takes advantage of disability. Rejection, blame and disbelief increase the victim's feelings of being used, trapped, powerless and valueless.

In conclusion, children with special needs are at increased risk when they are:

- In the care of adults who believe the myths relating to abuse.

- Ignorant of their rights and what constitutes reportable behaviour.
- Devalued and dehumanised by society.
- Not adequately protected by childcare, education and legal systems.
- Deprived of a personal safety programme in school.
- Deprived of information about their bodies.
- Heavily dependent on adults for daily care and personal hygiene.
- Deprived of affection and approval at home.
- Overprotected, with few opportunities for independence and problem-solving.
- Unable to give or receive communication about sexual matters.
- Lacking confidence and the opportunity to complain.
- Unable to distinguish between appropriate and criminal touching, due to the volume of touching involved in their daily care.

In addition, child victims with disabilities are further disadvantaged because they are the ones most likely to be:

- Abused by people in a caregiver role.
- Disbelieved or ignored when they report it.
- Interviewed by professionals who have no specialist skills in communicating with children with special needs.
- Deprived of justice and therapy, increasing the risk of further abuse, severe emotional disturbance and re-enactment of the abuse with other children.
- Obliging to the sexual demands of their peers without contraceptive protection.

They are also more likely to suffer violent and prolonged abuse by multiple offenders. In general, the more serious the disability, the more vulnerable the child is. See one of my other books *Developing Personal Safety Skills in Children with Disabilities* published by Jessica Kingsley (London), for more ideas on how to help children with disabilities protect themselves.

Fortunately, most special education units now take child protection seriously. Parents should ensure that they are informed about what is taught and how they can reinforce the safety strategies at home.

HOW CAN YOU TELL IF A CHILD HAS BEEN SEXUALLY ABUSED?

Physical signs of sexual abuse

There are some physical indicators of sexual abuse that a parent can identify. There may be love bites, redness restricted to vaginal or anal openings (not spread widely as in a nappy rash), soreness, tearing and bleeding, unusual enlargement of the vaginal or anal opening or internal damage. Oral sex may leave the child with a throat or mouth infection or successive mouth ulcers that can't be explained. There may be blood on underwear and the child may find it uncomfortable to walk or sit. Young children may have bruises on the inner thighs or in unusual areas marking where they have been held down. Usually parents note a cluster of signs suggesting something is wrong and there may be verbal and behavioural hints too. The thought of sexual abuse is so horrific that adults tend to search for other explanations dismissing multiple signs as 'He's growing up I suppose'.

The assessment of these signs requires specialist skills that your family doctor is unlikely to possess. Police or your child abuse helpline may be able to refer you to a specialist assessment service which is usually located at your nearest children's hospital. Alternatively, take your child to the emergency unit of the nearest children's hospital.

Sexually transmitted infections

Sexually transmitted infections (STIs, formerly referred to as sexually transmitted diseases or STDs) are usually indicators of child sexual abuse. New Zealand health statistics suggest that up to 13 percent of sexually abused children and young people are infected. They include gonorrhoea, chlamydia, syphilis, HIV and genital herpes. Chlamydia is the most common STI contracted by children and young people in Australia. It can affect the penis, cervix, fallopian tubes, anus, throat and, in rare cases, the eyes. Chlamydia can cause serious long-term health problems, such as pelvic inflammatory disease and infertility if it is not treated quickly. It is passed on through unprotected oral, vaginal or anal sex with an infected person, that is, sex without a condom. A pregnant woman can also pass it on to her baby during childbirth. Seventy-five percent of sufferers show no symptoms.

For girls, symptoms can include:

- Vaginal discharge
- Frequent urination
- Burning sensation when you urinate
- Itchiness
- Bleeding and/or deep pain during sex
- Bleeding between periods
- Painful periods
- High body temperature
- Abdominal pain

Boys with chlamydia may complain of:

- Frequent urination
- Burning when they urinate
- Watery discharge from the penis
- Burning and itching around the opening in the penis
- Pain and/or swelling in the testicles

Genital herpes is another common sexually transmitted infection caused by the herpes virus. It is characterised by fluid-filled, painful blisters in the genital area. Further information about these diseases can be found on the internet.

Abused children may ask relevant questions, such as: "Mummy, do I have to keep secrets?" or "If I tell you a secret will you promise not to tell?" (You could respond by saying, "I can't make that promise because secrets that make children worried sometimes have to be told to get help.").

> Parents think of secrets as nice surprises that must be kept, not realising that the question could be hiding something more sinister.

Tell your children that they only have to keep good surprises about birthdays and presents but they must tell you about secrets that make them sad or worried. Bad secrets must always be shared and we must never keep secrets about wrong touching.

"Is it alright for Uncle X to do funny/silly things?"

(*Most parents reply along the lines of, "Of course it is OK if he makes you laugh." The child goes away confused and the abuse continues. Ask what uncle is doing before you comment. You can't assume that your child's definition of silly is the same as yours.*)

"Do I have to go to Granddad's/scouts/school today?"

(*Before saying yes, find out why your child is reluctant to go there.*)

When children ask these casual but very important questions, most parents assure them that Uncle is always being silly, that we all have to tolerate teasing, tickling and silly games and that grandpas and uncles love them and will be upset if they don't visit. When children are terrified of an abuser in the family, they may be too afraid to tell anyone until they are in a safer environment. When abuse has been disclosed, parents remember the hints that children gave and suffer enormous guilt.

The strong message here for parents is to **listen to children carefully, especially if your instincts tell you that something is wrong or has changed.** Put your own feelings aside and ask questions in a calm, clear manner. Don't ask vague questions, such as, "Did he touch you?" because young children don't associate touch with having to provide oral sex. If we don't respond to children's veiled cries for help, they believe they are helpless and hopeless and become even more psychologically damaged. However unreasonable it may seem, your lack of protection may also be held against you in years to come.

Behavioural signs and possible effects of child sexual abuse

Child victims tend to attract the attention of their parents by changes in their behaviour. Some will become angry, belligerent and destructive. Others will become quiet and withdrawn. Not all behavioural changes are specific to sexual abuse. In other words, they can be due to other factors. However, victims usually present several signs simultaneously along with emotionally disturbed, changed behaviour. Some of the common signs and effects are listed here.

- *A sense of shame.* Sexual abuse not only violates the child's trust but creates deep feelings of shame which negatively affect the child's life. Shame makes children hide away. Abusers deliberately cultivate shame because it keeps victims silent and cooperative. Girls abused by family members are often told that it was their sexy appearance or behaviour that led to their abuse. They are told they are 'worthless sluts' and 'dirty whores' who deserve all they get. Boys are labelled as 'poofs', 'homos' and other derogatory terms. Children accept highly damaging, repeated shaming.

- *Deterioration in school performance.* Diminished concentration affects progress especially in mathematics and reading. It is no coincidence that large numbers of abused children end up in special education. On the other hand, we occasionally find victims who excel at their studies despite abuse, because they feel safe at school and spend more time involved in school-related activities.
- *Social isolation.* Abusers typically isolate victims from support by destroying their trust in protective adults, indicating that those adults don't love them. An insidious trick is to claim that the mother knows and approves of the abuse or that she will be angry and reject the victim if she hears complaints about this 'special' relationship. By making the child feel unsupported and dependent on him, the abuser gains power and control.
- *Withdrawal from social contact and interaction.* Victims may suddenly spend a lot of time in their bedrooms and become anti-social. Old friends may be abandoned without explanation. Some victims think, "If they find out what's happening, they won't want to be my friend anymore". Some withdraw almost completely due to disassociation (see below) or the persistent use of the freeze/alarm/fear/terror response that is associated with Post Traumatic Stress Disorder (PTSD).
- *Dissociation* is the term used when victims separate their minds from their bodies during the abuse. Some describe this as like floating close to the ceiling. They can see what is happening to their bodies below but they don't feel anything. Dissociation can continue for years after the abuse ends.
- *Helplessness.* Children are inherently helpless and subordinate to adults. Any attempts they make to

protect themselves are mostly overridden, leaving them feeling that they have to tolerate the intolerable acts.

- *Night fears/terrors, refusal to go to bed, sleeping disorders or nightmares with flashbacks of the abuse.*
- *Eating disorders.* This includes overeating, bulimia and anorexia nervosa. Some victims gain weight, sometimes to the point of obesity, hoping to appear sexually unattractive to abusers.
- *Anxiety and regression.* Abused children are often anxious. Anxiety is linked to the abuser and the environment where the abuse occurs. Common indicators are a return to immature behaviour, such as bedwetting, thumb sucking, temper tantrums, destructive behaviour, clinging to trusted people and separation problems.
- *Fear and distrust.* The child fears and distrusts familiar people in previously enjoyed situations. This includes a sudden refusal to attend school or club meetings or see previously popular relatives or friends. A sudden change is likely to be due to unpleasant experiences. Investigate calmly.
- *Sadness.* Young victims are often sad-eyed, quiet and withdrawn. Some let their hair slip over their foreheads to avoid eye contact. Forced smiles may be evident in photographs. They find it difficult to discuss their sadness.
- *Anger and defiance.* Some victims, especially boys, hide their feelings behind a fragile mask of cheerfulness, toughness, anger, defiance, anti-social behaviour or indifference.
- *Obsessive behaviour.* This can be a defence mechanism, for example, over-eating or wearing ugly clothes to avoid being viewed as sexy or insisting on wearing several pairs of underpants as a means of protection. An obsession with showering may arise from the child feeling dirty as a result of abuse.

- *Inappropriate sexual behaviour.* Some abused children re-enact sexual experiences with dolls, animals, adults or other children. Some may behave sexually with members of the same sex as their abuser because they have learned that this is how to please adults. This places victims in danger of multiple abuse. The adult thinks, "She knows what it is about — she's asking for it". Whereas the child thinks, "Why is this always happening to me? Why am I different?" Sexual misbehaviour is a reflection of the child's environment. Those who exhibit sexual knowledge beyond their years may have been abused directly or through exposure to excessive amounts of sexual violence or pornography or by living in a highly sexual environment. Inappropriate behaviour is also likely to re-occur after a victim has seen the case worker or has come face to face with the abuser. The source of the problem needs to be investigated calmly and sensitively. Victims need to be assured that they no longer have to behave sexually to please adults.
- *Substance abuse.* Drugs, alcohol and solvents of all kinds are widely misused by abused children and young people. Abusers introduce them to make the victims more compliant. Older children use them to stifle bad memories or as an act of defiance.

It is important to consider the possibility of abuse as a factor when a child or young person engages in drug or alcohol abuse or sniffs solvents. Drug abuse can ultimately lead to committing violent crimes.

- *Suicidal thoughts.* Victims of child sexual abuse are at high risk of self-harm and may contemplate, plan or attempt suicide. Threats should be taken seriously and professional help sought. Don't dismiss it as an attention-seeking ploy.

- *Panic attacks.* The victim experiences severe discomfort, palpitations, sweating, trembling, nausea, shortness of breath, dizziness and more.
- *Self-mutilation.* The victim slashes arms and wrists with knives or razor blades. Occasionally the genital area may be targeted. Slashing is strongly indicative of past or present abuse. For some, it reduces tension. It can also be a form of self-punishment or, paradoxically, it restores contact with reality. It can be a physical representation or a distraction from the emotional pain that is being experienced. Child abuse should always be considered a possibility when a young person exhibits self-destructive behaviours.
- *Mutilating others.* Both girls and boys abused by males have been known to mutilate the genitals of younger boys.
- *Arson.* Children normally experiment with fire but interest is limited. Abuse victims are the ones most likely to be involved in burning schools, their foster homes and setting bush fires, particularly during fire ban periods.
- *Cruelty to animals.*
- *Developmental delay.* The trauma of abuse can affect the development of the child's brain in the early years.
- *Post-traumatic stress disorder (PTSD), depression and other mental illnesses.* PTSD is an anxiety disorder arising from factual and emotional memory. Previously referred to as 'shell shock,' it is often suffered by war veterans. Symptoms can appear years after the events. Common symptoms include the traumatic replay of the abuse in their daily lives, separation or stranger anxiety, avoidance of situations that give reminders of the abuse,

hyper-vigilance, exaggerated or impulsive behaviour, sudden anger or violent outbursts, nightmares, phobias, intrusive recollections, chronic fatigue, sleep problems, depression, physical pain, guilt and self recrimination, nervousness, anxiety, loss of interest and loss of concentration due to impaired memory.

- *The Stockholm syndrome.* This relates to the emotional bond that some victims form with their abusers, protecting them from police and the justice system. Children trapped in abuse do whatever they can to survive. Sometimes the only mechanism available is to identify with and protect their abuser. This explains why many deny they were abused and continue to protect offenders years after the abuse ended. Victims who exhibit the syndrome convince themselves that their abuser loved them and acted in their best interests. They exaggerate and are grateful for acts of kindness shown without realising that these were part of the seduction process and had a sinister purpose. With that framework, they deny that the abuse was harmful even when it was violent.[39] They focus on the abuser's needs and may see the world from the abuser's perspective. They find it difficult to escape from their abusers when opportunities arise. With the abuser as their role model, they are then at risk of becoming the next generation of offenders.[40]

Recent research has shown that there is a link between child sexual abuse, mental illness and behaviour problems in adolescence.

EFFECTS OF TRAUMA ON BRAIN DEVELOPMENT

Why does child sexual abuse have such a profound effect on the developing child?

American neurologist Professor Bruce Perry and other scientists have shown that traumatic experiences in early childhood have a damaging impact on the development of the brain. From birth, children absorb information from their environment. Put simply, their experiences contribute to how the brain is formed. Scientists often refer to the wiring of the brain. When babies are born, all the neurons are present but they lack the wiring to connect them. The child's experiences in the first three years of life determine how the brain is wired. With every experience, connections are formed and strengthened. These connections can't be created later. After the age of 10, our brains wipe out unused connections. It is a matter of "use it or lose it".

If basic needs are not met or the young child is traumatised by abuse, domestic violence, neglect or sudden separation and insecurity, the normal pattern of stimulation is changed and the brain may organise itself in abnormal patterns. This can result in behaviour problems, attention deficit and learning disabilities and addictive behaviours. It is no coincidence that a disproportionate number of abuse victims require special education. Sexual abuse can retard the child's development by rewiring the brain in such a way as to predispose the child to lifelong psychological problems. The impact varies according to the child's resilience, whether s/he is from a secure and supportive family or whether s/he has already had to cope in a dysfunctional setting.

When a child is stressed, cortisol — a hormone — is released and influences the brain's hippocampus. A child suffering from ongoing sexual abuse and trauma can remain in a perpetual state of fear and stress. Cortisol levels remains elevated and certain areas of the brain can be damaged as a result. Studies revealed that abuse survivors often suffer from poor impulse control, leading to acting without thinking, bullying, excessive fear, anxiety and an inability to control aggression. It has long been known that a large percentage of convicted criminals were victims of childhood abuse.

This is obviously a massive and complex subject. Interested readers may learn more by researching the Internet for related articles written by Professor Bruce Perry.

FACTORS THAT INFLUENCE A VICTIM'S RECOVERY

The severity of the abuse does not necessarily equate with the severity of the effects. Some children are more acutely distressed than others by what, to adults, may seem to be comparatively less severe offences, such as having their breasts fondled or kissed. Some of the issues that determine how well a child recovers include whether:

- It involves a breach of trust by the abuser; the most damaging abuse is that committed by a parent figure, someone loved and trusted or, worst of all, a priest who invokes God.[41]
- Secrecy or threats are involved.
- It is a single offence or continues over a period of time.
- The child reports it quickly and is believed and supported.
- The offender admits the abuse and apologises to the child.
- The victim feels guilty and blames him/herself instead of the offender.
- The victim believes he was chosen because he is gay.
- The victim enjoys the grooming process or some aspect of the relationship.

- Victims are blamed, for example, when the abuser is a priest who forces the child to confess the abuse as his sin.

Paradoxically, abuse by a stranger is likely to cause the least harm, given that it is usually a one-off crime, there is no relationship between abuser and victim, no breach of trust and often no secrecy and the victim is believed. In those circumstances, it is easier to affix the blame where it belongs — with the perpetrator.

YOUNG CHILDREN COMMUNICATE THROUGH DRAWINGS

Young, abused children rarely have the vocabulary, the ability or the confidence to disclose what is happening to them. Some may communicate their feelings and experiences through their drawings. There may be several significant features such as:

- Sexually explicit pictures, indicating that the artist has a sexual knowledge beyond his/her years.

  Stay calm, take a deep breath and ask the child who the people are in the picture, what is happening in the picture? Where and when does this happen? Never express disgust, as that will silence the child. If the response suggests abuse by someone outside the immediate family, call the police and ask to speak to a child protection officer. If you suspect abuse in the child's immediate family, ring your child abuse report line.

- The abuser is drawn with very large hands or arms compared with other figures.

- The abuser has a huge, erect penis, which, in drawings by 3 to 7-year-olds, may resemble a third arm.

  Ask who the person in the picture is and where the artist sees him looking like this. Who else is there when this happens?

- The abuser has a self-satisfied and even sinister grin while the victim appears sad.

    Ask who the adult is and why the little person looks so sad. What is happening to make the child sad?
- An obsession with drawing genitals, possibly attracting your attention to them. The obsession suggests that something has happened to cause anxiety.

    Ask who showed them how to play this game. When and where do they play?
- Armless self-portraits, when the artist draws arms on pictures of other people. Missing arms suggests a sense of helplessness.

    Say "I'm really concerned about you. Something is obviously worrying you. Is it someone at home or someone at school? Is it a secret? Who else knows the secret? What will happen if you tell?
- Self-portraits lacking a mouth when the artist draws mouths on other figures. This may suggest that the artist has a bad secret and terrible things will happen if it is disclosed.

    Say, "I know you are worried about something bad. Let's talk about it. Who else knows about it? What did (that person) say would happen if you told?" This should indicate whether the problem is serious. Don't ask what the secret is.
- Faceless self-portraits and less sophisticated body shapes as the victim's body image deteriorates. Drawings of other people remain unchanged.
- Egg-shaped, open mouths with exaggerated, jagged teeth can be associated with oral sex. The mouths are very different from the line smiles drawn on other figures.
- Phallic symbols: drawings of clouds, trees or humans are given a penis-like appearance that makes viewers uncomfortable.

- Preschool victims may draw themselves attached to the ground for security while offenders are presented as free-floating.
- Drawings and writing that include references to love when abuse has been presented as "what people do when they love each other". Be concerned when children write love letters to adults.
- Offenders may be presented as scary monsters, witches, insects or snakes.
- The frequent use of angry colours (especially red, purple and black) when children have a wide choice of colours available to use.
- Victims often present their sexually explicit and important drawings to people whom they trust.

    Say, "That's a really interesting picture. Who is that person? What's s/he doing? Where do you see that?"

Samples of drawings from abused children

Abused children may draw pictures that are explicitly sexual, emphasising genitals. This boy victim drew pictures of football teams, all with outsize genitals. Despite being worried about his sexually problematic behaviour in class, the teacher did not notice the content of the drawings and merely wrote on every drawing, "Good try Paul".

*Although, often the 'clues' to look for are quite subtle,
other times children's drawings are explicit.*

*This child was being sexually abused by both her mother and
brother. The child shows that she can draw arms and legs,
as shown on brother and mother/monster, but her poor self-image
is reflected in her lack of face and limbs.*

This is a drawing of an abuser by a young victim. Note the size of the arms and inclusion of genitals and the smile on the abuser's face.

An armless self-portrait by a 5-year old victim.

Drawing by a sexually abused 7-year old boy who was developmentally delayed. The teacher wrote the text but didn't ask the artist why he was afraid.

An example of phallic symbolism, where the abused child draws a picture that includes sexual symbolism.

Chapter 6

What You Need To Know About Child Sex Offenders

D o you think you could spot a wolf in sheep's clothing?

Many parents think they would recognise child sex offenders by their appearance. They say, "We don't have someone with a mental illness in our family," or "My child is safe because we don't know anyone like that," assuming that offenders can be identified by their appearance.

Forget about the stereotypical dirty old man in the raincoat. The person who sexually abuses children is more likely to be a familiar face: a relative, neighbour, family friend, older student at school, cousin, teacher, sports coach, club leader or religious figure, who uses sophisticated techniques to gain your trust and unsupervised access to your child.

There is no single profile of a child sex offender but there are some reliable indicators. This chapter will assist you in identifying them and improving the protection level of your family.

CHILD SEX CRIMES ARE DENIED

Child sex abuse is the most loathed, denied, secret and hidden crime in the world. It is hidden because there is a great deal of shame attached to it — shame felt by victims, families and the organisations whose carelessness enables the abuse to occur.

Most offenders deny their crimes and delude themselves that they love their victims and have caused no harm. They have to believe this in order to continue damaging victims without being troubled by their conscience.

Offenders are also very afraid of being jailed. They are the most despised prisoners in the penal system and often experience violence perpetrated by male prisoners who may have murdered or raped old women but feel superior in the prison pecking order. Serial offenders who had received no treatment told me they were guilty of past offences to which they pleaded not guilty but claimed that "this time I didn't do it". When mixed with other criminals, sex offenders feel compelled to deny their sexual attraction to children for reasons of self-preservation. This is unfortunate because denial is contrary to rehabilitation. Paedophiles can reinforce each other's deviance in the confined environment of a jail. They share information about victims and create networks that continue long after they are released.

Such is the level of denial that only 15 percent of 558 convicted incest offenders admitted any wrongdoing when they joined a London sex offender treatment programme after being released from jail. Within a year, they'd admitted a total of 291,276 crimes against children. That is an average of 522 crimes per offender.[42]

Similarly, when 23 offenders joined an American treatment programme, they admitted committing offences against an average of three victims. However, when faced with a lie detector test, they revealed crimes against an average of 175 victims.[43]

In another study, 561 self-confessed American sex offenders admitted a staggering 291,737 crimes against 195,407 children before the age of 32, that is, an average of 520 offences and 374 victims per offender.[44] Men who abused boys outside their homes were most active.

To put this into perspective, 561 men abused so many children that we would need two sports stadiums the size of

Beijing's Olympic Bird's Nest Stadium to accommodate them. And yet, most victims believe that "it only happened to me and it happened because I'm bad". Furthermore, mothers of victims are apt to believe their partners who deny allegations or say the child instigated it and "it only happened once and it won't happen again". It is easier to believe that a child is lying than to accept that you are living with someone who views and uses children as sex objects.

> Given that (a) less than two percent of reported child sex offenders are convicted in Australia, (b) few offenders seek treatment without a court order and (c) child sex offenders offend well into old age, it is reasonable to assume that an abuser will damage hundreds, even thousands, of children in a lifetime. That is why it is so important to provide the best possible protection for our children.

MOST OFFENDERS START OFFENDING IN THEIR YOUTH

Psychiatrist Dr. Gene Abel and Nora Harlow studied 4,007 American, self-confessed child sex offenders, most of whom were men.[45] They found that 20 percent were committing offences against boys before the offenders were even 10 years old, 43 percent when they were aged 10 to 15 years and 13 percent when aged 16 to 19 years. This means that 76 percent were offending before they were aged 20. Men who abused girls (54 percent) started offending much later in life.

In their book, *Stop Child Molestation*, Abel and Harlow explain that a boy's first experience that is identified as 'sexual' is critical to his future development. In adolescence, the increase in testosterone leads to an intense interest in all things sexual. When their first experience involves children or being abused, their sexual thoughts and fantasies may include younger children, rather than girls their own age or the latest pop star. As sexual thoughts become linked to masturbation and orgasm, they solidify the perception of children as sex objects and increase the drive to child molestation. In other words, the real danger is the linking of sexual thoughts about children with experiencing an orgasm, which, in turn, leads to repetition. This is seen to be the major reason why child molesters remain child molesters.

Boys who fantasise about sex with children have no way of knowing the potential dangers they face. They are unlikely to tell you or even their friends about their fantasies and, over the years, they can secretly build up sexual desire for younger children, increasing the risk that they will become offenders.

How sexuality education can help

Abel and Harlow showed that the risks can be reduced if parents openly talk to pre-pubertal boys about their bodies, including wet dreams, their sexual thoughts, masturbation and orgasm. Parents should ask their sons to tell them if they start fantasising or masturbating to thoughts of their own abuse or sex with younger kids, versus the girl next door or the latest pop star. They need specialist help if they are fantasising about something sexual that happened to them when they were young. Abel and Harlow provide word-for-word examples of what to say. Adolescents usually know that paedophiles (often referred to as "dirty old men") exist but have no idea that this predilection can start at their own early age. They also need to know that, if they become attracted to children, there are people who can help and that this is the time when help is most likely to be successful.

Unfortunately, we have a poor history of talking about sexual matters with children and when boys signal that they have an unhealthy interest in younger siblings or other children, teachers and parents and school managers tend to make excuses on their behalf while avoiding the problem. Instead, they say:

- He's a good kid.
- He's never been in any trouble.
- He's too young to be interested in sex.
- It's just normal experimentation/curiosity.
- The complaint was exaggerated.
- The kid made it up.

The misconception that a good teenager from a good home could never have a sexual interest in children is widespread. Teachers have been only too willing to write off sexual abuse, even rape, as "boys will be boys". Consequently, the people who care most about the vulnerable boy collude and prevent him from receiving help.

Most cities now have treatment programmes for juveniles who exhibit inappropriate sexual behaviours. New Zealand has community-based programmes for youths and even pre-school children. Contact the children's mental health service in your state for information.

It must be emphasised that the majority of male victims do not become abusers, but Abel et al. (US) and Bentovim's (UK) findings that one in four to five male victims becomes an offender is far too high to ignore, when you consider the long-term, harmful effects on both themselves and their victims. We need to focus more on prevention.

FEMALE OFFENDERS

Comparatively little is known about female offenders. That is because they are less accessible to researchers than men, given that few are jailed. Society has a history of minimising their offences and taking them less seriously than offences by men. When men abuse girls, the girls are viewed as victims, but that isn't necessarily the case when the roles are reversed and women abuse boys. The award-winning film, *The Reader,* featured explicit sex between a boy and an adult woman. Would that have been accepted had the adult been a man?

Male victims seldom regard what happens to them as abuse until they are older and realise that they were used. The public view is likely to be that the sex was consensual or even beneficial. While addressing a group of predominantly male psychologists on this subject, one audience member put up his hand and stated that he had been sexually abused by a woman when he was 8 years old. Immediately there were loud guffaws throughout the audience, with men calling out, "Half your luck," "Have you got her phone number?" and "Can I have her name?" That alone demonstrated the point being made. Would they have roared with laughter had it been a woman in the audience who said she had been abused at that age? The answer is very likely no. Add to the fact that these were psychologists, from whom one would expect a more mature and empathetic response, it is clear that this attitude is indeed an entrenchment of this attitude.

In recent years, a number of female teachers have been convicted of sex offences against under-age male students, but radio talk-back programmes demonstrated that men are not convinced that this is harmful. However, as the film, *The Reader,* revealed, abuse by females can be as psychologically harmful as abuse by males, given that there is usually an abuse of power and a breach of trust, which negatively affects the victim's development. Women abuse fewer children than men and those who do mostly abuse boys. Mother-son abuse is especially damaging because it often continues into adulthood and involves long-term control over the victims' lives. Adolescent male victims lose their childhood.

The characteristics of female offenders usually include:[46] [47]

- A traumatic childhood history of sexual abuse.
- Membership of dysfunctional families.
- A history of aggression and anti-social behaviour.

- Often younger than adult male offenders when caught.
- Blaming men for what they do.
- Extremely possessive attitudes towards victims.
- Engagement in more than one form of abuse and use of distorted thinking to rationalise their behaviour.
- Committing multiple offences, but with fewer victims than men.
- More relationship-driven abuse than male offenders; female offenders deny abuse and present themselves as loving partners of lonely youths, pleading that a special bond existed and they were the only ones who understood the boys.
- Abusers who, similar to male offenders, tell themselves that their victims need them and that they are performing a valuable service.
- The use of threats when victims show signs of asserting their independence.
- More than one-third choose victims with intellectual disabilities; worse, our research established that social workers and some parents turned a blind eye to women in their late 20s and 30s having sexual relationships with developmentally disabled boys as young as 13, victims who referred to these adult women as their girlfriends.

Occasionally, girls who were abused by men choose to abuse younger boys for revenge. Like their male counterparts, female offenders groom and impose secrecy, isolating victims from family and friends. Females are also likely to use verbal coercion, engage in mutual masturbation, share pornography and play sex games. They use the same stages of grooming victims as males, preferring young adolescents with high sex drives and a need for independence. These boys are easy prey.[48]

International research confirms that from 20 to 25 percent of all child sexual abuse is committed by females. In the author's own research with 198 male victims and 84 sex offenders, 23 percent of victims and a startling 50 percent of convicted male sex offenders reported that they were introduced to sex prematurely by older females. With the exception of two who had been abused by their mothers throughout childhood and adolescence and one whose older sister engaged him in sexual acts, these victims did not define the behaviour as abuse simply because it didn't hurt. Most involved pleasurable genital manipulation and the receipt of oral sex. The damage was caused by the premature sexualisation of the boys who became obsessed with sexual thoughts. Five- and 6-year-olds were unable to concentrate at school, were reprimanded for sexual behaviour and subsequently singled out and abused by more violent male predators.

The research suggests that, overall, female and male offenders follow similar patterns of abuse. In American studies, 8 percent of female perpetrators were teachers and 23 percent were babysitters. Research on teen and adult female perpetrators showed that many suffer from low self-esteem, antisocial behaviour, poor social and anger management skills, fear of rejection, passivity, promiscuity, mental health problems, post-traumatic stress disorder and mood disorders. Some say that female offenders are likely to be influenced by male co-abusers but none of the offenders in our Australian study were accompanied by men.

Findings tell us that we should question our assumptions about the safety of female child-minders and ensure that children are well informed about what constitutes appropriate and reportable behaviour when left in the care of other people.

PAEDOPHILES

Paedophiles stem from all educational, socio-economic, ethnic and religious backgrounds. They can be government ministers, Anglican archdeacons, Catholic monks and priests, bishops, diplomats, TV personalities, teachers, doctors, police, lawyers and even members of the judiciary. The majority of paedophiles are overwhelmingly male but female paedophiles are not unknown.

The word *paedophile* is commonly but wrongly used to refer to all child sex offenders. The definition of a paedophile is someone who is *only or predominantly* sexually attracted to children and should not include those who are also sexually attracted to adults. It is not a crime to be a paedophile per se but it is a crime when those inclinations are acted upon. Once they offend, their behaviour is criminal and usually habitual.

Paedophiles constitute a minority of child sex offenders. The majority of offenders live in heterosexual relationships and give the appearance of being caring — and often religious — family men.

Paedophiles are attracted to specific age groups

Paedophiles usually abuse children within a specific age range and a preferred gender. The preferred body shape is usually that of a child younger than 12. Boys are abused more frequently than girls at a ratio of two to one. Girls are more likely than boys to be abused at home. Paedophiles who were themselves abused by males tend to abuse only boys and those abused by both men and women abuse both boys and girls. Few boys are abused only by women.

The paedophile is not attracted to the real child. Some are attracted to innocence and want to be the first to destroy it; others prefer children who have already been abused because they feel less guilty if they are "not the first".[49] Children are attractive to them because they are powerless and offer no threats to the paedophile's immature personality. The paedophile feels omnipotent and gains satisfaction from being in complete control. As victims mature and begin to make demands, they are usually abandoned. Rejection and abandonment can lead to mental illness in the victim.

Paedophiles relate well to children

Paedophiles consistently seek the company of children or young people and relate to them in an adolescent fashion. Their immaturity makes them very popular because they provide fun, both communicating and playing at the child or young person's own level. They seek employment with and volunteer for any activities that involve their targeted age group and which provide opportunities for unsupervised contact. Some loiter around amusement arcades, schools, swimming pools, parks and places frequented by school truants and children during school holidays. Because they are immature themselves, they can be especially skilled at relating to children and making them feel special and valued.

Be very suspicious when someone is perceived as a Pied Piper who attracts children to his home. Paedophiles deliberately offer activities that appeal to youngsters. Their homes are often like miniature amusement parks, complete with pets, pinball machines, kids' favourite pop music, model railways and jukeboxes. They may perform as clowns or magicians or possess an aquarium or aviary. Offenders let boys drive their cars or boats illegally. They ply them with drugs, cigarettes, pornography and alcohol. They make boys feel privileged and grown up, and alienate them from their parents, providing activities and substances banned at home. They convince themselves and their victims that they love them more than their parents do, but, while real love puts the child's needs first, paedophiles block out the long-term damage they inflict on young lives in order to satisfy their lust.

Their ability to relate to children makes paedophiles exceptionally good teachers, youth pastors, sports coaches, camp leaders, counsellors and youth workers. Colleagues admire them and rarely suspect that their enthusiastic volunteering has any devious purpose. Their skills are also used to befriend new victims via the Internet. Paedophiles don't relate satisfactorily to adults because adults don't reaffirm their narcissistic image. Most live alone or with their mothers or, because they can't share their interest in children with their peers, they find the company of other paedophiles who reinforce the normality of their behaviour.[50] They are typically full of self-pity when caught.

Paedophiles have a persistent behaviour pattern

Most paedophiles abuse children well into their old age. Their interest in sex with children is obsessive. It dominates their thoughts, fantasies and lives. Some are sexually excited by memories of their own childhood abuse, re-enacting what happened but reversing roles, placing themselves in the role of abuser. Paradoxically, although he may have already committed hundreds of crimes, when first convicted, the serial paedophile is likely to be described by the judge as a 'first offender' and given a light sentence or good behaviour bond, neither of which may incorporate treatment.

In April 2009, a UK media source revealed that, despite the habitual and serious nature of the crime, more than 200 convicted paedophiles escaped with "a slap on the wrist" while cautions were handed out to 206 others who raped or used children for sex. In addition, 35 convicted offenders were given community service orders. Opposition spokesman Dominic Grieve commented that, while the government made loud noises about "cracking down on paedophiles," 54 percent of those *found guilty* escaped prison. "The public will be shocked to learn that law enforcement is at its most lax in protecting the most vulnerable in our society," Grieve said. While prison may not 'cure' a paedophile, it does reduce the time and opportunities available to re-offend.[51]

The inadequacy of the justice system makes it all the more important that we take steps to help our children to stay safe.

Paedophiles rationalise their crimes

Paedophiles rationalise their crimes and view the children as equal sexual partners. They totally ignore their victims' protests, using their authority, power, coercion, tricks, lies, blackmail and threats of violence to gain control.[52] By ignoring differences in size, knowledge and development, they retain their omnipotent, grandiose self-image and assume that, because their victims do not reject them, the children are responsible for what happens to them. In addition, they choose to misinterpret normal behaviour: a 3-year-old was alleged to have actively sought sex and was "asking for it and wanted it" when she placed her hand on the offender's thigh.

When girls reveal that their mothers' partners have abused them, the men invariably claim that their victims enticed them, that it was 'a moment of weakness' and assert that it will never happen again. Unfortunately, many mothers accept the explanation and reject their child, causing serious psychological harm.

Paedophiles manipulate everyone responsible for children's safety

Paedophiles not only fantasise about manipulating children, they fantasise about manipulating the parents and other adults responsible for the children's safety. They plan conquests in detail for months, even years, in advance and gain satisfaction from every small success along the way. Some paedophiles control several victims simultaneously. They use competition, peer pressure, child and group psychology, motivation techniques, threats, tricks, bribes and blackmail. Paedophiles continually recruit new victims to replace older ones. A paedophile child minder who is left to undress, shower or put children to bed will almost certainly abuse them. They are skilled at identifying sad, lonely, vulnerable, needy children who lack self-esteem and will respond to being treated as 'special'. They are often attracted to kids who remind them of themselves when they were molested.

Skilled offenders are patient, taking as much time as necessary to develop an emotional bond with the desired child. They brag that, given time, they can abuse any child they choose. They often have several lined up at different stages of seduction. They may keep records, some claiming to have abused hundreds or even thousands of boys. The image of the dirty old man in the raincoat is unfortunate because paedophiles succeed by being personable and charming, meeting the needs of children and *their parents and carers and* developing their trust. They present an image of respectability and trustworthiness so that, when a child seeks help to stop abuse, the global reaction is, "I don't believe it. I know him. He wouldn't do that". The skilled predator produces a string of reputable witnesses to vouch for his good character in court.

A West Australian teacher was convicted of offending against children in his junior primary class. Parents obviously didn't realise that child sex offending is very different from stealing a car or shoplifting when they told TV interviewers that they would welcome him back because he was a wonderful teacher, had obviously made a few mistakes but had served his debt to society and deserved another chance. Using the same rationale, the teachers' union successfully argued for the reinstatement of a junior primary teacher in New South Wales. As the school principal was not informed of the teacher's criminal convictions, due to his 'right to privacy,' she was unable to make an informed decision about his employment; he went on to abuse almost every child in his class.

Suspicions are usually offset by the person's status in the community. People think, "Why would a professional risk his career and freedom to have sex with a child?" It often doesn't make sense. It is much harder to report a lawyer who is chairperson of the school council than it is to report the school cleaner.

Paedophiles develop an image of respectability

Paedophiles deliberately target single mothers who are fooled by the fact that the men "get on really well with the kids" and behave in an exemplary fashion until trust is established. They are perceived as ideal father figures. They may move in with or even marry women specifically to access their children. They help with chores around the house and act as babysitters. Paedophiles may also adopt or foster children.

These predators have no conscience and show no remorse. They are difficult to detect because they are like chameleons, adapting to different environments and becoming whatever the targeted children, their parents or employers need at that time.

The early clue is their love of rough, boisterous play, tickling and massage especially with boys. This can become extreme and make you feel uncomfortable even before it becomes sexual.

Most parents ignore their gut feelings because they don't know what to say and are afraid of being mistaken and embarrassed. Furthermore, they don't want to upset the child who has probably developed affectionate feelings for this person.

Perpetrators are often active in religious organisations and they work hard to establish a reputation as outstanding community leaders; when suspicions arise they exhibit righteous indignation along the lines of, "How dare you suggest such a terrible thing after all the hard work I've put into this community? You will hear from my lawyer." Community members then defend the paedophile and ostracise his accusers.

Paedophile teachers are often seen as the best teachers their school has ever had. They volunteer for additional duties, sports training, camps, drama and choir rehearsals. Although single, they may buy a mini-bus to transport children home 'safely'. They gain the trust of parents and management so that security is relaxed. They test limits to see how far they can go. At the same time, they develop a supportive network of staff to vouch for their good character in court if they are caught.

High-status paedophiles require dual personalities to do what they do. For example, how does a paedophile judge sentence paedophiles for committing the same offences that he's committed without having a conscience? How can a priest commit sins with altar boys in the confessional? Their obsession with sex is such that one paedophile priest told the researcher that even the knowledge that the sin would send him to hell would not have been enough to deter him from abusing children.

So, how does one spot the predator?

Before they trust Mr. Nice Guy, parents and school staff should ask themselves why he elects to spend most of his free time with children rather than with adults. Why does someone whose work involves children also volunteer to take them for swimming, drama, choir, camping and sports training before and after school?

Does the well-practiced smile disappear when you say, "OK, I'll join you?" Paedophiles present the image of being the most caring staff members or volunteers the school has ever had but that is just part of their modus operandi to lower people's guards and develop trust.

Remember: If people seem too good to be true, they probably are! Never lower your level of security just because children like someone.

PEDERASTS

Pederasts are exclusively male and are as obsessed with sex and behave in the same way as paedophiles; however, they are attracted specifically to boys, aged eleven to eighteen years. The most dangerous period is eleven to thirteen years. Like paedophilia, the disorder is almost always obsessive and consumes much of their lives. They are usually unable to find sexual satisfaction with adults. Sex with children is less threatening because they are in total control.

Boys confuse pederasty with homosexuality, assuming that "dirty old men" are all gay. A homosexual is someone who is sexually attracted to persons of the same sex and roughly the same age. Society is confused by the fact that some pederasts live together, pretending to be gay, when, in fact, their sexual preference is for boys.

PAEDOHEBOPHILES

Paedohebophiles are sexually attracted to children with a body shape normal to those of less than eleven years *and* pubescent girls aged nine to sixteen years *and* boys aged eleven to sixteen years. These offenders are frequently married and bisexual. Their partners are likely to be passive female survivors of childhood abuse who have no high sexual expectations or needs. If the men have a sexual performance problem, their partners are likely to blame themselves. Some child molesters marry for convenience or as a cover. They download child pornography and have sex with anybody or anything. There is a relationship between domestic violence and child sexual abuse.

SEX OFFENDER NETWORKS

It is now easy for child sex offenders to join networks, both local and worldwide, through the Internet. Secret clubs exist to support members' criminal behaviour and share victims, images and information. International paedophile clubs are advertised on the Internet. Some are said to have more than 5,000 paying members.

Members of local networks tend to be middle class, often high-profile businessmen and professionals. It is also common for one offender to have control over a group of children. There are informal groups where several members abuse a number of children. This was noted in the evidence presented to the *South Australian Inquiry into the Sexual Abuse of Children in State Care* (2008). Commissioner Ted Mullighan commented that South Australians would be shocked to learn that the abusers occupied high profile, high status positions.

Victims trapped in networks are often subjected to sadism, torture and appalling degradation as well as rape. They may be forced to sexually abuse each other for the gratification of the adults. There are groups of molesters who are psychopaths and simply feel entitled to treat children as sub-human, gaining pleasure from their pain and powerlessness. Narcissistic predators think they have the right to do whatever they like and get away with it.

INDICATORS THAT WARRANT CAUTION

Be cautious if you note a cluster of indicators such as someone who:
- *Has an excessive interest in children,* boosts children's egos and relates to a child at the child's level.
- *Manipulates situations to develop your trust and create opportunities to be alone with the child.* They will explore the adults' needs and meet them, such as by repairing

cars, computers or houses to develop 'friendship' and trust. If you are a single parent or a mother whose male partner is often away, the offender may offer to take your son fishing, sailing, camping or participate in other male pursuits. You may not realise that you are a pawn in a carefully calculated plan to make you relax your safeguards.

- *Introduces wrestling and boisterous play that involves excessive tickling or massaging.* This is prevalent in the abuse of boys. Ignore laughter and put a stop to this type of play. Be assertive. It is all too easy for hands to slip under clothing in this type of play, which is, of course, why they do it.

- *Provides special treats.* Predators buy children's affection with flattery, attention, treats and expensive gifts that you can't afford. Be alarmed when someone gives gifts and tells a child to keep it secret.

- *Has a special relationship with a child.* Attentiveness is the most common technique used in seduction. Victims love and perceive offenders as their best mates. With such positive feelings they fail to report offences.

- *Takes lots of photos of children, either fully or partially dressed.* Sex offenders collect vast stores of photographic images. He may morph children's faces onto nude bodies in sexually explicit poses that are used for sexual fantasies or sold as pornography and distributed on the Internet around the world.

CHILD MOLESTERS IN THE FAMILY

Children's carers have the opportunity as well as the authority to manipulate and terrorise children to engage in sex. The majority of offenders live in heterosexual relationships presenting as normal, caring parents. To sexually molest their own children, they have to ignore the incest taboo that normally provides protection. It is widely thought that step- and de-facto parents, mothers' boyfriends and fathers' gay partners present greater risks than do the children's own fathers.

Although a small percentage rape their sons, incestuous fathers are more likely to abuse their daughters. Paradoxically, those who do abuse their sons often present a decidedly macho image. A man who was abused by his father and older brothers throughout his life from the age of 5, decided to leave his wife and children to adopt a gay lifestyle at the age of 40. He called a family meeting to make the announcement. His father was outraged and told him not to darken the doorstep again because "We don't want any bloody poofters in this family." The hypocrisy escaped him.[53]

Incestuous fathers are often rigid, religious and authoritarian, convinced that they own their wives and children and can use them as they wish. As victims reach puberty, the offenders tighten the reins and restrict their freedom. They often pretend they are providing sex education or are protecting daughters from rough, randy youths or preparing them for marriage.

Incestuous fathers were often raised in low socio-economic, dysfunctional families with a history of violence. They create opportunities to be alone with victims. For example, they teach the children to drive the family car and encourage mums to take evening jobs or go to church to get them out of the house. Molestation usually occurs when the mother is absent or in hospital, dies or the father is subject to great stress. The abuser may make his victim feel special and powerful as a wife replacement. This alienates siblings and increases the victim's dependency on the abuser. On the other hand, he may control her through violence and fear, telling her that she is a useless, worthless slut, whore or bitch, who is incapable of doing anything without him. Over time, she believes him.

The sex-offending father figure is often perceived as a dominant, overly protective, strict character, while the mother presents as a shadowy, background figure. He is sometimes called the perfect patriarch, presenting a mask that hides aggressive dominance. He volunteers at school, attends parent information days and is likely to read the lesson in church. Quite frequently, the mother was herself an abuse victim. Accustomed to a dominant male, she chose a partner not unlike her own abuser.

Father-daughter incest offenders may also abuse nieces and nephews, their children's friends, grandchildren and others outside the family. If the abuse isn't stopped, it can continue until victims are adults. As some victims go on to abuse their own children, very unsafe, incestuous families are created and more and more members become both victims and abusers. It is important to remember that child sex offenders offend well into old age. They exercise control by telling victims that what is happening is normal but must remain secret because no one else will understand. This causes confusion. Some use threats and violence, especially the threat that, if the child does not cooperate, a younger sibling will be abused. Years later, victims learn that their sibling was being victimised at the same time and their sacrifice was in vain.

Threats can include the death of their mother, siblings, themselves and beloved pets if they tell. The threat and the secret can be as psychologically damaging as the sexual acts themselves. The damage is exacerbated when the children are told their mothers know about the abuse and say it is OK. Similarly, they are harmed when mothers disbelieve or completely ignore children's disclosures, turn away and behave as if they haven't heard. Some mothers choose to support offenders and send victims to live with grandparents while the abusers remain unpunished in the children's homes. This is especially damaging when the abuser is not the child's own father or he warns the child that, "If you tell, you'll be sent away for being a bad kid," and then it happens. These children are justifiably angry and few grandparents know how to handle their angry behaviour. Unsupported, some resort to placing their emotionally damaged and difficult grandchildren in foster care, where they become even angrier and often finish their schooling in special education.

Children who seek help from trusted family members are sometimes abused again by opportunists who think "s/he knows what this is all about so it doesn't matter". This abuse of trust has devastating consequences for a child's development.

If you have the misfortune to learn of a child that has been abused, it is vital that you believe the child, phone your child abuse report line and provide support for the child. Do not cross-examine the child. Say that you know how upsetting this must have been, but that they are not alone and this has happened to other kids and you are really glad that s/he has told you. Say that it is never a child's fault when this happens and that grownups (or older kids) know that they aren't allowed to do these things with kids.

PORNOGRAPHY IN SEX-OFFENDING

Child sex offenders may overcome inhibitions by using alcohol, drugs and child pornography that confirms their perception of children as sex objects. They collect pornographic literature and videos and keep diaries of conquests which are their most treasured possessions.

Downloading child pornography is not a victimless crime; COPINE research undertaken by the University of Cork for the European Union showed that three-quarters of downloaders admitted also to abusing children just before or after viewing. Child pornography is used for:

- Sexual fantasies and masturbation.
- Showing targeted children images of deviant sex to desensitise them and normalise abuse: "Look, everyone

does it. They even publish magazines/make films. Didn't your parents tell you? Why don't we give it a try?"

- Controlling children by taking sexually explicit photos of them using a webcam or by morphing the young person's face onto obscene pictures and then threatening them that, unless they comply with demands, the images will be sent to their parents or posted on the Internet.
- Gaining sexual satisfaction from reminders of their own sexual encounters.
- Sale or exchange with other predators or to collect as a means of joining paedophile clubs that require thousands of new images to gain membership.

Collectors conceal their obsession by downloading child pornography at work or when female partners are in bed. What is alarming is that many of those convicted in recent police swoops were in professions involving the care and education of children. The FBI reported that, with just one exception, all were men. There are more than 200,000 child pornography websites on the Internet. Every image represents an abused, degraded and exploited child.

There are support services available for men who become obsessed with pornography.

STAGES IN PREDATORY GROOMING

Grooming is the word used to describe the seduction methods used by child sex offenders to gain the trust of potential victims, their parents and adults responsible for their safety, prior to introducing sex. American author Carla van Dam published two books on grooming methods used by offenders. She suggested that if parents and professionals who work with children understood how predators operate, there would be fewer crimes.[54]

Most offenders follow a process for selection and preparation before engaging in criminal conduct. Several steps have been identified:

Step One

A desired child is identified. Vulnerable children include those who have family problems (or think they have) or lack an involved father figure and want to be loved, noticed and valued. The offender then sets out to get to know the child.

Step Two

The predator finds ways to get to know the parent. They may offer to baby-sit or find other ways to be alone with the child. I was once called to a primary school in a poor area with a high percentage of children from mother-led, single parent families. Sixty-five children were known to have been sexually abused by men who presented themselves as ideal lodgers and baby-sitters. Because victims were too young to be cross-examined in court, reported abusers were never prosecuted. Offenders remained free to move from household to household to abuse more children.

Step Three

Paedophiles provide activities that appeal to children. *Be suspicious when they behave more like big kids than adults.* Older boys are given access to dirty talk, cigarettes, pornography, beer and drugs that make them feel adult.

Step Four

Offenders test the boundaries of the adults to find out what they can get away with. If there is no parental or other adult interference, their risk-taking behaviour escalates. One childcare worker painted flowers on children's bare bottoms, engaged in excessive tickling and boisterous play, attached phallic balloons to the ceiling of the centre, introduced sex talk with staff and some parents and was allowed to take children to his home to look at pets. He was not challenged because he was overtly gay, popular with the kids and was perceived as cute and amusing. He was eventually convicted of crimes against 10 children.

Without a child protection programme that alerts them to grooming tactics, boys are unlikely to resist a fun-loving adult. Stroking and tickling can progress to beneath the shirt to nipples and, if there is no resistance, into pants. It is crucial that children recognise the moment when touching changes from fun to wrong and says, "Stop that! It isn't allowed!" (And then escapes and reports to a trusted person who will help). You and the child are in a difficult situation because the typical perpetrator takes umbrage, pretends it was an accident and tries to make you feel guilty and embarrassed for overreacting.

If the child ignores the first sexual touching, the abuser takes this as permission to proceed. The child is then viewed as an equal partner and both are blamed.

Step Five

The next step is the social isolation of the child. Offenders refer to a girl as "my little princess" and, in families, they become "Daddy's special girl" as the father chooses their company over that of siblings. This makes others jealous. Similarly, victims are isolated from their protective parents with, "This is our special secret" or, "Don't tell Mummy about this. She knows already and says it is alright". When paedophiles use sex education as the cover for sexual abuse, they pretend that parents have been remiss because they haven't taught the children about sex.

Step Six

The last step is to make victims feel responsible for their own abuse to ensure they keep it secret. Typically, boys accept genital fondling and oral sex but want to opt out when the abuser says,

"You've had your fun. Now it's my turn," and abuse becomes obnoxious, uncomfortable or painful. The typical response is, "You should have said no in the first place. You didn't. You're a bad kid and you'll get into big trouble" or "You know you wanted it. You liked it. It is your own fault". That is most effective when the boy's body responded to sexual touching, as most do.

Then there are threats: "They'll send you away if you tell." Father figures may say, "I'll go to jail and your mum won't have any money and you won't have anything to eat or anywhere to live," and even, "I'll kill myself" (or the entire family, plus pets). This puts an intolerable responsibility on the child.

In paedophile networks, children are abused after being given drugs or alcohol. Rohypnol is used to make them drowsy and forget what happened. Even if they remember, children think they can't tell their parents because they engaged in forbidden behaviour, such as drinking beer, smoking marijuana or looking at pornographic material. They don't want to get in trouble or upset their parents.

If they disclose abuse and you react in an emotional, angry, shocked, unpredictable way, it may well be the last time you ever get a window into what is happening to that child.

Children will never initiate questions or disclose personal information if they suspect that you can't handle it.

Boy victims are usually abandoned by the age of 17. The abuse of girls, especially by father figures, can continue into adulthood.

HOW SEX OFFENDERS CONTROL CHILDREN

Tricks: To make children cooperate when they wouldn't otherwise do so.

Bribes: To persuade children to do something they would not normally do by offering something attractive in exchange for sex, such as a new bike.

201

Giving the child banned substances, such as cigarettes, drugs, alcohol and pornography, which can then be used as a threat when children want to opt out: "What will your mum say when she knows you've been drinking beer?"

Threats: Something terrible will happen if the child doesn't keep the behaviour a secret. Those who don't groom their victims must resort to terrifying them to ensure compliance. Victims protect offenders long after the abuse ends because they remain afraid.

Secrecy: When victims are told, "This is our special secret. You mustn't tell anyone. They wouldn't understand". Parents teach children to keep secrets, especially family secrets, assuming that secrets are generally nice things to have. Victims then keep the abuse secret, even if they know that what happened was wrong.

Persuasion: Coercion, inducement and enticement are commonly used: "I thought we were friends. This is what people do when they love each other."

Dependence: Victims are made dependent on the abuser for their emotional needs.

Authority: Children dare not defy authority figures, which include priests, teachers and parent figures. Factors are heavily weighted against the child. The victim will not easily overcome superior knowledge, physical strength and skill. Personal safety education can help by alerting children to wrong behaviour, hopefully enabling them to stop and report abuse in its early stages.

Pornography: Initially, offenders may produce copies of sexy magazines and ask whether the child has a boy/girlfriend and whether they've had sex. Explicit child pornography is then introduced. They may leave it in a place that will catch the child's attention. They introduce pornographic videos and then suggest re-enacting what was seen in the movie.

Victims involved in the creation of pornography are told to smile. This is because offenders can use it to point to other victims and say that what is happening is enjoyable. Offenders try to convince boys that sex with men is more enjoyable than sex with girls.

> Children should be warned to get away as quickly as possible when an adult or older person introduces sex talk or inappropriate pictures in magazines, the Internet or other media.

Parental approval: Children are confused when paedophiles befriend parents who then let them go to sports, fishing, camping or boating trips with the offender. When the paedophile's behaviour changes, they think, "It must be OK because Mum let me go with him."

Role reversal: Girls keep abuse by father figures secret because they are made to feel responsible for keeping the family together. This is very harmful. They remain silent because of shame, self-blame, a sense of entrapment, fear of being disbelieved or the threat of removal from home if the abuser is a family member.

Shame: Girls used for sex by parent figures are brainwashed into believing that they are unworthy of respect and have no rights.

Declarations of love: Male offenders outside the family may convince girls that they are in love and want to marry them when they reach 18, (even if they are already married). This has been especially prevalent in the abuse of girls on overseas student exchanges and by staff in boarding schools.

STRANGER DANGER

Focusing only about abduction from strangers, parents often think they don't need to worry about child protection because, "We always know where the kids are" and "We take them everywhere."

It doesn't occur to them that there are paedophile teachers and paedophile clergy, church workers and, more often, child-molesting relatives and neighbours.

Some mothers have said, "We don't need to teach safety skills because we trust everyone here."

The stranger isn't the greatest danger

Although we have known for more than 30 years that strangers are responsible for comparatively few cases of child sex abuse, parents, police, media and some teachers continue to deliver the dangerous stranger message. For many children, this is the only child protection message they hear. And yet, as long ago as the late 1970s, police records showed that only six percent of reports of child sexual abuse involved strangers. Most of these dangerous strangers take steps to get to know future victims and their parents so that they can abuse them repeatedly. Furthermore, children under the age of 10 don't understand what the definition of a stranger is. They envisage a stranger as an ugly male who wears a black balaclava, leers and steals children from their beds. The problem for children is that anyone who does not fall into this stereotype is assumed to be trustworthy.

Children abused by strangers usually experience single, non-violent offences and, ironically, they tend to cause the least amount of harm because there is no relationship involved. Children are more readily believed when they report strangers than when they report people who are trusted by their parents or members of the community.

PARENTS WHO ALLOW CHILDREN TO SEE PORNOGRAPHY AND SEX AT HOME

Some parents engage in sexual activities when children are present. This constitutes child abuse because hearing strange sounds and possibly seeing a male on top of their mother makes youngsters fearful. They think that Mum is being hurt.

Some parents allow children to see pornography in the home, excusing their behaviour with "they are too young to understand". Wrong! Children learn from everything they see and hear. From pornography they learn inappropriate sex roles. Girls may think they have to behave sexually and boys may learn that it is OK to tie girls up and rape them because that's what men do in pornography and the girls appear to like it. Researching with boys, some 5 to 8-year-old told us that their dads showed them pornography on the Internet, telling them that this is what real men like and it's fun. This again constitutes reportable child abuse.

Children anxious about sexual matters may simulate what they see with other children. Acting out fears reduces children's stress; for example, children who have been in hospital often play at 'nurses and doctors' after they return home. Children in war-torn countries pretend they have guns and shoot the bad guys or they hold out their arms sideways to simulate aircraft dropping bombs. However, when young children act sexually outside the home, it elicits emotional responses from both adults in charge and other parents and creates more victims. It can trigger an official enquiry by child protection services and trauma for the children.

For all these reasons, if you must have pornography in your home, keep it under lock and key and carry the key with you. Evidence that another child is being exposed to sexual activities should be reported to your child abuse report line.

RISKS TO CHILDREN IN RELIGIOUS ENVIRONMENTS

You may be shocked to learn that extra vigilance is necessary when children, particularly young boys, attend church-related activities. Religious institutions have a long history of forgiving and supporting reported child sex-offenders, shuttling them from parish to parish and school to school.

Even recently, Catholic priests convicted as serial offenders have been allowed to continue teaching and performing pastoral duties with children from 5 to 7 years old after being reported to bishops or released from jail. Neither parents nor congregations were made aware of their criminal histories.

It is on public record that 203 clergy offenders in Australian churches were convicted of sexual offences against children between 1990 and 2008. In a public statement, one victim wrote:

"The church's philosophy of putting priests on a pedestal and the teaching that everyone must 'forgive' those who wrong them creates an ideal environment for child abusers. Forgiveness as taught by Christ does not mean glossing over heinous offences, but bravely facing the facts. While Christian forgiveness leaves the ultimate punishment in God's hands, it is not inconsistent with action in the courts." (Mykah, 2 September 2008).

Churches offer a psychological hiding place by providing absolution for what the church defines as a sin when, in fact, it is a crime. Sex offenders can confess on Sunday and re-offend on Monday, with the expectation that God will forgive them again a week later. One priest admitted in court that he had confessed to child sex offences 1,500 times and been forgiven every time. Furthermore, although clergy are mandated to report child abuse in South Australia, admissions made in the confessional remain secret.

Churches are vulnerable places because they welcome volunteers with open arms. Police checks are seldom conducted and supervision is often superficial. Churches enable predators to access well-behaved, often naïve, respectful youngsters who are organ scholars, altar boys and members of choirs, Sunday schools and youth groups, as well as those in church schools. Child sex offenders specifically target the children of families most devoted to their church. They gain the parents' trust, certain that if they are caught red-handed, the parents will sacrifice their children to protect the good name of their beloved church. Parents may report sexual crimes to a bishop but they seldom inform police.

In her remarkable book, *Hell on the Way to Heaven* (Random House 2010), Crissie Foster shows how, on a daily basis, the powerful and feared Father Kevin O'Donnell was able to remove children from their school and take them to adjacent premises to be abused. Foster shows that O'Donnell was able to abuse children for fifty years and was protected by the Catholic Church. When devout Christian parents hear that a priest is a child sex offender, they are shell-shocked. They held the priest in awe, viewed him as next to God and welcomed him into their homes. They find it difficult to face reality or accept that their trust was misplaced.

Although he pleaded guilty to sexual offences against a large number of children, parishioners continued to proclaim O'Donnell's innocence, suggesting that he only pleaded guilty out of the kindness of his heart to protect children from having to give evidence. Two of the Foster's young daughters were victims of O'Donnell with tragic consequences. Once the truth was revealed, the Fosters began a battle to find out how this could have happened. The Church offered silence, lies, denials and threats. Their chilling story made national and international headlines.

Recent court cases have shown that victims' parents make it easy for priests to have access to their children. Some felt privileged that the priest showed a special interest in their child. Some offenders abused sick children in their beds while supposedly praying for them. Those who admitted their crimes often blamed their victims.

Parents who reported abuse to senior clergy were told, "Leave it with me and I'll deal with it". Abusers were merely moved to a retreat, another parish, a South Pacific Island or some other remote, developing country where they could damage more young lives with little risk of prosecution. When we interviewed 198 Australian adult male childhood victims, 59 percent of those who were abused at age 11 to 15 years cited religious figures as their abusers, 29 percent were Catholic priests, one-third were monks in residential schools, 10 percent Christian Brothers, 10 percent church youth leaders and 10 percent other clergy.[55]

American research shows that clergy abuse is even more damaging than abuse within the family because it involves both spiritual and psychological abuse. Furthermore, victims of clergy abuse are the ones least likely to be believed and supported.[56]

While little if anything has been done to reintegrate and compensate victims and their families, it is important to note that churches have policies to welcome back convicted child sex offenders on the grounds that "they have the right to receive God's blessing" and their unsubstantiated belief that returning to the Church will deter them from re-offending.[57]

> Church communities are especially vulnerable because they take people on trust, think the best of others and practice forgiveness. Child sex offenders are adept at manipulating and charming people to get what they want.

Clergy's offending patterns

The sexual abuse of children by clergy follows patterns:

- The priest is perceived with awe as "next to God," which places him in a unique, powerful position, causing immense fear and confusion for the victim.

- They choose as their victims compliant children of devout parents who are honoured that their son (typically) receives special attention. Parents unwittingly facilitate abuse by permitting overnight stays and encouraging special relationships.
- Victims are shocked and freeze when sex is introduced.
- The victim is under tremendous pressure to keep the abuse a secret.
- The child may be terrorised and threatened with the wrath of God or confused when told that God specifically chose him to provide sex for the priest.
- The victim is given the impression that the abuse is his/her own fault and s/he is a sinner. The child may be forced to confess the abuse to the very person who committed it, reinforcing the message that the child is to blame.
- The victim is protective of church-going parents.
- When abuse has been revealed to church administrators, their response has seldom been responsible and sensitive. The parents' trust in bishops has made way for manipulation and intimidation, leading to further damage to children.
- A community that is uninformed about the dynamics and long-term damage caused by child sex abuse supports offending clergy and church workers and denigrates victims and their families.

Despite the widespread publicity given to reports of child sex abuse, the idea that clergy can harm children is often still completely alien to those responsible for their safety.

Pederasts in church youth activities
While both Roman Catholic priests and monks have, in the past, used their authority to abuse children in boarding schools

and elsewhere and were often sadistic and violent, Protestant offenders had less authority and were more likely to resort to the grooming methods commonly associated with paedophilia. Adelaide Anglicare worker, Robert Brandenberg, ran the Church of England Boys' Society (CEBS) for 37 years. Parents, including members of the clergy, sent their sons, thinking that membership would be a good thing. They did not know that, in actuality, it accommodated a three-state paedophile network. The published history of CEBS in Tasmania includes at least four clergy who were subsequently charged with child sex crimes. Hobart's former Archdeacon, Louis Daniels, pleaded guilty to 13 counts of sex offences against young boys between 1973 and 1993. Abuse survivor Steve Fisher said that priests would go to each other's homes, taking boys with them to be sexually assaulted. Victimised by the Rev. Garth Hawkins, Fisher alleged that the paedophile ring involved doctors and MPs as well as priests.

In 2003, the author was invited to provide seminars for Tasmanian clergy and parishioners who, uninformed about the nature of sex offences and the grooming methods used, refused to believe that their beloved Archdeacon was a sex offender leading a double life.

Robert Brandenberg gained everyone's trust. He asked parents' permission to take groups to 'footy' matches. Some were suspicious about a single man spending all his time with kids and, when their sons returned home, they asked if everything was 'alright'. They learned the hard way that young people don't associate 'alright' with sex. Assured that everything *was* 'alright'", they relaxed and, when Brandenberg sought permission to take boys to prepare a rural camp, they agreed. Parents assumed that there was safety in numbers but they were wrong. *It is as easy to abuse a group of boys as it is to abuse one.* Those who resist are humiliated, "What's wrong with you? Everyone else is doing it. It is fun. You're weird". Children don't like being different from their peers and they join in, however reluctantly.

Brandenberg was the typical pederast who made his home attractive to boys with pinball machines, sex talk, alcohol, marijuana, pornography and popular music. He took kids to Chinese restaurants and let them drive his car illegally. He also had a spa pool that he used to persuade new victims to undress. Typically, he increased his supply of victims by encouraging boys to bring friends, knowing that boys don't tell if that means 'dobbing' in their mates.

Brandenberg abused boys in his home, his Anglicare office and at three camps in South Australia and interstate. He displayed photographs of an estimated 200 victims on a 3 x 1-metre notice board in his home.

"It was a trophy room, there were about 200 photographs of boys," one victim said. "He used to brag about how many he had done it to and then dumped." Brandenberg apparently drowned himself in a local reservoir after being charged with offences against 26 boys. It was later estimated that he had raped more than 200 boys aged 7 to 15 years.

In 2003, the rector of the parish and the ordained brother of a victim revealed that, for four years, they'd raised concerns about Brandenberg's victims with Anglican authorities to no avail. They persisted in seeking an inquiry and the synod eventually agreed. Police set up a task force to investigate 65 complaints involving 17 different child sex offenders connected with the Anglican church.

A sad aspect of this offending is that parents believe they are giving their sons the best opportunities for character-building when they encourage them to join youth groups attached to churches. Quite clearly, children need a sound understanding of what constitutes reportable, wrong behaviour and how to stop and report it before they join groups given that there is no safety in numbers. Without knowledge, all children are vulnerable.

Victims try to protect their parents

Victims of church-related abuse, the majority of which are boys, seldom tell their parents or, later on, their spouses. Men think there is nothing to gain from exposing their victimisation. As children they think they won't be believed and as adults they don't want to cause distress. If they seek therapeutic counselling, they keep it secret. A typical comment is, "My parents had several jobs so I could go to a good Catholic school so as to avoid sex, drugs and bad influences and, despite their efforts that's exactly what I got. I don't want them to know about this — they would be too distressed — there's nothing they can do about it now and it would be of no benefit to tell them."

Interestingly, the Internet has been a key factor in *reporting* offences committed by clergy. Victims find each other and give mutual support. However, when stories are published, some re-live the trauma and develop post-traumatic stress disorder. Others develop incredible rage, especially when they learn that there were other victims and were not the 'special' children they were purported to be. It is common for victims to ruminate about their sexuality, tending to blame themselves for 'letting' it happen or not reporting it.

Apart from fear and shame, victims have had to deal with a hostile church hierarchy. Those who made reports to bishops were often treated as victimisers. In some religious organisations, victims were made to forgive their abusers publicly but the abusers did not have to apologise to them.

Predators in religious schools

How safe are children in religious schools? Recent court cases showed that some pederast priests have been allowed to continue both priestly and teaching duties years after being convicted of molesting boys. Father John Denham was still working in Sydney parishes six years after serving a two-year prison sentence (2000) for sexually abusing a student at a boys' college. The priest was reported in 1978 and was transferred to another school where parents were unaware of his history. Ten years later he was chaplain at Waverley Christian Brothers College. In 2006, he did relief work in understaffed parishes. No alarm bells rang to warn parents and children to be cautious.

On August 14, 2008, just a month after the Pope's visit to Sydney, Denham was charged with another 30 child sex offences against boys as young as 11. Furthermore, his superior, the former head of the school, was charged with perverting the course of justice. Case after case confirm that school principals have ignored parents' reports of sex offending even when teachers were witnesses. In one Christian school, the whistle-blowing staff member was sacked and the victims expelled; the principal later pleaded guilty to sexually abusing students.

From 1979 onwards, three paedophile teachers were apparently reported to the principal of Canberra's Marist College. One, Paul Lyons, committed suicide when charged in 2000.[58] Another, Brother Kostka, allegedly threatened his victims with expulsion if they went to the police. The victims said they remained silent because they realised that being expelled would disappoint their parents who worked so hard to send them to this exclusive private school. Staff thought it odd that students had free access to Kostka's study but they said nothing, even when Kostka told colleagues that he enlisted boys to go to his bedroom to wake him up each morning. One mother stated she had complained to the headmaster that Kostka was taking boys into his office, sitting them on his lap and masturbating. The headmaster is said to have reported it to the provincial head of the Marists. Police were never informed.

One victim said he reported Kostka because he was concerned about the monk's behaviour with another young boy. The victim said he returned to the school several years later and told another headmaster of the abuse. Again, the police were not informed. The victim met senior Marist, Brother Alexis Turton, who assured him that Kostka had retired to their Mittagong farmhouse. The victim's brother visited the farmhouse and found Kostka running a drop-in centre for boys.

There is widespread agreement that, when those in authority turn a blind eye, offenders become more daring. Five of the Marist monks' victims are known to have committed suicide. Kostka was asked to leave in 1992 but it was not until 2007 that the school finally asked victims to come forward.

Unfortunately, these stories are not unusual. The strong message for parents is to report suspicions and sexual crimes to police, not head teachers or clergy. Churches and schools have a long history of ignoring allegations and moving clergy and monks to other areas when complaints arise. Given the publicity and massive compensation claims paid to victims, one might expect schools to be safer places than they were a few years ago but it is clear that parents can't afford to be complacent. Furthermore, the child protection protocols of some prestigious schools show that managers have learned nothing from experience. Despite mandatory reporting laws that require reports to be made directly to child protection services and police, the school protocols instead demand any reports of abuse be passed on to departmental heads, school principals, the Professional Standards Committees, bishops and archbishops, not police.

Church responses to victims

Parents who reported abuse by clergy, monks and teachers have found that churches responded more like businesses than Christian services. Not only are their financial assets protected by teams of legal advisers, but their responses have been dictated by insurers' lawyers who ordered archbishops not to apologise to victims or accept any responsibility for abuse by clergy.

At times it seems that churches have yet to recognise sexual abuse as intrinsically evil and condemn its perpetrators accordingly. Authorities have typically minimised their causal role in harm by devaluing and blaming victims. Thus, they have been able to view the children, not their abusers, as endangering their institutions by having exposed the crimes.

Churches are using legal devices to avoid responsibility in court for young parishioners abused while in its alleged care. In 2008, Australian Marists announced that they would use a legal precedent known as the Ellis case to avoid paying compensation to a large number of boys abused by their monks and priests in schools. Those who try to take civil action against the Church may find them denying that the criminal priest technically was employed by the diocese, asserting he only served God. This position maintains that it was God that appointed the priest in question, signed his contract of employment and paid his salary and taxes. Anglicans and the Salvation Army have employed the same argument.

Victims not only deserve compassion but also expressions of moral indignation.

All Australians should be concerned about the fact that the quality of justice for child victims depends on who employed the rapist. Victims hoped that this response would change after the Pope's public apology in Sydney in 2008. It didn't.

CHILD SEX ABUSE IN ELITE SPORTS

The problem of child sexual abuse in sports has been recognised by both the Olympic Committee and the Australian Sports Commission. Sexual harassment and sex abuse happen in all types of sports and at all levels, with a greater prevalence in elite sports. Members of the athlete's entourage who are in positions of power and authority appear to be the main offenders. Victims do not complain because they want to achieve their performance goals and the coach is perceived as crucial to that. Research also demonstrates that sexual harassment and abuse in sports seriously and negatively impact athletes' physical and psychological health. They can damage performance and lead to athlete drop out.

Based on this information and in its role of promoting and protecting the health of athletes, the IOC Medical Commission held a conference on 'Sexual Harassment & Abuse in Sport' in October 2006 in Lausanne. A panel of participants composed of leading sports psychologists, sociologists, psychiatrists and policy experts from around the world, as well as an elite athlete advocate, attended to review the scientific literature and to produce safe guidelines for the prevention of and early intervention in cases of sexual harassment and abuse in sports. The Australian Government Sports Commission website provides details of international publications relating to this issue. However, there have been problems in local clubs, too.

In 2004, a 60-year-old former junior sports coach in a small town in Victoria was jailed for 15 years for sexually assaulting young boys over a 20-year period. Twenty-six young men made 109 allegations of rape and sexual abuse. Despite the strength of the evidence, some local residents told media that they supported the accused because he had "served the football club well" for many years. Others said his criminal behaviour with boys was widely known but no one challenged him. They knew that large numbers of boys visited his house for noisy, alcohol-riddled, weekend parties but his status as a trainer insulated him from criticism.

In South Australia, parents trusted an Adelaide Magistrate when he wrote to them via their schools, using his Magistrates Court stationery, offering to transport their sons safely to a club for young lifesavers. No one seems to have been suspicious that, while the man was a club trainer, he couldn't even swim. This man is serving a 25-year jail sentence with more charges pending. Parents imagined (wrongly) that their children were safe because of the man's professional status and the fact that the boys were in groups.[59] This man demonstrated that no one can be trusted on the basis of their position in society and there is no safety in numbers.

CHILD SEX OFFENDERS ARE PROTECTED BY ADULT IGNORANCE

Those who emphatically pronounce that child molesters should be jailed and society throw away the key are often the first to defend offenders that they, themselves, trusted. An Australian Childhood Foundation study, *Out of Sight — Out of Mind*, showed that:

- Child abuse was of less concern to parents than the rising cost of petrol, transport problems and the state of footpaths.
- 31 percent of a sample of 720 adults admitted they would not believe children who confessed they'd been sexually abused.
- 16 percent were unclear about whether or not sex between a child and an adult constituted abuse.
- 43 percent couldn't hazard a guess at the number of reported cases of child abuse in Australia, while the remainder significantly understated the size of the problem.
- One in five respondents said they wouldn't know what to do in response to learning a child was being abused.

Similarly, a survey undertaken by the National Association for the Prevention of Child Abuse and Neglect (NAPCAN) with

21,000 respondents (2010) found that although 92 percent thought that child abuse is a serious problem, fewer than half would take any action when faced with clear evidence of sexual or physical abuse or child neglect. Reasons given for not reporting abuse included:

- Anxiety that they could be wrong (48%).
- Concerns about what might happen to them (44%).
- It's not their business (42%).
- Don't know what to do (38%).
- Don't want to cause problems for the child (33%).
- Don't want to upset the parents (30%).
- Don't want to admit things like that happen (22%).

These are disturbing examples of how negligent we are both as a society and as parents. We need to become better educated and proactive when it comes to protecting children. Clearly, we can't rely on other people, schools, the community, the justice system or anyone else to protect them. *We* have to take more responsibility. That means acquiring knowledge about offenders and how they operate.

In the United States, more than 80,000 cases of child sexual abuse are reported every year. Jennifer Freyd, an Orlando professor of psychology, showed her classes videos in which male and female victims described sexual offences committed by adults when the victims were as young as 9 years old. One hundred percent of her female students, along with 100 percent of male students who had experienced abuse, believed these victims' reports. Men who had no history of abuse did not. In other words, personal experience was essential for these men to believe that abuse occurred. This is a concern when such men serve on juries.

Freyd calculated that 86 percent of sex crimes against children are never reported to authorities and that men "just don't get it" unless they've been victims themselves.[60] Macho-type males believed that, if it happened at all, either the abuse wasn't harmful or victims must have wanted it. Freyd found that these attitudes discouraged victims from speaking out and allowed perpetrators to escape unpunished, leaving them free to repeat their crimes. It also has serious implications for using men on juries.

The findings suggested that educational efforts need to be more heavily focused on men and boys to help them understand that such acts commonly occur and can contribute to a number of societal ills. It is a concern that fathers don't get involved in child protection. They leave it entirely to mothers and are too disinterested to even ask what their children have been taught.

Mothers can be complacent, too

The complacency of mothers is often based on very unrealistic expectations. The average parent:

- Doesn't talk to kids about vulgar behaviour.
- Reprimands children for vulgar, inappropriate talk.
- Provides modesty training, teaching little girls not to reveal their underwear.
- Doesn't give children the vocabulary or permission to report abuse.

Nevertheless, some mothers say they don't need to do anything about child protection because *they* will sense when something is wrong. Nothing could be further from the truth.

Mothers also believe that their children will know instinctively that abuse is wrong and, without any previous conversations about the subject will report it immediately to them.

Interestingly, risks may even be ignored by mothers who were themselves incest victims, if they accept the blame for what happened. They deny that their children are at risk from their abuser because, "He knows that I know what he did, so he wouldn't dare touch my kids" In the meantime, offenders think,

"She knows what I did to her and yet she still lets her kids come to see me. I'm safe."

Adult incest survivors often say they protect their kids by accompanying them when they visit a paedophile grandfather or uncle, not realising that offenders are daring and find opportunities to offend when the parent is in the kitchen, the same car, same room or even the same tent. Offenders know that the more daring and the more bizarre the circumstances, the less likely it is that the child will be believed.

Some abused mothers trapped in violent relationships think that abuse is an unavoidable aspect of life and that kids have to learn to put up with it. Some know that nieces and nephews are at risk but remain silent because "it's not my responsibility," "it is none of my business," and they don't want to cause family upheaval.

Some Indian and Asian mothers say that their cultures prevent them from protecting their children; that is, they are unable to accuse someone who is senior to them in the family hierarchy such as an older uncle or grandparent.[61]

There is a clear need for school-based personal safety education programmes that involve both parent figures to provide better protection for children.

Child sex offenders are protected by family members

Child sex offenders and extended family members often use the same strategies to deny or minimise their offending. These are:

- *Physical denial.* Some family members provide false alibis for offenders, lying about their whereabouts at the time of offences to protect their family from shame and financial hardship if the abuser is jailed. Offenders and their supporters display righteous indignation and threaten to sue accusers, hoping to frighten them into withdrawing their statements. This kind of family support makes it difficult for offenders to seek and receive treatment.

- *Psychological denial* by proclaiming that the offender has an impeccable character and they are horrified that anyone would make such accusations. They protest without focusing on the offences.

- *Minimising the extent of offending.* "Yes, he/I touched the child but it was harmless and they're exaggerating. He/I would never penetrate a child." And when he has: "The child was old enough to know better. S/he could have stopped it if s/he wanted to."

- *Denying the serious effects of abuse.* "Yes, it happened but it was a long time ago. S/he should get over it and get on with his/her life" or "S/he wanted it/cooperated so it wasn't really abuse," or "It was at the lower end of the scale."

- *Denying the need for treatment.* Some offenders deny the need for treatment or, if under pressure from their lawyer, attend a session voluntarily and then claim that the therapist told them further treatment is unnecessary because they won't re-offend. They are lying. If they have been abusing children since adolescence, it will take far more than a single session to create a difference and re-programme their obsessions.

- *Denying responsibility for their behaviour.* They blame alcohol or their 'seductive' victims or 'frigid' wives.[62] Defence lawyers now encourage offenders to use the "I was a victim" excuse to reduce their prison sentences. We all have choices; past abuse is an explanation, *not* an excuse for abusing others.

- *Closing ranks.* Offenders orchestrate the shunning of relative-victims after abuse is disclosed. That is why those abused within the family need additional care and support and why professionals need to understand the extent of this phenomena. Professor Caroline Taylor believes that judges should take this behaviour into account, considering offenders actively use shunning as a threat to silence children or punish them for their disclosures. The fear of losing family support and connection can trap children into long-term victimisation. They (and their supportive parents) are ostracised by the very relatives who should be supporting them.

Family support can be very destructive when it protects offenders and stigmatises victims. A teacher groomed a victim's family so well that he married the boy's cousin. They built a luxurious house and had a baby. Concern about the baby led the victim to report the offences. For two years, the abuser was in denial. He sold the house to pay legal fees. The extended family blamed the then 11-year-old boy for not stopping the abuse. "You knew it was wrong," they said. "You could have stopped it. He's lost his house, thanks to you." When other victims came forward, the man realised that his protestations of innocence were doomed and changed his plea to guilty. He received a 10-year jail sentence. The extended family then ostracised the victim and his parents because the abuser didn't like being in jail. There was a clear need for individual and family counselling but nothing was made available.

A characteristic of child sex offenders is their ability to shift the blame to someone else and show no empathy for their victims. They are cowards. Sadly, their family supporters often follow their example.

In cases of abuse within the family, concerned members should seek and be automatically offered counselling at the time of the arrest, after the conviction and before the offender is released. Understanding abuse, abusers and family responses can help family members to circumvent this damaging dynamic.

For more information on child sex offenders, see Anna C. Salter's *Predators, Pedophiles, Rapists and Other Sex Offenders* published by Basic Books in 2004.

CHARACTERISTICS OF UNSAFE SCHOOLS

Whenever child sexual abuse occurs in a school, there is invariably a lack of emphasis on children's safety. At an elite Brisbane school, the abuse of boys by the school counsellor was common knowledge among older students. Some staff members were suspicious but remained silent because the offender often referred to his long-time friendship with the headmaster and how they attended the same church. Sex-offending teachers develop and flaunt the trust of school managers. If boys resist their advances, they are sent to the principal for trivial or concocted misdemeanours to demonstrate the abuser's power.

When children revealed that a teacher sexually abused the entire class of boys sent to him for remedial reading, the principal appealed to staff to keep the matter "within these four walls to protect the good name of the school". Fortunately, parents didn't agree with him and reported the offences to the police, only to discover that the teacher had recently been dismissed from a boys' boarding school for committing similar offences.

Schools that harbour sex offenders invariably lack child protection protocols and child protection curriculum, despite the fact that school programmes have been available in New Zealand and some Australian states since 1985.[63]

When teachers are prosecuted, school principals often act as character witnesses, assuring the court that the accused was the best and most popular teacher the school ever had. What these school managers fail to realise is that they are describing the typical paedophile who volunteers for any activity that provides unsupervised contact with children. He is perceived by the community as a hero and those who accuse him are vilified. Protective parents should ask for a copy of the school's child protection policy and regulations. If your children attend a private school, look very closely at the rules for reporting allegations of abuse. How is the child protected? Are police to be informed immediately if the abuser is a member of staff? What if a child is abused by an older student? Is the school really focused on protecting children? If not, why not? If you are not satisfied, contact the principal, the school council or the education authority.

CHILD SEX OFFENDER TREATMENT

Child sex offenders rarely admit to the damage they do to children. Some even argue that sex with adults is good for kids. Denial is likely to persist until offenders undergo an intensive treatment programme. Although specialist treatment has been successful in reducing re-offending, not all convicted child sex offenders have access to it. In 2008, it was reported that there were 125 child sex offenders incarcerated in South Australian prisons and only 20 per annum could receive treatment.

Some prisoners don't want to change. Some told the author that they intended to re-offend within a week of release. Some refused parole if it meant undergoing a treatment programme that was perceived as an uncomfortable 'guilt trip'.

There is no cure for paedophilia. You can't change a well-established, sexual attraction to children. Some paedophiles genuinely want to change, choosing to undergo hormone therapy (colloquially and unfortunately referred to as chemical castration) that reduces libido.

Some are concerned about their sexual attraction to their own children and want help but are too embarrassed to seek it and don't know where to go. Governments have spent millions of dollars on TV advertisements to stop domestic violence but not a cent has been spent on advertising treatments to put a stop to child sexual abuse.

FALSE REPORTS

Male teachers, parents and carers often worry about the risk of being falsely accused of sexual abuse. Fathers ask,

"Should I stop showering with the kids? Might I be accused of abuse?"

"Should I stop cuddling my kids?"

"Should I stop going around the house unclothed?"

"What if my daughter tells her teacher that I patted her on the bottom? Will she report me?"

False allegations of sexual abuse are rare and reports are investigated thoroughly before anyone is charged with an offence.

Affectionate parenting should never be changed for fear that someone might misinterpret it. To the contrary, when we asked 198 male victims what could have been done to protect them from abuse, they all referred to the need for physical affection (hugs, kisses, cuddles and approval) from their dads. The lack of it made them vulnerable to male predators. The second most important protection would have been information about their bodies, as available in the booklet, Secret Boys Business.

Parents can usually sense when children are uncomfortable about nudity and want privacy in the bathroom and bedroom.

However, to avoid false accusations, mothers and fathers who are separated and have new partners would be wise to use basic safety strategies for handling children, teaching them to clean themselves when using the toilet, drying themselves when having a bath or shower and sleeping in separate beds.

CHILD SEXUAL ABUSE IN THE LEGAL SYSTEM

With the exception of Western Australia, family courts are the responsibility of the federal government.

If children report sexual offences by a parent or parent's new partner, the safe parents may soon find themselves facing complex, conflicting procedures and responses that are inconsistent between state agencies and federal courts.

If child abuse victims are too young to be cross-examined by a barrister in criminal courts, their abusers are not prosecuted. Unless they are convicted of the crime, the allegations are unproven.

State child protection services may not substantiate abuse because:

- The child is considered to be too young to be assessed.
- The children reside with the safe parent and are perceived as safe, even though they have weekend contact with the accused parent or
- Sometimes children can't or won't immediately disclose abuse to officials, who are strangers to them.
- Resources are inadequate.

Protective parents then face a dilemma. If they do nothing, their children can be removed by state child protection services as being in need of care and protection. To avoid this, protective parents may turn to the family court to seek orders to stop or introduce supervised contact between the child and the accused parent, believing the court's first priority is to cater to the best interests of the child.

There is no automatic input from state agencies to family court matters. Family courts rely on evidence placed before them and lack the capacity to investigate allegations of abuse. In Australian amendments introduced in 2006 the law requires the judge to authorise shared parenting as a starting point, unless substantial proof of abuse of the child is entered into evidence. The protective parent may not necessarily be given legal aid because of "lack of merit" and may be manipulated into agreeing to allow contact on the threat of losing residency of the child. The court consultant may well decide that the safe parent (usually the mother) is mentally ill or vindictive and has coached the children to make the complaint of sexual abuse to stop the father from having contact. Appeals are possible, but are limited to legal issues and they are very costly. Some mothers have lost their homes in efforts to protect their children.

In 2000, the Chief Justice and three reviews and reports made recommendations to change the law so that children's safety would be prioritised. Fathers' groups responded by threatening the Labour Government that, if any changes were made, millions of fathers would vote Liberal. The Attorney General responsible for family courts responded weakly that it was "all a misunderstanding".

For further information on the family court, read Thea Brown and Renata Alexander's 2007 book, *Child Abuse and Family Law,* published by Allen & Unwin.

CONCLUSION

Although the picture presented is frightening, you can take steps to reduce the risks to your children without creating 'bubble-wrapped' kids.

The most important deterrent to offenders is the supervision of the child by knowledgeable adults who are forearmed and know how predators operate. It is also important to have an informed child who understands the difference between acceptable and reportable behaviours.

It obviously helps if you are alert to the grooming methods used by paedophiles but don't expect other parents to be as well informed as you. You may be a lone voice when others have been seduced by the charm and generosity of the typical paedophile.

Well-informed supervision exerts a restraining influence on potential abusers who specifically look for situations where parents, teachers and others responsible for children are trusting and negligent and where security is lax. Offenders seek arrangements that provide opportunities to be alone with children as minders or favourite 'uncles' (real or adopted) who are granted opportunities to read bedtime stories, for example.

Ask yourself why a teacher, sports coach, etc., would offer to babysit other people's children. What is in it for them?

Rely on your gut feelings. Be assertive. Ask why the teacher is allowed to keep children after school if there is no other adult present. Surely that is against the school's child protection policy? Ask for a copy of the policy and read it very carefully.

Report the sexual harassment of your child by staff or others responsible for their safety; harassment precedes abuse.

When Mr. Nice Guy steps over the boundaries and makes you feel uncomfortable, assert yourself. He may be OK but it's better to be safe than sorry. It makes sense to pursue your suspicions, not abandon them with guilty feelings because the suspected Mr. Nice Guy has charmed everyone else with his generosity and helpfulness. Always remember that if someone seems to be too good to be true, thet probably are.

A teacher, coach, youth worker or other professional has a defined role and responsibilities. Don't let anyone go beyond these roles to become a child's best friend, babysitter or de facto uncle/aunt. Offenders like to create relationships where your trust is such that you ignore your instincts and suspicions, ignore risky behaviour and give them the benefit of the doubt.

The temptation to overlook inappropriate behaviour is great when it involves an authority figure. You feel embarrassed, don't know what to say and fear what others will think if you intervene; it is probably a new situation for which you haven't had any practice. Stop boisterous play, massaging and tickling immediately. Take care that your own fear of embarrassment doesn't take priority over the child's safety. Trust your instincts and act on them without apology. Gut feelings are usually accurate concerning risky behaviour. Do not be put off by threats to sue you; you have legal protection when you report reasonable suspicions of child abuse to child protection services or police.

Never assume that children are safe in groups. Get involved in camps and make sure that your children are aware of child protection strategies before they leave.

Be aware of offenders' patterns of behaviour because the odds of a child being abused are increasing. After abuse is revealed, teachers and parents invariably recall warning signs that they ignored.

An important deterrent to offenders is to have well-informed, confident children who know their rights, can differentiate between appropriate and inappropriate behaviour and will turn to a protective and informed parent for help. Your children will encounter some form of sexually inappropriate behaviour whether it involves adults or other children. Knowledge is power. The next chapter provides ideas on how you can provide better protection.

Chapter 7

What You Can Do To Keep Kids Safe

This chapter explains what can be done to better protect our children. We don't want to make them fearful. We don't want to become 'helicopter parents' hovering to keep them safe. We want children to be aware of what is right and wrong and what to do when acceptable behaviour changes and becomes reportable. We want children to take note of and respond safely to creepy feelings, creepy people and wrong behaviour. We want them to develop good observation and problem-solving skills, skills that are valuable throughout life but are especially useful for staying safe in emergencies. We want them to be strong and confident in the knowledge that they have the right to be safe with people.

The chances are that you've taught your children to cross the road safely when you're not there to protect them. You've probably taught them to stay safe with heat, fire, water, sharp objects and electricity. If you have, you've already begun the kind of teaching you need to do to keep children safe with people.

You've probably recognised that you can't supervise your kids all the time and they need to know what constitutes acceptable versus reportable behaviour so that if they encounter the latter, they know what to do. Experts agree that the age of three is the best time to start. The later you leave it, the harder it becomes, because if the topic has previously been a taboo subject, both you and your child may be too embarrassed to engage in useful communications.

WHY PERSONAL SAFETY EDUCATION IS IMPORTANT

Although there are some good quality child protection programmes available for schools, they are not widely used and you can't rely on teachers to provide the information that children most need. History shows that, although they may talk about safety in general, they frequently omit the most important safety issues, including sexual misbehaviour and the child's right to say no to wrong touching. Some teachers lack the confidence to tackle sensitive matters and may fear that a comprehensive programme might result in disclosures of abuse that they would prefer to avoid. Some teachers are also survivors of sexual abuse who find that teaching safety strategies brings back upsetting reminders of their own experiences.

Parents need to talk to children about personal safety issues for several reasons:

- **Uninformed children are powerless.**

Sexual abuse is about sex and power. It involves the strong controlling the comparatively weak for sexual gratification. Children are especially powerless when they lack knowledge about what is reportable behaviour and how and when to report it. *Age-appropriate knowledge is a key to safety.*

- **Young children are incapable of judging the motives of adults.**

Young children take their concepts of what is safe and unsafe from adults. They turn to us for guidance. If we say, "Yes, it's OK. You're safe. There's nothing wrong," they accept our reassurances, irrespective of whether they like or dislike what is happening. They view the adult's character as 'good' or 'bad' based on their behaviour. For example, when the abuser says s/he loves the child and provides gifts, treats and attention, the abuser is perceived as a good person, regardless of the pain associated with sexual violation. Children under the age of eight trust all adults who look or seem kind. They are incapable of assessing adults' motives and don't recognise gifts as bribes. *This is why it is important that they know what is right and wrong behaviour and that you create and maintain an open relationship where they can safely come to you with concerns.*

- **Children associate goodness with obedience.**
Children think they have to obey adults even when they know that what the adult is doing or demanding is wrong. This helps sex offenders to offend with little risk of being rejected. Children are especially vulnerable when they've been trained to suppress their feelings to please others. They have to tolerate sloppy, wet kisses, bristly chins and too-tight hugs, for example, because mum says the relative will be upset if they don't cooperate. This gives kids the message that their own feelings don't count and they must put up with unwanted touching to please grownups. *That is opposite to the message that children need.*

- **Children don't know that sex abuse
is wrong and reportable.**
If children have not been taught what constitutes OK versus wrong, reportable behaviour, many regard sexual abuse as normal. This is especially likely when victims are boys and offences involve older kids, siblings, relatives or carers. Children view what happens in their families as 'normal' even if it is a crime. *Boys are abused at a younger age than girls and should be taught to value and take care of their bodies and be given age-appropriate information.*

- **Children are vulnerable in groups.**
There is an old saying that there's safety in numbers. We transport children to childcare, school, camps, clubs, choirs, sports,

scouts and church activities and assume that they are safe because of the presence of others.

Boys are especially vulnerable in all-male groups. It is comparatively easy for a sex offender to overcome the resistance of an uninformed child if he can show that what is happening is normal and that everyone else does it. Boys like to be the same as others and they are easily recruited with comments such as, "What's wrong with you? This is fun. You're weird".

A 7-year-old American girl was visiting her grandmother when a neighbour, Mr. Clark, invited her to join his own two sons and their friends for a picnic in the park. When Julie climbed into his mini-bus, Grandma said (as most of us do), "Be a good girl and do what Mr. Clark tells you to do". Fortunately, when Mr. Clark introduced sex, Julie refused to cooperate. When she returned to her grandmother's house, she gave a detailed description of what happened. Interviews with the other children not only confirmed Julie's evidence but told of previous abuse by Mr. Clark. Eventually he was convicted of offences against 38 local 7- and 8-year-olds. What was both puzzling and disturbing is why 37 children had cooperated with Mr. Clark but the American girl didn't. Why did children accompany him a second time without complaining to parents? Why did his two sons remain silent?

Julie had one advantage over the others. Her American teacher had told her class that "No one is allowed to play around or tickle the private parts of your body or ask you to touch theirs and that, if they do, you hold out your arms in front of you and raise your hands vertically to create personal space and say, 'Stop that! It isn't allowed!' Then tell your mum or someone you trust as soon as possible." And that's exactly what Julie did.

- **Uninformed children are confused by adults' sexual misbehaviour.**

Because parents reprimand them when they use sex-talk or show their bottoms when there are visitors, children are shocked and confused when adults introduce sexual behaviour and especially when an adult exposes himself. While offenders give assurances that there's nothing wrong, their behaviour indicates otherwise. They take advantage of the child's confusion to gain compliance. There is another conflicting message when the victim is told to keep the behaviour secret. Why would secrecy be necessary if what is happening is all right? School-aged children know that some kids behave indecently but they never expect grownups to be indecent because "they tell children off for being rude". *Children can accept and understand the idea that, if no one stops them, rude kids can grow up to become rude adults — and it helps to report and stop them.*

- **Children lack opportunities to express anxieties and fears.**

Parents underestimate children's fears. Children simply don't talk about them because, with the best of intentions, adults reassure them that "there's nothing to be afraid of" (when they are terrified), that "it doesn't hurt" (when they are in pain) and that the molesting relative causing their anxiety is really trustworthy and "you know he loves you and will be really upset if you don't see him" (or whatever they resist doing). Victims feel they must remain silent and tolerate the intolerable.

Ask your children what and who they are afraid of. Who gives them creepy feelings? Who is the rudest person they know? What do these people do to generate these feelings? Work out what you can do about it together.

- **Without personal safety education, young children are vulnerable to dangerous strangers.**

Despite knowing since the late 1970s that the stranger isn't the greatest danger to children, the media, parents, some teachers and police continue to give the 'dangerous stranger' messages: don't talk to strangers and don't get into a stranger's car. Had they taken the trouble to investigate, they would have realised that children younger than 8 (and some say 10) don't even understand what constitutes a stranger. They say he's half-human, half-monster. He looks ugly, sinister, has evil eyes, wears black clothes, drives an old black car and steals children from their beds. Five-year-olds say he takes them away and kills them and their mummies and daddies never see them again and their parents will be upset and cry. They say they have never seen a stranger in their lives except on TV but would know one instantly if they saw one. *The resulting danger is that anyone who doesn't look like this sinister creature is deemed to be trustworthy.*

Paradoxically, while parents avoid providing safety strategies because they "don't want to scare the kids," children 6 to 9 years old have nightmares about dangerous stranger-monsters. Some girls of 7 to 9 years of age are so anxious about them that they are nervous visiting the homes of relatives and friends because dangerous strangers might be hiding there. They are anxious when walking to and from school if male drivers pause in driveways to let them walk past. The driver is assumed to be sinister if he smiles. Younger children are afraid to tell a shop assistant in a department store that they are lost because, "she might take me to a stranger". Instead, they look for any adult with a smiling face and ask them to take them home. Yes, a stranger.

> The dangerous stranger message can be hazardous because if adults don't resemble the stereotypical, ugly monster of their imaginations, children trust them. Most strangers are helpful and if children need help, for example, when lost in a shopping centre, at a Christmas pageant, show or sports event, they will need the ability to choose the safest stranger to assist in the particular set of circumstances.

With parents' cooperation, numerous TV programmes have demonstrated that, despite the parents emphasising that strangers are dangerous, kind-hearted children will accompany the first stranger who seeks their help. On one programme, a 12-year-old climbed into the back of a van to pick up a parcel for an actor who pretended to have a bad back. A very capable six-year-old girl virtually climbed into a TV crew's car to show directions on a map. Her older sister ran indoors to tell her mother but left her little sister behind. A six-year-old and a two-year-old gave their names, chatted to and walked off happily with an elderly actor who sought their help to find an imaginary, lost puppy. Their mother assured interviewers that she had taught the girls to avoid 'bad men' and they would stay safe. While their mother was in a shop, several children from the same family left the shopping centre to help the actor (who feigned a disability) to carry his groceries to his vehicle. The sad thing was that the most helpful children were most vulnerable, especially while playing close to home. In four days of filming, only two children were suspicious enough to seek their parent's advice.

Most strangers are helpful but we do need to develop a sense of caution. Instead of talking about strangers, we should ask children to imagine what someone could do in a variety of (potentially dangerous) situations, rather than ambiguously refer to dangerous people. Strangers are successful because they use charm and appeal to children's needs or willingness to help, not because they are ugly monsters.

Using examples of potentially dangerous situations, ask "What if...?" and "Just suppose..., what would be the safest thing to do?" emphasising situations rather than people.

- **Without safety information, children believe they have to keep the bad behaviour of adults a secret.** Children are usually taught that secrets must always be kept, especially family secrets. Uninformed adults assume that children's secrets are fun ones, not realising that child sex offenders depend entirely on secrecy to continue their crimes without risk of prosecution and punishment.

School programmes teach children to keep good surprises (such as holiday and birthday presents) and tell bad secrets that make them sad or worried. Unless you are involved in a school programme, you may inadvertently undermine what is being taught by assuring children that they have to keep secrets, especially family secrets. Children become confused when receiving these conflicting messages, concluding that they can only tell kids' secrets or nice secrets that make people happy and they have to keep bad secrets because they make people sad.

If such a policy is too hard, adopt: "We only keep good surprises about special days like birthdays (that someone will learn about later) but we must never keep secrets about touching/bodies and secrets that make us feel worried, sad or scared."

Without your help, children think that if they tell a secret about abuse they will be punished both by you and the abuser who created the secret. This is because (a) the behaviour was naughty; (b) they would have to talk about stuff that is naughty which is, itself, possibly naughty; and (c) they would be disclosing an adult's secret (also naughty). Without prior evidence of your willingness to support them, children believe that you would inform the abuser that they told the secret. *This is why it is so important for parents to be involved in personal safety education, both at home and at school.*

Without correct vocabulary, victims only give hints about abuse.

Abused children may give hints

Some children don't have the knowledge or language to report sexual abuse. They may give hints by disclosing abuse in the third person. They pretend that it is happening to a friend. This is their safest way of acquiring information for themselves. They test you out to see if it is safe to make a disclosure. They watch to see how you respond. With the benefit of hindsight, parents remember vague hints such as:

"I don't want to go to Grandpa's anymore." (*Ask why.*)

"I don't like the games he plays." (*Ask what and how they play.*)

"I don't like the way he teases me." (*Ask how he teases.*)

"He plays silly games with me." (*Ask how they play them.*)

"I don't like the babysitter. She's mean." (*Ask, "What does she do that you don't like?"*)

"Uncle X wears funny underpants." (Ask, "*When do you see his underpants?*")

"I don't like his pee-pee." (*Ask, "Did he show it to you? Where did you see it?"*)

"I don't like the way he tickles me." ("S*how me where he tickles.*" *If the tickling is harmless, promise to have a word with the tickler*).

"I don't like playing horsey with him." ("*What do you have to do when you play?*")

"I don't like his milk/ice cream. It is yucky." (*Ask where it comes from.*)

"Mummy's boyfriend hurts me when I'm in their bed. (*Ask where he hurts and what he does.*)

"I've got a secret." (*Ask, whether it is a happy secret or a sad one.* "*Would you like to tell me your secret?*" *If not,* "*What will happen if you tell me the secret? Who else knows it?*")

A boy overheard his dad say that he would kill anyone who touched his son. The boy asked his teacher what happens to people who kill someone and she replied that they go to jail for a very long time. Because of that, he kept his abuse secret for many years.

If your child suddenly decides that s/he doesn't want to visit someone or do something previously enjoyed, sit down quietly and find out why.

Listen carefully to your children, especially if they are looking sad or their behaviour has changed. Ask questions calmly to find out what is happening.

Victims often think they are reporting abuse when they give hints. Our failure to understand is interpreted as an unwillingness or inability to help. Their sense of helplessness and hopelessness then increases.

Unless you have demonstrated to your children that you will protect them, they may not believe that you will do it

Children think that if they tell you about sexual misbehaviour, you won't believe them. Twenty-six percent of 5- to 9-year-olds involved in research with 375 children said they had asked a parent to help them to stop uncomfortable and unwanted touching by an adult and their pleas were ignored. Children sought parents' help to stop excessive tickling and sloppy kisses from relatives and granddads rubbing their whiskery chins against their faces until it hurt. They were accused of whining, being "a misery" and told that the adults would be upset if they didn't cooperate. Little girls living in hotels had to put up with unwanted contact with intoxicated customers because "mum says we can't afford to upset regular clients". From age 5 to 9, children had already cynically concluded that parents couldn't be trusted to protect them from unwanted touching by adults, that parents don't listen to kids, that grownups don't believe kids and that adults stick together.

To keep children safe, that image must be changed. Don't give children the notion that their feelings don't count and they have to put the feelings of their relatives and other adults first. That message plays into the sex offender's hands. When your kids don't want to be kissed, tell your relatives that they are still loved but your children are growing up and are at a stage where they just don't want to be kissed. Ask them to respect that.

SKILLS NEEDED TO STAY SAFE
FROM SEXUAL PREDATORS

American and New Zealand research findings have shown conclusively that the children who have the best safety knowledge and safety skills are those in a comprehensive and explicit school programme with their parent's involvement. However, any programme is better than none. Children learn not only to avoid dangerous situations but they help brothers, sisters and friends to stay safe, too. A survey of 2,000 children for American Scouts showed that information doesn't always protect your child against abusive behaviour; some victims simply freeze. And we must never underestimate the power and force, the tricks and attractive baits that offenders use to trap children. However, with an explicit, open, honest and comprehensive approach that provides activity, repetition and reinforcement, victims are more likely to stop abuse quickly by reporting it. They then feel good about their involvement and this reduces psychological harm.

Our interviews with 84 convicted child molesters confirmed that they avoided confident, well-informed children because they are the ones most likely to recognise their tricks and report them.

Please note that a school programme does not eliminate parental responsibility for child protection, neither does it make children responsible for protecting themselves. It has to be a combined effort.

To create safer children, we must help them to:

- Develop confidence and strength of character.
- Engage in open communication; let them know they can talk to you about any situation (and promise you won't get mad).
- Remember their name, address and phone number and how to contact you when you're not at home.
- Know how to contact a trusted adult if they are scared.
- Know the correct vocabulary for their body parts, including penis or vagina, so that they will be understood if they report sexual misbehaviour at school, etc.
- Know that their breasts, buttocks and genitals are private. Private means, "keep out, don't touch, it's mine, you're not allowed, etc."
- Understand that their mouths are private, too and no one is allowed to put anything "yucky" or "stinky" or any part of their body into the mouth.
- Know that no one is allowed to tickle or play around with these private parts and attempts to do so must be reported to you.
- Tell you secrets that make them feel sad or worried, etc.
- Recognise, escape from and report sexual misbehaviour, irrespective of who the perpetrator is — even if it's someone they know and like.
- Recognise, escape from and report potentially dangerous behaviours.
- Get away from people and situations that give them creepy feelings.
- Avoid and tell you if kids or adults introduce dirty/rude talk and rude pictures, given that these are commonly used to groom children for abuse.

- Improve children's decision-making and problem-solving skills using role play: "what if..." and "just suppose..." questions to work out the safest thing to do in a variety of potentially dangerous situations.
- Develop observation skills by playing I-Spy and car-spotting games to draw attention to different makes of cars, registration numbers and descriptions of people.
- Develop independence with safety.
- Answer the phone safely when at home alone.
- Take safety precautions when using the Internet and other technology.
- Report sexual misbehaviour to you or a teacher if at school.
- Know how to telephone police and a children's helpline.
- Keep on reporting until someone listens, believes and helps.

Safety rules often conflict with common parenting practices. Use what we call 'teachable moments' when you are with young learners. In other words, without being paranoid, use opportunities to draw your child's attention to safety issues in your daily lives around the house, when you go to school, a shopping centre, the park or a sports event. Use children's interactions, their questions and responses to highlight issues such as different feelings, different touches, rules about touching, emergencies and disclosing secrets while keeping good surprises about birthday and holiday presents and surprise parties.

If your child's school has a personal safety programme, get involved

Participate in your child's school programme so that you can:

- Learn what is being taught from week to week and reinforce safety messages and strategies at home.
- Become sufficiently well informed to communicate with children about sexual misbehaviour so they can confidently turn to you if they have concerns.
- Respond to children's hints and disclosures about sexual misbehaviour supportively and effectively.
- Learn to change parenting styles if those used might increase children's vulnerability to abuse.
- Provide opportunities to talk to staff, other parents and possibly local child protection personnel.

Without your involvement, you can inadvertently undermine what is being taught at school by:

- Teaching children that, to be good, they have to obey adults.
- Giving children silly names for genitals that no one outside the family will understand if your child tries to report sexual misbehaviour.
- Assuring children that all secrets must be kept.
- Punishing children when they choose the wrong moment to practice being assertive, by saying no when told to go to bed or switch off the computer. (Say, "We want you to say 'no' if somebody is giving you a wrong touch or seems creepy but there's nothing creepy about switching off your laptop".)
- Telling children to "be good and do as (e.g., the childminder) tells you".
- Not encouraging boys to express their feelings.
- Dads depriving boys of physical affection in the mistaken belief that affection will make them 'sissies'.

Involvement in the school programme is vital for child safety. It has to be a community effort involving mums and dads, teachers and carers, to change from passive observers to active participants.

Using services for children with special needs

Given that children with disabilities are at highest risk of abuse, both at home and at school and that abusers may be carers or volunteers, as well as older students, make it your priority to seek:

- Child protection information, to be read by all staff, visitors, school bus drivers, parents and everyone involved in the school or centre.
- A child protection policy that everyone in contact with children must read and agree to.
- Child protection curricula that is explicit and rule-based (not feelings-based) and using activity learning methods such as role-play, puppets and practice.
- Evidence that there is appropriate supervision, especially in boarding schools, changing rooms and toilets, because inadequate supervision has been cited as a major factor in child sexual abuse in education settings.

The protection of children with disabilities requires the cooperation of everyone involved in their care. It is obviously difficult for parents to participate when children are boarders, the parents work full-time or live far from the school. In those circumstances, extra efforts must be made to maintain ongoing communications with staff. When parent participation is limited to attending a single information session, it has little impact.

Schools should be made aware of your needs if meetings are planned at inconvenient times, a crèche is needed to enable you to attend, you have transport problems or you feel uncomfortable on school premises because of your own negative experiences and would prefer to meet in a local community centre.

Parents might also ask schools to:

- Establish a parents' group where you can share information and concerns.
- Avoid using jargon in communications and ensure that written information is succinct.
- Introduce a buddy scheme where parents support each other and share transport.
- Take into account local customs and avoid meetings that clash with popular social activities and late-night shopping.
- Consider holding separate sessions for dads/father figures, if their attendance is typically low.
- Use languages appropriate to the community for child protection posters and advertising on ethnic and community media.
- Recruit expert help to communicate with parents who are deaf or have non-English-speaking backgrounds.
- Display relevant children's child protection-related work at meetings.
- Arrange separate meetings for different language groups and involve bilingual speakers as necessary; and, most important.
- Supply a child protection library for parents to access.

If your child's school does not have a child protection/ personal safety programme, talk to the school principal/ head teacher, school council, Parent Teacher's Association or the chief executive officer of your Education Department. It is possible that they don't understand its importance. If the school has a programme but hasn't involved parents, explain to the school why your involvement is important, sharing the information on these pages. Ideally, schools will distribute weekly information on what has been taught, why and how you can help.

Questions that are frequently asked about safety education:

Won't a personal safety programme place an unfair responsibility on children to protect themselves?

No, quite the reverse! We, the adults, place unfair responsibility on children if we send them out into the world when they're unable to differentiate what does and doesn't constitute reportable behaviour and how to report this.

Won't a child protection programme make children fearful?

Programmes have been in American schools since the 1970s and Australian, New Zealand and Canadian schools since the early 1980s, with no evidence that they create fear. Road safety programmes don't make children afraid of travelling and a lesson in water safety doesn't make children afraid of water. By the same token, a developmentally appropriate personal programme does not make children afraid of people; on the contrary, when children understand their rights and are assured of parental support, their confidence increases. Surveys of New Zealand parents showed that relationships with children were more open, honest and less fearful after involvement in a school programme. Staying safe with others is just one of many skills that children need for survival.

Aren't these children too young to use the correct anatomical names for genitals?

Ask yourself why, if it's OK to teach children that an eye is an eye and an ear is an ear, they should be given different, silly names for genitals. The message that this conveys is that genitals are invisible and un-mentionable and that parents won't be able to cope with children's concerns about them. This is the opposite message to the one needed for children to stay safe.

To make children safe, don't you have to talk about deviant sex?
In these programmes, we give children guidelines on handling the most common forms of sexual misbehaviour sometimes experienced at school. Without information, they are likely to be confused about what constitutes normal and reportable behaviour. Child protection education is about safety.

Will information make children distrust their parents?
Paedophiles have been spreading this fear for the last 35 years because they have everything to gain when parents fail to teach their children safety skills. If all children had access to these programmes, the paedophiles' supply of victims would be reduced and their safety and anonymity would be at risk. If you let children know that you are there to help and that you will believe them and not blow a fuse if they disclose 'sex stuff,' they will trust you more, not less.

Is there a risk that safety education will interfere with the free expression of affection in the family?
No, quite the opposite. Child protection programmes encourage parents to provide more physical affection, especially for boys. A lack of it increases their vulnerability to predators.

> Boys need tenderness and as many hugs and as much attention and overt approval from their dads as their sisters do. Paedophiles and pederasts are successful because they boost boys' egos, provide physical contact and make them feel loved and special.

Will the programme teach children to challenge adult authority?
One of the most common fears is that, if we teach children to say no to adults, they will challenge authority and become perpetually disobedient. Personal safety programmes tell children that

they can say no when they feel unsafe or someone does or wants them to do something wrong. Of course young children will make mistakes when they first practice saying no, but with your help they soon learn to differentiate between situations in which they can and should say no as distinct from situations they simply dislike.

Chapter 8

Developing Children's Safety Skills

TALKING ABOUT TOUCHING

One of the most difficult skills to teach children is how to tell the difference between acceptable touching and reportable, wrong touching. This has to be tackled conscientiously because it is the central goal of personal safety education. We have to be clear and use children's language because there is often a vast difference between what we say and what children hear and understand. They can't take vague hints and transfer them to sexual experiences with people they love. If children can't make the critical distinction between acceptable and wrong behaviour, their safety is jeopardised. In other words, to stay safe from sexual abuse, children must understand that no adult or older kid is permitted to touch, tickle or play around with children's genitals or ask children to play around with theirs and that kids of any age are not allowed to touch them against their wishes.

Some programmes refer to good versus bad touching. Please, don't talk about 'bad' touching because children associate 'bad' with spanking or hitting and bad people. Sex offenders try to give the impression that they are generous and caring. Also, children don't associate providing oral sex with touching, because they relate touching to hands, not mouths.

In addition, sexual touching is presented by the abuser as fun, affection, a game, 'what real men do' and it can be exciting.

An additional reason for not using the bad touch concept is the risk that, by identifying sexual touching as bad, children may acquire negative attitudes toward their own bodies.

For these reasons it is better to refer to right and wrong touches, having previously pointed out that kids can touch their own bodies and will want to share them with someone special when they grow up.

Brainstorm positive aspects of touching

For the touching concept to be effective as a tool for child protection, we make children aware of different kinds of touching in their day-to-day environment by using puppets, stories and books. Ask children to think about:

- How we touch for communication.
- How we touch when we greet relatives and people we know.
- Different affectionate touches.
- Supportive and comforting touches.
- Touches for reassurance.
- How people touch when they are winning at sports.
- What they know about sexy touches.
- Creepy touches.
- What types of touching your child likes and dislikes. Make it clear that we don't have to tolerate touches that make us feel uncomfortable. Ask, what can we do about it?
- Touches we need.

In addition:

- Tell children that sometimes we like being tickled and stroked but our feelings can change. If they change, we have the right to stop the touching.
- If the touching changes from good to worrying, creepy or scary, that can be stopped, too. For example, if someone tickles us and then puts their hands under

our clothes, that is a wrong touch and not allowed. We have to say, "Stop that. It isn't allowed!" using a big, loud voice and then get away and tell someone. (You need to practice this approach.) It doesn't matter who is doing it: it can be your best friend's dad, your neighbour, your favourite uncle. They have to keep to the rule: no touching the private parts of your body.

- Ask about any instances when touching started out feeling good but changed and they wanted it to stop. What did they do? What could they have done?
- What can someone do if the person giving the wrong touch doesn't take any notice? Suppose he says, "Don't be a wimp. You know you like it. You were laughing".
- What if the person said, "I wouldn't tell your mum, if I were you. She won't believe you"?
- What if that person said, "Don't tell anyone. It is our special secret. You'll get into big trouble if you tell"?
- What if the person said, "I thought we were friends"?

Ask children, "Why do you think a grownup would want you to keep wrong touching a secret?" (The abuser exploits the fear that the children think they've done something wrong and are scared that they'll get into trouble.)

Note that adults, especially relatives and friends, often find it amusing when children tell them to stop tickling. They don't take it seriously and tickle all the more.

It is very important that you support your child and ask the tickler to desist. Relatives may be offended unless you explain that your child is involved in a personal safety programme.

Teach children to look people in the eye and say, in a big strong voice, "I didn't like it when you did that. Please don't do it again".

Except when children are controlled by fear and terror (as happens when trapped in paedophile groups and parent-child incest), most sexual touching feels neither bad nor unsafe in its early stages. Criminal touching is difficult to stop because it starts with good touching that children like, such as cuddles, kisses, massaging (especially boys), overt favouritism and treats. Older siblings have introduced sex after taking little brothers into their beds to comfort them after nightmares. The victim is confused and wonders if the wrong touch was accidental. That is a deliberate ploy. If the child gives the adult the benefit of the doubt and says nothing, the abuser views this as the child being cooperative and abuse becomes more serious. Another difficulty is that adults are judged on face value and children won't suspect ulterior motives when an offender pretends to love them.

> Without a clear understanding that adults and older kids are never allowed to touch, tickle or play around with children's buttocks, breasts, genitals or mouths, the messages will be lost.

Some programmes tell children that no one is allowed to touch them unless they *want it and agree to it*. That is helpful for preventing guilt in normal same-age sexual experimentation but the message is obviously confusing and dangerous if children are faced with sexual touching by older youths or adults. Even if sexual touching feels good, it constitutes a crime.

WORRYING OR CONFUSING TOUCHES

Abusers of boys invariably involve them in boisterous play that makes witnesses feel uncomfortable but, because the child seems to enjoy it, nothing is said. Touching becomes worrying when it doesn't match our expectations. When the behaviour has never happened before, it creates a confusing mix of pleasant and anxious feelings. Anxious children freeze. Anxiety is inevitable when genital fondling results in arousal, accompanied by feelings that what's happening is wrong.

Touches are worrying when we are not sure of the toucher's intentions. Confusion is especially likely when the toucher is saying something that contradicts the behaviour, for example, when the child is told that "everybody does it" but, simultaneously is told to keep the behaviour secret or bad things will happen. There is also confusion when a beloved adult is violent and causes pain, while assuring the child that what is happening is "great". Typically victims think there must be something wrong with them because they were hurt and don't think it is at all great. The abuser also puts the blame on the victims for his own pain, saying that he will enjoy being raped if he just relaxes and it will get better with more practice. Sadly, victims accept these explanations and tolerate pain as the price they have to pay for the relationship with someone who meets their emotional needs.

Activities to reinforce messages about touching could include:

- With young children, make a *Touching Book*. Talk, write and draw about different touches: "Touching I like" and "Touching I don't like."
- Use photos and pictures from magazines and books to demonstrate both good, safe touches and wrong touches. How can you tell that it is a good touch? Point to touches that are obviously unwanted or unsafe. What could someone do to stop wrong touches? What could a child say to get help to stop the touch in the picture?
- Discuss how it feels when you get a wrong touch. When do you see/get wrong touches?
- Ask, "What does a creepy touch feel like? Have you ever had a creepy touch? Who gives creepy touches? What happened?"
- Ask your child to think of all the different kinds of touches that there are — pats, cuddles, hugs, punches, scratches, squeezes, hits, handshakes, high

fives, pushes and shoves, kisses, strokes and caresses, massages, prods and pokes, pinches, sexy touches, kicks. Ask how someone might feel when receiving different touches. Identify everyday, mutually enjoyable touches and wrong and unsafe touches. Who gives good touches?

- What can someone do if they get a wrong touch that feels scary or creepy?

It is important to make children aware that good touches can change to wrong touches and that, when they do, kids have the right to say "Stop that! It isn't allowed!" They also have the right to stop any touching they don't like. When you play rough or tickling games with your children, tell them, "I want you to say 'stop' when you feel uncomfortable". Make sure that you and other relatives stop immediately if they tell you to stop! Give the message that children don't have to put up with unwanted or uncomfortable touching by adults.

Try these exercises:

- Brush your child's hair. Say, "I want you to yell 'stop' as soon as it gets uncomfortable". Brush more vigorously until you get the instruction to stop. Watch the child's face in the mirror to make sure that s/he said stop at the precise moment that it looked as if it became uncomfortable.

- Read, *My Grandma is Coming to Town,* by Anna Grossnickle Hines, about a young boy whose grandma is visiting for the first time in a long time and he's uncomfortable about having to hug her. Discuss why he might not want kisses and cuddles and might not want to sit on her lap. How did he show that he didn't want to do this? Is it OK for a boy or girl to say no to being cuddled and kissed and hugged? Why? ("It's my body and I'm the boss of it.") What could the boy do instead of being kissed and cuddled that won't upset Grandma? What could the boy say to Mum or Dad to get help? What could Mum say to Grandma to make her understand without being upset?

- Discuss how someone could solve a problem involving an adult giving a creepy touch. Responses could include saying, "I don't like being kissed (or squeezed or hugged) anymore," and moving away; saying, "I only shake hands now"; or "I don't want to be tickled," and move away; teach your child to tell you.

- When you take a child to the doctor, talk about the touching that a doctor is allowed to do but add that the doctor is required to have a parent or a nurse with him. Most doctors now seek a child's permission to touch the body.

- Practice what you teach. Ask children if they want to be cuddled and hugged and ensure that other family members give them a choice. Reinforce the message that rules about touching apply all the time, regardless of who the toucher is. Tell your child that "some grownups don't know about the touching rules. They didn't have them when they were kids and you may have to tell them". Emphasise that rules apply whether they are at home, at school, at Granddad's house, in public toilets, on a school bus or in a taxi — wherever they are.

- Let children know that you will help them to stop any touching they don't like and that they can tell you if they aren't sure about touches that feel creepy.

- Practice saying "No!" and "Stop that! It isn't allowed!" in a big, loud voice.

DISCUSS RULES ABOUT TOUCHING

Even 5-year-olds know there are 'rude', naughty kids. Explain that if we don't stop them, they might continue behaving in this way until they become 'rude' adults. You can tell your child that adults who give wrong touches and do sex things with children know that what they are doing is wrong. Because they are scared of getting into trouble, they tell kids to keep their behaviour secret. Unless we report them, they'll carry on doing it, upsetting lots and lots of little kids. The only way to stop them is to tell Mum or, if it is at school, tell the teacher, then police.

How would you contact the police? (Ensure that your child knows the procedure for dialling in an emergency.)

What if the teacher said s/he didn't believe you? Who else could you tell?

Suppose that s/he listened but took no notice? What else could you do?

How would you know when to stop telling?

Few children think they can talk to teachers about sexual misbehaviour. They say that teachers can't help because they don't know the person involved or "they don't know where I live". They view teachers' powers as limited to their classrooms.

Conclude with the fact that we touch things all the time and that most touches are good, safe touches, but it is important to know what to do if they change and become wrong or creepy touches.

USING PUPPETS OR DOLLS TO DEMONSTRATE WANTED VERSUS UNWANTED AND WRONG TOUCHING

Use puppets for scenarios that involve unwanted and wrong touches. The puppet tells the child what happened and asks the child for advice on what s/he should do to resolve the problem. The following are examples:

- Female puppet says, "A boy at school pulls my hair. It really hurts. Does he have the right to pull my hair?" Ask, "Did the puppet want to be touched? Does she have to put up with this? What can she do to try to stop it from happening again?" What should she say to get help from someone? Who could she talk to?

- Puppet says, "I was having a drink at a friend's house when her dad knocked the glass and spilt orange juice down my t-shirt. I think he knocked it over deliberately. He told me to take off my shirt to dry it and he started wiping me down with a towel, touching the private parts of my body. It made me feel uncomfortable. I didn't know what to do." What should she have said? Who should she have told?

- A male puppet says, "When one of Dad's workmates came to the house, he sat me on his knee and gave me a creepy feeling. The man says he's going to see me again. What should I do? What should I say? Who should I talk to?"

- A male puppet says, "A big boy at school put his hand down my pants in the school toilet and now I'm scared to go to school. I know you kids have some good ideas. Maybe you could tell me what to do."

- A male puppet says, "I've got a problem at school. A big boy unzipped his pants and told me to touch his penis. Can you tell me what to do?"

Work through these scenarios with your child:

- Tara's aunt takes her to netball every week. Tara likes going to netball and likes her aunt but her aunt is always kissing people. Tara's aunt is kind and buys her ice creams but Tara hates being kissed. Her aunt gives those wet, sloppy kisses on her mouth. Tara hates it so much that, when her aunt phones now, Tara pretends to be sick. That's a pity because Tara likes netball — as well as ice creams and treats.

  "What's wrong with you?" Mum asked crossly when Tara said she didn't want to go. "You know she loves taking you out and she'll be upset if you don't go."

  "But I don't like the way she kisses me," Tara said.

  "Of course she kisses you. She loves you. She'll be upset if we tell her to stop doing it. We all have to put up with things that we don't like."

  Is Tara's mum right?

  Does Tara have to put up with being kissed?

  Tara doesn't want to upset her aunt but she wants the kissing to stop. She wouldn't mind a hug, but she'd prefer there were no kisses.

  What can she do?

  What can she say to her mum?

  What do you think her mum could say to her aunt?

  What could Tara say to her aunt?

  Tara's mum could explain that Tara is growing up and no longer likes to be kissed. We have to respect children's feelings so she should ask her to make do with a hug instead. If her mum won't help her, Tara could say "Aunty, I love you to bits and I love coming out with you but I don't like being kissed now that I'm growing up."

- Mark was kicking a ball around in the park with his friend when some big boys said they would give him some money to go into the men's toilets. That gave him a creepy feeling. What should he say? What should he do?

Mark should listen to his creepy feeling, get away quickly and tell someone. He could phone the police if he has a mobile phone. He should take a description of the big boys: how many there are, what they are wearing and what they look like. And of course he should tell his mum.

- Bill is Mum's boyfriend. Mum thinks she's really lucky because Bill and her son, Luke, get on really well. Bill loves playing rough, tickling games on the floor and Luke likes it unless it goes on for too long. Bill massages Luke's back and he likes that, too. One day Bill put his hands under Luke's shirt. Luke got a creepy feeling and wasn't sure whether Bill was supposed to do that. What do you think? What should Luke do?

- The man next door invites Emma in to play computer games. Should she go?

    She asks her mum and her mum says yes. Suppose that, when she's playing on the computer, the man lifts up her t-shirt and touches her underneath it. Is that allowed? What should she do? What should she say?

    Ensure that your child says, "Stop that! It isn't allowed!" Suggest that Emma should go straight home and tell her mum and that she should not go there again.

- Uncle Tony is Andrew's favourite uncle. They play rough and tumble and tickling a lot. One day they are on the carpet and Uncle Tony slips his hand into Andrew's pants. Andrew jumps up, holds out his arms and shouts, "Stop that! It isn't allowed!" Uncle Andrew says, "Sorry, it was an accident. You mustn't tell anyone about this. You'll get into trouble." What should Andrew do?

Ensure your child knows that Andrew should ignore the plea for secrecy and tell his mum what happened.

Suppose that Andrew's mum said, "No, I don't believe you. You must be mistaken." What should he do? What should he say?

> A New Zealand programme, Kid-power, uses role-play to enable children to practice responding to adults who put pressure on the child, such as:
>
> "I thought you loved me."
>
> (Answer: "Yes, I love you, but it isn't allowed.")
>
> "But I thought you were my special friend."
>
> (Answer: "Yes, I am your friend, but it isn't allowed.")
>
> Escape and tell. Practice is especially important for children with learning disabilities.

RECOGNISING AND RESPONDING TO FEELINGS
INTRODUCE LANGUAGE TO EXPRESS FEELINGS

Child protection programmes emphasise the importance of helping young children to become aware of and extend their vocabulary to express their feelings so they can respond safely to potentially unsafe situations. They should begin to recognise what it is to be happy, sad, worried, angry and that something is yucky and creepy.

Early childhood centres often make a 'Feeling Box' which contains materials with different textures that give differing sensations, ranging from sandpaper of various grades to hessian, steel wool, dough, plasticine, a pan scourer, a nail brush, velvet and silk. You can include something 'yucky' to emphasise that yucky feelings are different from others.

For sighted children, make a hole in the top of the box just big enough for a hand to go through. To prevent children from seeing the contents, attach a toeless sock to the hole. They then push their hand through the sock to reach the materials to be touched. The child is asked to describe the feel of the first object to be touched. Is it a soft, rough, nice touch or a worrying touch that they don't like?

Some people use yucky substances such as manufactured slime, dough, plasticine, pretend spiders and obnoxious substances found in novelty shops. Ask children to describe how they feel before and after they put their hand in the box. Do feelings change when they remove the object and see what it is? Is that a good feeling or a yucky one? Which parts of their body tell them that it is yucky? What do they want to do when they get that feeling?

When they react negatively to pretend creepy-crawlies, ask how they felt when they picked up what they thought was a real insect. How did their feelings change when they found it was plastic? Which parts of their body told them that they didn't like what they were holding?

In addition, you can:

- Provide a variety of activities that enable children to express feelings appropriately.
- Play different kinds of music: happy, sad, loud and soft and discuss how it makes children feel.
- Discuss colours and how they make children feel.
- Designate a grumpy corner where children go to simmer down.
- Provide a stamping mat for stamping out angry feelings.

An extension of this activity is to provide small containers which hold safe odours such as herbs, lavender, disinfectant, ginger, garlic and fish. Chart which smells give good feelings and which give bad feelings. Blindfolds are often used for activities to develop senses, but be aware that some children may panic when they lose their sense of control.

Understanding your children's feelings is important. You need to know what is happening in their lives and acknowledge that their world can be frightening and worrying. For example, when children complain that pebbles hurt their bare feet on the beach, agree with them that pebbles can hurt. If you don't, they will argue indefinitely to convince you that you are wrong.

Agree that situations can be scary and then ask for suggestions as to how they can be changed. Most children are afraid of darkness, shadows, rustling trees outside bedroom windows and nightmares. They imagine that murderous monster-stranger-robbers are coming to kidnap them. Many problems can be easily resolved by buying a torch or a night-light that doesn't cast shadows, for example.

With the best of intentions, parents give assurances that there is nothing to worry about when children are terrified. Surveys have shown quite consistently that parents underestimate children's fears.

Emphasise that there are things adults can do to help when they are sad, angry, worried or afraid. Encourage children to express and respond to feelings appropriately. This is especially important for boys. Those who grow up unable to express emotions are disadvantaged in relationships. Help children to identify feelings when opportunities arise. When they resort to aggressive behaviour, it is usually because they lack the knowledge and skills to achieve their needs by acceptable means.

When a dispute occurs, stop the action and tell the participants that they will each be heard. Encourage each child in turn to explain what happened in terms of their own feelings. For example:

"I was upset because he took my doll and I thought he might break it and I wouldn't get it back."

Each child is asked how s/he would like the situation to be handled better next time.

- Ask the aggressor if s/he is aware of the relevant rules of behaviour.
- What were the aggressor's needs?
- How could his needs have been met in a more appropriate way?

Victims are then invited to comment on the aggressor's suggestions. How do they feel about them? Can they suggest other methods? Ideally the adult gains a consensus and the participants are asked to verbalise the agreement they just reached. Initially the process is slow, but once the procedure is learned, children will resolve situations by themselves and reduce future opportunities for friction.

Brainstorm what we can do when we have bad or sad or angry feelings.

Look at pictures of people in magazines and books and discuss what kind of feelings they are having.

Help children to identify unsafe, scary, creepy feelings

When there is no adult encouragement for children to express fears, they keep them to themselves. They don't realise that, if parents knew they were afraid, they could help. Unless they are involved in a school's child protection programme, few kids realise that parents can replace a babysitter who misbehaves.

Our research has shown consistently that few parents know what and who their children are afraid of. They underestimate children's fears because they don't talk about them.

Children are also great protectors of parents. They disregard their own feelings to protect ours. That makes them very vulnerable to exploitation. For personal safety, it helps if children can recognise and tell you about creepy, worrying and confusing feelings. This can't be taught in a few minutes; children need opportunities for practice in their day-to-day lives. It is also an advantage if you can take action to make your child feel safer, both at home or at school.

When children of six to eight years of age visit a zoo, they often have subsequent nightmares about large mammals and snakes. Some say they are afraid of people who dress up with masks and pretend to be ghosts, disguising their identities. They are especially frightened at Halloween and worry about violent television and adults fighting.

Draw children's attention to the warning signs that their bodies give when they experience worrying and creepy feelings.

> The central message is that, when we identify worrying or creepy feelings, there is usually something that we can do to make ourselves feel better and safer.

Make a Feelings Book

Borrow and read books about feelings from the library. Help your child to create a *Feelings Book* which contains writing and illustrations with pages labelled as follows:

- I feel safe when…
- I feel unsafe when…
- I feel frightened when…
- I feel happy when…
- I feel sad when…
- The person who makes me feel happiest is…
- The person who makes me feel the most scared is… (*Ask why.*)
- I feel pleased when…
- I feel sad when…
- I get a creepy feeling when I'm with… (*Ask why.*)
- I feel uncomfortable when I'm with… (*Ask why.*)

- I feel comfortable when...
- I feel grumpy when...
- I feel angry when...
- I feel most scared when...
- The creepiest person I know is... (*Ask why.*)
- When I get a nasty text message I feel... (*What does that feel like?*)
- I feel a little bit scared when... (*Ask what they can do about it*)
- I feel really scared when... (*Ask what they can do about it*)
- I feel scared when other kids...
- I feel scared when adults...
- I feel scared in the dark when... (*Ask what they can do about it*)
- If I feel scared during a thunderstorm, this is what I can do to stay safe...
- If I feel scared watching TV or a DVD or video, this is what I can do to make myself feel better...
- If I feel anxious about the way that a grownup behaves to me, this is what I could do to make the feelings go away...
- I feel cross when...
- I feel worried when... (*Ask what they can do about it*)
- I know other kids who feel scared when...
- This is what I can do to stop scary feelings...

With this exercise you will learn a lot about what is going on in your child's life. Do not deny your child's feelings and say, "There's nothing to be afraid of". Sympathise by saying that you can understand that it must be awful to be in that situation and you want to help. Discuss each item in turn. Ask why that person is scary. What happens that makes the child scared?

Point out that everything we hear gives us feelings.
Say, "Sometimes we like what we hear and want to hear it again and again."

Some sounds are scary and some are too loud.

When we get bad feelings, we want them to stop.

Ask what are some sounds that your children like or don't like to hear.

Everything we taste gives us feelings.
Say, "Our bodies give us lots of different feelings. Some are bad feelings and we want them to stop. Everything that we taste and eat gives us feelings. Everything we lick or swallow or put inside our mouths gives us feelings."

When we get good feelings we say, "That was yummy" and ask for more. When we get yucky feelings we say, "Oh, yuck! That's gross". Nobody wants yucky feelings.

"Remember, nobody is allowed to put yucky stuff in our mouths. What could someone say if a bigger person tries?"

Discuss what children like and dislike tasting. Make a list of tastes that give you good feelings and tastes that give you bad feelings.

Emphasise that everything we see gives us feelings.
Say, "Sometimes we like what we see and watch. Sometimes we don't like what we see."

Ask what your child likes to see and doesn't like to see.

Young children are usually afraid of what they see on TV but don't think to change the channel.

Sometimes we get sad feelings.
Say, "Tell me, what makes you feel sad?"

It helps to share your troubles with someone.

If you feel sad, tell someone about it.

Tell someone who will listen and help.

Sad feelings often go away when we share them.

Who could you tell?

Draw a picture of a face with sad feelings.

Please note that older children should especially be encouraged to share sad feelings with you because predators specialise in making potential victims feel that they understand them better than their parents do.

Sometimes we get creepy feelings.

Say, "Some people are creepy."

Some people do creepy things.

What gives you creepy feelings?

Who gives you creepy feelings?

When does this happen?

What can we do if someone gives us creepy feelings?

Sometimes we feel angry.

Say, "Everybody feels angry sometimes."

It is OK to feel angry but you should tell someone about it.

It is best if we share angry feelings, not keep them to ourselves.

Who makes you angry?

What makes you angry?

What can you do to make yourself feel better?

Sometimes we get yucky feelings.

Say, "Yucky feelings are bad feelings."

They make you feel a bit sick inside.

Have you ever had a yucky feeling? What happened?

What did you do?

What gives you yucky feelings?

Who gives you yucky feelings?

Yucky feelings tell you that you don't want to be there. You want to get away.

They make you want to say, "Ugh! Yuck! That's gross! Go away and leave me alone."

What can kids do if something happens that gives them a yucky feeling?

Suppose it is a grownup?

Sometimes if you tell someone about it, they can help you to stop yucky feelings.

Who could you tell?

Remember, you are the boss of your body and if someone gives you that yucky feeling, say "Stop that!" and then get away and tell someone who will help.

People are not allowed to do yucky things to kids.

Can you draw a picture of a person's face that tells you he's getting a yucky feeling?

Sometimes we feel scared.

Say, "What sort of things make you feel scared?"

It can be scary if someone pushes you into the swimming pool and you can't swim.

It can be scary if you are crossing the road and a car comes towards you at a fast speed.

People can make us feel scared, too.

What can you do when you get scary feelings?

When you feel scared, tell a parent or someone you trust. It helps to talk about it. Tell someone who will listen.

Who could you tell?

Sometimes we feel confused.

Confusing feelings are especially difficult to explain to children at the lower end of the developmental scale and yet they are likely to feel confused when they encounter sexual misbehaviour. While their instincts may tell them there is something wrong, the abuser gives assurances that everything is alright and normal, and the children don't know what to do. Most victims feel powerless.

270

Discuss scary feelings

If someone feels scared in the house alone, what could they do?

If someone feels scared in bed in the dark, what could they do?

If we are scared in a thunderstorm, what could we do to make ourselves feel safer? (Never stand under a tree or use an umbrella outside because of the risks associated with lightning.)

If a grownup or bigger kid makes a child feel scared, what can s/he do?

If a kid feels scared watching TV, what should s/he do?

What does it feel like when a mouse runs out of a cupboard?

What would it feel like if there was a cockroach in your bed?

We all get scary feelings and we can do things to make them go away.

Sometimes we're asked to do something that doesn't feel right. Sometimes other kids or grownups ask us to do things and we get a funny, worried feeling; it doesn't feel right.

If someone asks a child to do something that doesn't feel right, what can s/he say?

What can s/he do?

If you have a worrying or confusing feeling, you can say: "Please stop that. I don't like it." (Or "Stop that! It isn't allowed!")

Get away.

Tell someone.

Who can you tell?

Which parts of your body might tell you that it is not OK?

If the person doesn't take any notice when you say "Stop," tell someone about it. Tell me or someone who will help you.

And if they don't take any notice, tell me or telephone the Kids Helpline.

Sometimes we feel unsafe.
Children don't relate the word 'unsafe' to sexual misbehaviour. They associate unsafe with riding a bike without a crash helmet, driving too fast and not obeying traffic lights.

Children take their concept of safe and unsafe from adults.
Use:
- I feel safe when...
- I feel a bit unsafe when...
- I feel very unsafe when...

Seek lots of examples and in each case ask what your child could do to feel safe again.

Sometimes it feels scary but it's fun because we know that we are really safe. For example, when you go on the roller coaster, it can be scary but it is also fun.

Which parts of your body tell you that it is scary?

Ask about scary things that are fun, such as bumper cars and roundabouts at fairs. Riding on a swing is exciting but if someone swings you too high, swinging becomes scary. What are your scary feelings telling you?

Sometimes people make us feel scared.
What sort of things make you feel scared?

Sometimes it is OK to be scared. When a grownup pretends to be a lion and chases you around the room, it can be a bit scary. You feel scared but its fun and you know you're really quite safe.

If there's a big, loud bang outside, it's OK to feel scared until you know you are safe.

Our bodies give us scared feelings to tell us that we're not safe.

What sort of things make you feel scared? What else can you think of?

Discuss what can be done to make them less scared.

Emphasise that we all get scared or anxious or uncomfortable feelings but there are things we can do to make them go away.

Good feelings can change and become worrying ones.
Ask your child to think about times when something started out feeling good but changed and s/he wanted it to stop. What happened? What did s/he do?

The classic example is when someone pushes you too fast on a swing and you suddenly fear you might fall off. Which parts of your body tell you that it is no longer safe?

To stay safe, children need to know that the initial acceptance of someone's behaviour isn't binding; in other words, we can go along with something to start with and then suddenly change our minds. It's OK to change our minds. In some situations, we may have to do that to stay safe. This is very difficult for children to understand. Child sex offenders know this and take full advantage of it.

Sometimes we feel good and we don't want those good feelings to stop.

It can be fun to wrestle with someone you like.

It can be fun to be tickled by someone you like.

Chasing and tickling can be fun.

But we don't want to wrestle or be tickled or chased all the time.

Tickling hurts when it goes on for too long.

When wrestling is rough, we want it to stop.

Just remember: you're the boss of your body and you can say, "Stop that! I don't like it," or "Stop that! It isn't allowed!" Get up and hold out your arms, back away, get away and TELL.

Let's practice.

Sometimes we like to be touched or tickled, but then the touching changes and we want it to stop. Has that ever happened to you?

What can kids do if someone gives a worrying, confusing feeling?

Emphasise using eye contact and a big voice. Practice yelling.

Suppose that the other person doesn't want to stop doing it. "Come on, you know you like it. Stop being a wimp." What could a child do to make it stop?

Look at pictures of people in magazines and books and look at their facial expressions to discuss how they are feeling.

Be prepared for children to misuse, "I feel upset," when they don't get what they want.

Say, "How would you like to feel? What can you do so that you don't feel sad/upset/angry, etc., anymore?"

Extend the process by linking feelings with actions: "I feel a bit sad because..., so I'll go and...to make me feel happy again."

Encourage children to express their own feelings and consider the feelings of others when faced with conflict-ridden situations. When opportunities arise, ask, "How did you feel when Brent snatched your iPod? Brent, how do you think Darren felt when you snatched his iPod? Did you have the right to do that? How could you have handled that better? Darren would you have lent Brent your iPod if he'd asked you nicely?" If the answer is no, ask why not. If the answer is yes, then say, "OK, Brent, ask Darren if you can borrow his iPod for a few minutes and thank Darren for being helpful." If necessary, use a timer.

When children resort to aggressive behaviour, it is usually because they lack the knowledge and skills to achieve their needs by acceptable means. When a dispute occurs, stop the action and tell all participants that they will be heard. Encourage each child in turn to say what happened and how they felt about it. For example:

"I was upset because he took my crayons when I was using them and I was afraid he wouldn't give them back."

Ask children in turn how they would like the situation to be handled next time: e.g.,

"I want him to ask me nicely."

Ascertain whether participants are aware of the relevant rules of behaviour. What were their needs? How could they have met their needs in more appropriate ways?

Can they suggest better methods? Ideally, the adult gains a consensus and the participants are asked to verbalise the agreement they reached.

Use puppets to talk about feelings in different situations. The puppet asks the child for suggestions to resolve problems in a variety of situations:

- The puppet tells the child that a big boy said he will give him (the puppet) a beating at lunchtime in the playground and he feels scared.
- How would the puppet feel? What can he do to feel safer?
- It is lunchtime. The puppet says he went to his bag to collect his lunch and found it had been stolen. How will he feel? What can he do?
- The puppet tells the child that he lost his mum in Kmart and couldn't find her. What would that feel like? What could he do?
- A woman with a big smile sees him crying and says she'll take him home.
- How do you think he feels? Should he go with her? What should he do?

Use traditional cautionary tales and stories to discuss feelings. How do you think the bears felt when they returned home and found that Goldilocks had eaten all the porridge and broken their beds and chairs? Did Goldilocks have the right to go into someone else's house? Did she have the right to eat their food, sleep in their bed and break the furniture? Why not? And how do you think Little Red Riding Hood felt when she saw the wolf in Grandma's bed? Should Little Red Riding Hood have walked though the forest all by herself? Discuss how we know when we are scared. Which parts of the body tell us? Ask what sort of things make your child scared.

Our bodies give us scary feelings to make us take action to make ourselves safe again.

Other ideas:

- Draw or paint pictures or make masks depicting angry, sad or worried faces.
- Use a mirror to practice making a sad, grumpy or happy face.
- Introduce the notion of what is confusion and discuss what to do in different, confusing situations.
- Practice other ways of saying no without using words.

Encourage the appropriate expression of feelings.

As stated earlier, when children become aggressive, it is usually because they are frustrated and lack the vocabulary or the knowledge and skills to achieve their needs by acceptable means. When a dispute occurs, stop the action and tell the participants that they will be heard. Never get into arguments about who started it. Encourage each child to explain what happened in terms of their *feelings.*

"I was upset when..."

"I was angry when..."

Discuss how needs could have been met in appropriate ways.

Ask whether the aggressor had the right to do what he did. Is that what the other child wanted? Would the aggressor want another child to behave the same way to him?

Brainstorm what we can do when we have angry or unhappy feelings.

Ask what kinds of things make us feel sad, angry, worried, stupid, lonely, scared, fed up, anxious, envious, guilty or disappointed.

Ask what we can do when we get each of those feelings.

Discuss alternative ways of handling problems.

IDENTIFYING EMERGENCIES AND SOLVING PROBLEMS

Teach your child about emergencies (and how to respond to them)

The safest children are those who can think of different, safe solutions to potentially dangerous situations. Without training, they tend to give up if their first idea doesn't work. If one solution resolves a problem, a child will try to use this same solution to resolve all problems, even unrelated situations. For example, when schools teach children to go to a Safety House if they feel unsafe, children will suggest that as the solution for when they are lost in a department store or central shopping area, where there are no Safety Houses. Similarly, when fire officers taught children to "stop, drop and roll" if their clothing caught fire, they offered that as a solution for all types of dangerous fire situations, even when it was obviously inappropriate. Children need practice in thinking through the safest thing to do in a variety of situations.

Teach children observation skills

Play '1 Spy' when out in the car. Play car-spotting games. Encourage children to identify types of vehicles, descriptions and registration numbers. Play the party game where you present several items on a tray, remove the tray and the child has to recall what was there. Teach children how to describe

277

people and what they are wearing. *Good powers of observation are an asset throughout life.*

We often hear of people trying to abduct children outside schools and how the adults who witness these incidents never think to note the description of the vehicle. Observation skills are taught in New Zealand primary schools to enable children to report people who harass or try to abduct them.

Teach children what constitutes an emergency

Ensure children know they can shout, scream, make a fuss and telephone parents, police or other services in a variety of circumstances.

Show your child how to get help in an emergency. Show them how to make a phone call (a) from home, (b) on a mobile phone and (c) a public phone with or without money or a phone card. Ensure they can furnish their full name and address.

Even if your children carry mobile phones, take them to a public phone and teach them how to use it to make a reverse charge call, a free emergency call or a call requiring money or phone card. At home, practice with an unplugged or toy phone, with you acting as the operator. Ensure that your children know the circumstances in which police, fire and ambulance services should be called and that they can provide their own names and addresses, as well as details of the location of the problem. Emphasise that they must only call the fire service if there is a real fire. Ask what might happen if someone called the fire service and there wasn't a fire. What would happen if there was a fire in our house but the fire service had gone to another house because someone called the fire service for a non-fire emergency? What do you think might happen?

By using "what if...?" scenarios, you can explore how your child might respond in the event of an emergency.

Help children to develop problem-solving skills and persistence

We can't protect children from every possible dangerous situation they might encounter but they have a better chance of staying safe if they can think of potential solutions to various unsafe situations and not give up if the first attempt fails. The following hints are provided to help develop problem-solving skills:

- Identify problems that are relevant to your child.
- Frame questions around the problem and ask, "What if...?" Have them suppose a certain situation and ask, "What could someone do to stay safe?" or "What would be the best thing to do if...?"
- Use a third party approach when appropriate. Ask "What could someone do?" rather than "What could *you* do?" as the child will be less afraid of being wrong and make suggestions more openly.
- Use brainstorming methods to generate a list of possible strategies or solutions. Ask, "If that didn't work, what else could someone do?" and "Can you think of something else they could do?"
- If a child provides an unsafe response, don't get upset or correct them. Instead, ask, "What do you think would happen if someone did that? Would that be a safe thing to do? What else could happen? Can you think of anything else that he could do that would be safer?" For example, if you ask what a 5 or 6-year-old boy could do if he came home and found the house locked, he is likely to say he would break a window and climb in, without considering the ramifications. Boys are also likely to say they would defend themselves by kicking someone in the groin when, in reality, children don't resort to violence against an abusive adult or bigger aggressors, even when they've been taught self-defence. Praise your child for trying hard and praise them for making sensible suggestions.

- What if the first person you told didn't believe you. What else could you do? What if the second person said, "You're making that up"? What else could you do? Read the story, *Nobody Listens to Andrew,* by Elizabeth Guilfoile. In it Andrew finds a bear in his bed when he gets home from school. When he tries to tell his mum, dad and granddad, nobody listens. They are all busy. Andrew eventually says (in a big loud voice), "Mum, Dad, I've got something really important to tell you," and everyone stops and listens. This theme can be adapted and varied. Children seldom realise that it is not a good idea to give important information when the adult is obviously very busy. Discuss when would be the best time to tell you something really important. Bath times and bedtimes are usually favourites for special conversations.

- Teach children not to give out personal information to anyone on the phone or Internet. Never tell someone your address, phone number, email address, what school or sports club they attend or where and when their parents are at work. It is particularly important to remind children of this when using chat rooms. They may think they are communicating with same-age friends when, in fact they could be criminals.

- Other useful stories for demonstrating persistence include:
  - *Hattie and the Fox* by Mem Fox.
  - *Possum Magic* by Mem Fox.
  - *One Duck Stuck* by Phyllis Root
  - *Wilfred Gordon MacDonald Partridge* by Mem Fox.
  - *Little Red Hen* an old folk tale available from multiple authors.
  - *Are You My Mother?* by P. D. Eastman
  - *John Brown Rose and the Midnight* Cat by Jenny Wagner.
  - *Franklin the Turtle* series by Paulette Bourgeois

Depending on the age of your child, ask whether different situations are emergencies and what he/she should do and say. If your child gives a silly answer, ask them, "Would that be really safe? What else can you think of that might be safer?" Praise children for their efforts.

Ask children what would be the best thing to do if they were at home alone and in a variety of situations using the "just suppose" or "what if" scenarios:

- What if Mum went to the shop and accidentally left the cooker on with the frying pan on top? There are flames coming out of it. Is that an emergency? What should the child do? Teach children NOT to throw water on a chip (oil) or frying pan fire. Use a fire blanket. Keep the fire blanket where it is accessible and show your child where it is. Give reminders from time to time. Some homes have a fire extinguisher. Keep it in good condition and accessible. Some fire services teach children to "stop, drop and roll" if clothing catches fire. Unless you discuss different situations and options, these children assume that they have to do this when anything catches fire. Alternatively, they would leave the house immediately without taking a cordless phone to contact the fire-brigade. Some fire services tell children to wait at the end of the drive. For farm children, drives can be extremely long.

- Ask, "What if there was smoke coming out of the stereo or TV? I'd gone to see the next door neighbour. What could you do?" Find out what your child knows about electrical fires. Would s/he think to remove the plug to cut off the power? Remember that it is unsafe to throw water on electrical appliances that are plugged into the wall. Use a fire blanket.

- In the event of an open fire, "What should someone do if a burning log fell onto a rug and it started smouldering?"

- If your child wears a nightdress or other clothing near an open fire, "If someone got too close to the fire and their clothes started to burn, what should she do? (Stop, drop and roll; as running feeds the flames.)
- Just suppose that a dog bites your friend's arm and it's bleeding really badly (send for an ambulance by dialling 000 or the appropriate number in your country and practice what you would say).
- What if your friend's big brother suggests that you drink his parents' alcohol? (Discuss ways of rejecting this.)
- A girl's grandma falls on the floor and the girl can't wake her up (practice sending for an ambulance).
- Someone phones when you're at home alone and says you've won a free holiday. He asks for your parents' credit card number.
- Someone you don't know phones when you are at home alone and says something rude. (Put the phone down, leave it and walk away until he hangs up. Ask your parents to contact the phone provider.)
- Mum left the washing machine on and it's flooding the kitchen. (Is the plug in the sink? If so, take it out. If not, switch off the machine at the wall and mop up the floor, as wet floors are dangerous.)
- The babysitter offers you a pill and says it will make you feel great.
- A woman comes to the door and says she's being followed by a creepy man and wants to come in to use your phone. (Ensure that the child doesn't suggest inviting her into the house. Why wouldn't this be a safe thing to do?)
- Someone phones and asks to speak to your mum but she's out shopping. (Suggest delay tactics e.g., "Mum is in the bath. I'll get her to ring you back," and take the caller's number. Never indicate that the child is alone

at home. Indicate that it's OK to tell a little lie to stay safe.)

- There is a car accident. When a boy gets closer he sees that people are bleeding. There are no adults nearby. What should he do and say?
- A man with a limp asks a girl to help him to carry his groceries from the supermarket to his car outside. What should she do?
- You are outside your house with your friend when a man asks you to help him to look for a lost puppy. He shows you a photo of a pup and says he is an off-duty policeman. What should you do?
- A man talks to you in the street and asks you where you live.

In what circumstances should police or other emergency services be called?

Don't talk about dangerous strangers. Children will need help from strangers in emergencies, the challenge being to choose the safest person to approach. Furthermore, children realise that adults talk to strangers every day and suffer no harm.

Young children don't understand what the definition of a stranger is and devious strangers pretend to be friends. Children under nine years of age think that strangers are evil-looking, male monsters who wear black balaclavas and leer. They will trust anyone who doesn't fit that stereotype. It is better to help children to think about potentially dangerous situations rather than identifying dangerous people.

Use "What if..." questions, involving a wide variety of possible situations. "What if someone asks you to go with them (to buy a toy, see a pet, etc.), what should you do?"

Suggest that older children ask three questions:

Will Mum know where I am if I go?

Will I be able to get help if I need it?

Do I feel comfortable about this?

If you don't get a 'yes' to all three questions, don't go. If you want to go, say, "I'll have to go and ask Mum first."

If there is an emergency, is it alright to:

- Interrupt an adult's phone call?
- Ask for help from someone you don't know?
- Dial 000 (Australia), 111 (New Zealand) or 999 (UK) and ask for help?
- Go into the school staff room at lunchtime and ask for help because someone has been injured?

Ask, "Can you think of other emergencies?"

What rules do you think you could break in an emergency?"

If your child doesn't remember your address, sing it to a tune, such as, "London Bridge is falling down," for example:

"I am living at seven-teen, seven-teen, seven-teen,

I am living at seventeen Morton Drive.

Morton Drive is at Norwood, at Norwood, at Norwood.

Morton Drive is at Norwood and that's where I live."

Suggestions for scenarios to develop problem-solving skills

When role-playing or using puppets to ask questions, follow these simple guidelines:

- Try not to answer for your children. Give them all the time they need to respond.

- Give your child time to look at the problem from different angles, so that they can gain a more complex perspective.
- If necessary, gently guide them towards appropriate answers and praise them when they arrive at an acceptable response.
- Never make it a chore; make it fun and interesting.
- Ask open-ended questions, e.g., "What do you think might happen if...?" rather than questions that can be answered with a yes or no.

Discuss every situation. Ensure that children link the emergency to the available services and assistance. Some children automatically suggest calling police in all situations, but don't necessarily know how to do it or what to say, if they had to do it.

More scenarios for discussion:

1. *A girl is sitting on a bus and a man sits next to her. She feels uncomfortable because there are lots of empty seats but he has chosen the one next to hers. He sits very close and she feels even more uncomfortable. Then he puts his hand on her bare leg. She feels extremely uncomfortable. What could she do?*

Most children responded to this question saying that they wouldn't know what to do. A few would get off the bus, despite the fact that it wasn't their stop and they would have a long walk home, assuming they were close enough to find their way home. No one suggested telling the bus driver. No one suggested telling their parents when they got home.

Possible solutions:

Take the hand off your leg and shout, "Stop that! It isn't allowed!" The chances are that the man would get off the bus at the next stop. (Ask, "What else could she do?")

Stand up and go to the front to tell the bus driver.

Get a description of the man.

Phone the police on a mobile phone or when you get home.

Phone your parents and/or tell your parents when you get home.

2. *The rain is pouring and you're getting wet when a car pulls up and the driver (whom you may or may not know) calls out, "Your mum sent me to collect you. She's not well. Jump in. You'll catch a cold."*

   Would it be safe to go?

   Why?

   Suppose that the driver says, "I know where you live. I'm your new neighbour."

   Would it be safe to go?

   Suppose that the driver says, "I'm a friend of your mum/dad."

   Would it be safe to go?

   Why?

   What if the driver is a woman? Would it be safe to go with her? Just suppose you see other kids in the car. Would that make it safe to go?

   Why?

   Some families introduce a secret code to be used if someone is authorised to collect a child in place of the parent.

3. *A boy is looking at toys in a big department store while his mum joins the queue to pay for a book. It is Christmastime and there are toys everywhere. The boy goes to a nearby counter to look at Nintendo games. When he turns round, he can't see his mum anywhere.*

   What would be the safest thing to do?

   Most children say, "I would stand still. Then I would ask a kind person with a smile on their face to take me home."

   Ensure that one of the options mentioned for getting help in a big shop or supermarket is to tell a shop assistant and ask for a lost child announcement to be made.

Next time you go into a supermarket, point out the PA system.

If a young child says, "I'd go to the car-park and wait by the car," or "I'd look for a kind lady," ask whether that would really be the safest thing to do. What might be safer?

Don't dismiss suggestions as silly or dangerous but, instead, ask, "What do you think could happen if you did that?"

4. *There are thousands of people at the Christmas street parade. When Jack and his sister, Chloe, turn round, they can't see their parents. Chloe starts to cry.*
   What would be the safest thing to do?

There are police at street events but children don't perceive the police as child-friendly. Discuss options and ensure that your child understands that police *can* help. Explain how. When in town, show your child how to differentiate a police officer from a security person in uniform.

5. *Billy is on his way home from school when a man he's seen before says, "I've got some kittens in my house. If you'd like to choose one, you can take it. Come and have a look." Billy would love to own a kitten but he hesitates because his mum doesn't know where he is. "Come on," says the man, "I'm not going to eat you. If you want one, you'll have to come and choose it."*
   What should he do?

6. *Emma's mum gets a new babysitter. Mum works late on a Thursday night and she leaves her phone number for emergencies. The babysitter says he's got some pictures to show her but she has to keep it secret. He opens his wallet and takes out sexy (dirty/rude) photographs.*
   What should she do?
   What else could you do?

Maybe Emma could ring her mum on a mobile phone from the bathroom.

(Does your child know your mobile phone number or have it programmed into her phone?)

Maybe Emma could get help from a friend or neighbour.

What should Emma say to the babysitter?

What should the child say to her mum when she comes home?

(Ensure that a clear report is provided and the child doesn't just give hints. Most children say, "Mum, I don't like the babysitter," or "The babysitter was mean/rude," but they don't give a clear description that would enable you to understand the problem).

Do children know their parents' mobile phone numbers?

7. *A man is sitting in a car close to your house. He lowers his car window and says, "Do you like chocolate? Just come over here and I'll give you some." He opens the car door. Jack loves chocolate but the man gives him a creepy feeling.*
What should he do?

Apart from shouting "No, thank you," stepping back and running away, does your child suggest taking a description of the vehicle and the man? Does your child suggest reporting to you what happened?

8. *What can you do to stay safe if someone knocks on your door when you're at home alone?*

9. *What must someone do if they are at home alone and hear glass breaking? It sounds as if someone is trying to get into the house through a window.*

Much will depend on whether there is an alarm system with an emergency button, whether the child has access to a phone to call police or whether there is another door for the child to leave the house.

10. Your friend calls. He says his mum is asleep and he can't wake her up. What should he do?

11. Suppose some kids you know come up to you and say:
   "How about some beer?" What would you say?
   Suggest saying, "No, thanks!"
   "OK then, want to smoke some weed?"
   Suggest saying "Forget it!"
   "Come on, try some. Everybody does it."
   Suggest saying, "I've made a decision not to do drugs."
   Back away while making direct eye contact.

> Explain to your children that negative peer pressure comes from kids who don't feel good about themselves. They try to get others to go along with what they are doing because they feel uncomfortable and want support.

12. For boys: Suppose that a Year 5 boy is in the school toilets. There's a bigger boy there and he says; "Come here, kid and give me a wank."
   Is that allowed?
   What should the younger boy do?

13. A 15-year-old girl is waiting outside the shops. Her dad hasn't come to collect her when he said he would. A man she knows offers her a lift home and she accepts. On the way, the man stops the car, puts his arm round her and says, "You are really very sexy and I want to make love to you." She is scared and doesn't know what to do. What should she do?

14. A man standing by a van says he has some great games in the back of his van and invites a boy to go inside to choose one. What should the boy do?

15. *You just missed your bus and there won't be another for half an hour. A car pulls up with a woman driver and she says, "Jump in. I'll overtake the bus and you can get on it at the next stop." Should you get in the car?*

16. *A child is at home alone and a man says he needs to come in the house to check the electricity meter. Should the child let him into the house?*

17. *Someone you chat to on the Internet wants you to send them a photo of you. Should you send one?*

18. *Someone you chat to on the Internet wants you to give your email address. Should you give it to them?*

19. *What if you see a gang of big boys coming towards you. What could you do?*

20. *A man is staring at you and follows you round the supermarket. What could you do?*

21. *A car full of big boys crawls alongside a boy (or girl) walking along the footpath. They call out for the child to get in the car. What should he/she do?*

22. *Someone stops a girl in the street and says, "Did you know you could earn a lot of money as a model? I'd like to take your photograph in my studio." What should she do?*

Always emphasise that, if your child makes a mistake and encounters a problem, you need to know. Assure your child that we all make and learn from mistakes and you won't be angry.

SECRETS THAT SHOULD BE TOLD

Both juvenile and adult sex offenders rely on secrecy for their own safety. They may refer to what they are doing as "our special secret" or they may just say, "Don't tell anyone because…," "Don't tell anyone or else (*this*) will happen," or "If you tell anyone, (*terrible things will happen*)."

Children need to understand that there are two kinds of secrets:

Good surprises

We refer to the good ones as good surprises that we keep until a certain day, such as a surprise party or a present for a special occasion. Good surprises are the ones we find out eventually when the time is right.

Bad secrets

Bad secrets are the ones that we're told we can't tell anyone ever. They give uncomfortable and worrying feelings. It is a bad secret when someone says, "If you tell, you'll get into big trouble."

"If you tell, I'll beat you up."

"If you tell, no one will believe you and your mum will be mad."

"If you tell, the police will take you away."

Ask, "Have you ever had a bad secret?"

People who give kids bad secrets are cowards. They do it because they know they have done something wrong and they are scared of getting into big trouble. If we keep bad secrets, they'll just keep on doing wrong things.

It is a bad secret if it is about something yucky or creepy or it hurts.

A bad secret is when you're told you have to keep the secret forever.

A bad secret is when you feel worried, unhappy or scared.

It is bad when you are the only one who knows the secret.

It is bad if someone says they will give you money or something you'd like if you promise not to tell the secret to your mum or dad.

It is always a big, bad secret if it is about being touched.

It is a big, bad secret if it is a bigger person and involves sex stuff.

It is a very bad secret if it is about an adult sharing beer, cigarettes, dirty talk or rude pictures with kids.

Always tell bad secrets. Bad secrets must be told.

Who could you tell?

Just suppose that person wasn't listening; who else could you tell?

Just suppose that the second person didn't believe you; who else could you tell?

Bad secrets must always be told.

Present different scenarios to establish whether your child can differentiate between a good surprise that can be kept and a bad secret that must be told.

Beware of tricks

We saw in the section on grooming that child sex offenders use tricks to gain the trust of parents and children. Paedophile strangers and juvenile offenders may trick children into accompanying them.

Discuss tricks.

There are funny tricks that make you laugh, but there are also bad tricks.

Find out what your child knows about people who play tricks on kids.

What do they do?

Why do they do it?

Some are mean tricks to make us do things we wouldn't do if we knew what would really happen.

Children's stories are full of examples of characters being tricked. Read the story, *Sitting Ducks,* by Michael Bedard or view the DVD, Volume 1, available from ABC Bookshops and libraries. This shows how an alligator acted in a friendly way while he was really only thinking about catching a duck for a delicious meal. See how the ducks are tricked into believing that they can't fly away. There are movies and other stories that demonstrate tricks. The witch in *Snow White* was presented as being pleasant while scheming to harm her. In the *Lion King*, Scar tricks Simba. In the story of *Aladdin*, Jafar tricks Aladdin.

Tell the story of the Gingerbread Man where the fox tricks the gingerbread man into thinking he'll be safe when he carries him across the water on his back.

Tell them that even grownups get tricked sometimes. A man pretended that he had a big business that made lots of money. He persuaded people to lend him millions of dollars, pretending that they would get more money back than they'd lent him because he was selling things all over the world. Later they found out that the man was lying. He didn't have a business. He stole their money and left the country. That was a very mean trick.

Kids trick other kids, too. A girl took her new purse to school for Show-and-Tell. She loved it because it was a present from her aunt for being a bridesmaid at the aunt's wedding. A new girl, much bigger, said she wanted it. She grabbed it as they left school and said she'd give her $20 for it. She didn't give her any money and the girl who lost it didn't dare tell her mum because she thought her mum would be cross. That was a bad trick.

What should she have done?

CHALLENGES INVOLVED IN PROTECTING CHILDREN WITH DISABILITIES

Most special education services now teach personal safety skills. When children attend special units from distant suburbs, parents may have little communication with school staff. It is important that you are well informed about what the school is teaching about safety and how you can help on a week-by-week basis. This could be achieved using email or teleconferencing.

Bear in mind that children (especially foster children) with disabilities may have:

- Already learned to comply passively with all adult demands.
- Developed a poor body image and poor concepts relating to personal space, increasing their vulnerability to abuse.
- No awareness of their rights.
- Already been sexually abused or have faulty or no knowledge about their bodies; this is especially likely if you are now fostering this child.
- Had few opportunities for independence.
- Feelings of shame, guilt, low self-esteem, social isolation, all of which make them vulnerable to abusers who pretend to love them.
- Over-protective carers who do everything for them (because it saves time and it's easier), depriving them of opportunities for independence.

Young and disabled children are incapable of judging adults' motives and collusion between an offender and an accomplice is beyond their imagination. This demonstrates the need for children to practice assessing situations rather than trying to identify dangerous people.

Emotionally deprived and disabled children are made more vulnerable by their desire to please and be accepted. They can't conceive that carers could do bad things to them.

When starting personal safety education, bear in mind that a child may have experienced sexual molestation without knowing that it was wrong.

Additional challenges when children are hearing impaired

Because learning is predominantly visual, visual materials such as posters, pictorial cards, social videos, DVDs and puppets are needed to reinforce safety concepts for children with hearing impairments.

In addition, please note that for hearing impaired children:

- Inadequate supervision has been cited as a critical factor in the sexual abuse of deaf children.
- Deaf and non-verbal children are often denied knowledge, resources and communication skills and may lack power in everyday life.
- These children often lack the means to communicate concerns.
- Both hearing and deaf teachers should be involved in school programmes; they are needed to provide material from a non-hearing perspective.
- Few deaf children have the opportunity to discuss sensitive, sexual issues with safe adults.
- Well-intentioned hearing professionals may select signs and ways of presenting information that don't relate to the ways in which children think. Children with a good knowledge of English often miss the subtleties of detail and innuendo used in oral presentations.
- There tends to be a much higher tolerance of touch in the deaf community than in the hearing community. The differences between acceptable and unacceptable

touching must be clearly illustrated and explained. This can be conveyed by using anatomically correct dolls, puppets and pictures.

- Deaf children abused at school are also likely to be abused around the home.

Many children now have technical aids which give them access to telephones. However, deaf and nonverbal children may not be aware of help-lines and how to seek help. An additional hazard for parents is the lack of specialist treatment facilities for victims of abuse with communication problems. If your disabled child has been abused, try to locate professionals who specialise in providing therapy for deaf children.

Provide opportunities to practice saying no in a big, loud voice. Deaf children are often told that their voices sound funny and, as a result, they are reluctant to yell. Deaf and intellectually disabled children need to be taught when and how to use other attention-seeking strategies for dealing with emergencies, such as what to do if molested by a passenger on a bus. In addition, self-defence training is an asset for these children.

Most parents are concerned about risks to children with communication problems. Hearing parents often respond by restricting the deaf child's freedom. If safety concepts are new to your child, you will need to use signs and examples until there is evidence that the messages have been understood. Allow children to show you the signs that they use for body parts and sexual touches and use them when possible using children's language and suggestions. You will facilitate communication and reduce feelings of discomfort.

When children have learning disabilities

To develop social awareness in children with disabilities, teachers and parent can practice some of the following:

- Standing at an appropriate distance from others when in conversation, i.e., providing personal space.
- Establishing appropriate visual contact without staring.
- Using appropriate language and topics of conversation.
- Learning and demonstrating a range of self-care procedures in different environments, such as locating and using a public toilet safely.
- Knowing the range of touches and in what circumstances it is appropriate to use them; for example, when to kiss, hug or shake hands.
- Demonstrate appropriate behaviour when rejecting friendship and intimacy, etc.
- Know how to make a complaint when something is unsatisfactory — people with disabilities are sometimes overcharged by unscrupulous people, including taxi drivers.
- Handling teasing and bullying.
- Travelling alone safely on public transport: how to choose a seat, who to talk to, what to do if they catch the wrong bus or miss their bus stop.
- Knowing when it is safe to provide a name and address.
- Knowing how to contact help services.
- Knowing what constitutes appropriate conversation. For example, a girl with a learning disability told everyone on the school bus that she'd been sexually abused.

When children have visual impairments

Visually impaired children need extra help to develop body awareness. This is necessary to teach safe, social behaviour that provides protection from the risk of abuse. Dolls should be selected for their realistic feel. Anatomically correct dolls with genitals, mouth, anus and breasts are a must for sightless children. They often lack a sense of danger and reject the need to close bedroom, bathroom and toilet doors as well as the outside door. They can be confused by demands for modesty and may refuse to conform to societal rules. They argue that everyone uses a toilet so why the fuss about closing the door. They don't understand why hair and grooming are important because, to them, voices are our most important feature. They may see themselves as asexual, ridiculing taboos and adult concerns. In addition, those with a poor self-image often engage in risky behaviour, convinced that no one would want to have sex with them because their bodies are imperfect.

When children have severe disabilities

Developing safety skills involves a focus on ways to increase independence, especially in matters relating to dressing, showering and hygiene, the development of self-confidence and self-esteem and the identification and rejection of inappropriate behaviour. Children who require assistance with toileting and hygiene need to know the difference between touching for cleanliness and touching for 'fun'.

Unfortunately, there is a tendency for carers to do everything for severely disabled children because teaching them to do things themselves can be very time-consuming and frustrating. Many severely disabled children have to tolerate staff touching parts of their bodies that would not be permitted in non-disabled society. The goals of personal carers must be to provide the necessary help while respecting the young person's privacy. When they need help that involves touching intimate places, the child should be given a choice and asked, "Do you want me to do that for you or would you rather do it yourself?" The sexuality of young people must be acknowledged and respected if we want adolescents to respect the sexuality of others.

Be careful when putting your child's name on clothing and school bags. If the name is visible it could enable a predator to be on a first name basis immediately. For more information, I have written a book specifically on this topic: *Developing Personal Safety Skills in Children with Disabilities* published by Jessica Kingsley (London) and available via the internet.

TIPS FOR KEEPING KIDS SAFE

- If your children walk to school, walk with them and point out places where they can get help, if necessary. If they ride to school on a bus, accompany them to the bus stop to make sure that they get on the right one. If they miss it, they may be tempted to accept a lift.
- Ask older children to check in if they change their plans.
- If your child arranges a sleepover, contact the child's parents.
- Don't talk about 'dangerous strangers'. Focus on potentially dangerous situations and how to avoid or resolve them.
- Don't rely on a programme that relies on feelings for telling children what is inappropriate, reportable behaviour, such as the American Protective Behaviours Programme promoted in Western Australia and Queensland. Feelings are unreliable to determine what constitutes reportable behaviour. A rules approach is more reliable.
- Don't refer to 'good' versus 'bad' touching; refer to good and wrong or creepy touching because children may not view genital fondling or the receipt of oral sex as bad. 'Bad' touching is often perceived as smacking and hurting.

- Young children and those with intellectual disabilities learn through doing. They need activities to learn. For example, if you want to help them to stay safe from people in cars, use a driver and a car and teach them to physically move back away from the vehicle when someone stops to ask the way. Practice. Also use puppets, stories and role-play. A puppet tells a story and asks the child for advice on what would be the best thing for him or her to do.

- Both young and learning-disabled children need to practice thinking about safe responses to a wide range of potentially hazardous situations. They find it difficult to transfer information from one setting to another. For example, if taught that they can go to a Safety House for help, they will suggest Safety Houses as the solution to all their problems, even if they are at a concert or a sports event. A concept must be taught and reinforced in many different ways, with time for revision and repetition. Check children's learning using "What if..." And "Just suppose that..." or "Let's pretend that..." scenarios. Ask "What could someone do about it?" and make it a game when you are out with your children.

- Instructions and questions must be clear. Use short, simple sentences. Avoid either/or questions and those that can be answered with just a yes or no. Remember that children do not understand vague hints. Information has to be broken down into small segments for young and learning-disabled children. They also need regular opportunities for practice and repetition.

- Children don't associate having to provide oral sex with 'touching'. They view touching as involving hands, not mouths. Secondary school children commonly refer to 'wanking,' 'head jobs' or 'blow jobs' in their everyday conversation.
- Rehearse safety skills so that they become second nature.
- Explain to older children how offenders lure or groom victims using alcohol, cigarettes, drugs, pornography and sex talk to reduce resistance.

Additional books to read include:

Cuddle Time, by Libby Gleeson, published by Walker Books, London (2004).

Developing Personal Safety Skills in Children with Disabilities, by Freda Briggs, published by Jessica Kingsley (1998).

I Don't Like Kisses, by Ricki Mainzer, The Five Mile Press, Vic (1992).

Our Granny, by Margaret Wild, Omnibus South Australia (1993).

Sally's Secret, by Shirley Hughes, Random House (1992).

Sloppy Kisses, by Elizabeth Winthrop, Aladdin Paperbacks (1990).

Teaching Children to Protect Themselves, to use with children ages 5 to 9, by Freda Briggs and Michael McVeity (2000).

What's Wrong with Bottoms, by Jenny Hessell, published by Century Hutchison Australia (1987).

Willy the Wimp; Willy the Champ; Willy and Hugh; and *Willy the Wizard* series of books by Anthony Browne, published by Random House Children's Books.

Books in the Franklin the Turlte series, information can be found in: (www.treehousetv.com/parents/tvShows/franklin/books.asp)

Please note that, while some of the older publications may no longer be available in bookshops, they may be available online.

WHEN YOU SUSPECT OR LEARN THAT A CHILD HAS BEEN SEXUALLY ABUSED

Although it can be exceedingly difficult, the first thing you must do is put your own feelings on hold. Don't appear shocked or upset; stay calm and matter of fact and keep your tone conversational. If your child sees that you are horrified, s/he will close down and you may never hear what really happened. Children are sensitive to parental distress and usually hide the worst information to protect you if they think you can't cope with it.

Say, "I'm so pleased that you told me. It must have been very worrying for you. I am really sorry that it happened. It is never a child's fault when this happens. Grownups (or older kids) know they are not allowed to do this. Unfortunately, it does happen sometimes. But don't worry, there are people whose jobs it is to help children stop this sort of behaviour. I think we need to tell them because we don't want this person upsetting other children. S/he needs help."

Congratulate your child on being strong and having the courage to tell you. This is especially important if secrecy and threats were used.

Never say, "Haven't I told you not to walk through the park...?"

Never say, "Why didn't you tell me sooner?"

Never say, "Why didn't you just say no?"

Never say, "You must be mistaken. He wouldn't do things like that."

And never, never say, "I don't believe you."

If you do any of these in a moment of shock, please apologise as quickly as possible to your children and affirm that you believe them.

Report suspicions or disclosures of abuse to the child abuse report line or police. Ensure that your child knows that someone will want to talk to them about it and that it's OK to talk about it.

Talk to child protection professionals about taking your child to see a specialist who can provide therapy, if needed.

When disclosures involve deaf and non-verbal children, request the child protection agency and police employ a suitably qualified interpreter. Problems may arise if interviewers are inexperienced in translating information about sexual misbehaviour, feel uncomfortable and subsequently transmit those feelings to the child. Find out whether your child would be more comfortable if you or another trusted adult were present during the interview. This can be helpful when assessment is urgent or when the child has an intellectual disability, multiple disabilities or a very idiosyncratic communication system that strangers may not understand.

Investigating suspicions

Parents often have a gut feeling that something is wrong but they don't stop to consider sexual abuse as a possibility. Some dismiss the behavioural changes with, "Maybe she's just growing up" or "He's just going through a stage". Some parents think that the child is just being naughty. Don't dismiss your gut feelings; they grow from disconnected observations over a period of time. Parents often do nothing because they don't know what to say and "don't want to put ideas into kids' heads".

If you are feeling uncomfortable about the inexplicable changes in your child, wait for a quiet moment and say: "I'm really concerned about you. You haven't been yourself lately. I don't like to see you looking so sad. I know that something's bothering you. Is it something or somebody?"

You could also ask:

- Is it happening at home or at school? (Or somewhere else?)
- Can you tell me about it or is it a secret?

If it's a secret, don't ask the child to disclose the secret.

- Well, it doesn't seem to be a happy secret and we don't have to keep secrets if they worry and upset us.
- Who else knows the secret?
- What will happen if you tell?
- Who said so?
- Is it a secret about touching?
- Can you point to where this person touches you?

The above questions are the ones most likely to reveal the required information without the child having to disclose the terrible secret.

You will learn who the problem person is and what kind of threat was made if the child were to tell anyone. If the child then reveals that abuse occurred, follow the recommended sequence.

If this method is unsuccessful, on another day ask your child if she would like to draw you a picture of your family and then talk about each family member. Who does the child like? Who would s/he like to take on a picnic?

Ask the child to draw a picture of the scariest person s/he knows. When it is finished, enquire very casually who it is and what that person does that is scary.

Ask for a picture of the rudest person s/he knows and the creepiest person s/he knows. What does that person do that's rude or creepy?

If children have difficulty telling you what happened, ask them to draw what happened — or *is* happening — that caused the anxiety. They often talk as they draw and you can write down what they say.

Assure your child frequently that s/he has done the right thing by disclosing abuse, but never promise that the act of reporting it will be sufficient to stop it.

Explain to the child that you will have to tell someone who is employed to help children in this situation. The victim is usually interviewed once or twice by a social worker and a police officer who specialises in this area of work. Sometimes there needs to be a medical assessment by a paediatrician or a psychological assessment by a psychologist who also specialises in this work. Assure your child that it's OK to talk to these people about what happened because they are there specifically to help any children who suffer this same kind of experience. When children have disabilities, it is important to educate interviewers of the different levels of understanding and your child's special needs.

Use open-ended questions

Although few cases involving young children ever go to court, you often hear people misguidedly say, "Don't question the child if abuse is suspected because you might contaminate the child's evidence and then the abuser will be found not guilty."

The reality is that, if you don't ask questions, you are unlikely to find out what happened and have the opportunity to help your child. Child protection services are unlikely to investigate a vague suspicion.

To avoid contamination of the evidence, use open-ended questions that provide the opportunity for a range of possible answers. For example, say, "Show me where he touched you," and not "Did he touch your penis?" Make an immediate record of what your child did and said when revealing sexual misbehaviour. Never promise to keep a bad secret.

When the abuser is a juvenile

Given that adult sex offenders typically start their criminal behaviour in childhood and adolescence, it is important that juvenile sex offenders are reported and taken seriously. They can cause as much damage and be as violent as adults and they need help. Never inform the abuser's parents. Don't merely report it to the school if it happened at school. Inform the police. Young sex offenders need to be assessed by child protection services and referred for therapy.

Supporting your child after the abuse

Stay close to your child after the disclosure to provide a sense of physical security.

Emphasise often that it is never a child's fault when an adult or bigger kid does wrong things.

Maintain normal, affectionate interaction with your child. Ask if s/he would like a cuddle. Some older children may resist being touched.

When a victim looks worried, say, "I can see that you're looking sad. Can we talk about what's worrying you?" Reaffirm to the child that you know s/he has had a very worrying time and has been very strong.

If victims behave aggressively, affirm that it's OK to feel angry with their abuser and suggest healthy ways to express their anger, e.g., with a punch-bag or clay to bash. They can also express anger with a therapist. Provide therapeutic play such as with water or sand, (both of which are soothing), hand painting, body painting and picture painting.

Victims need extra support when they must attend assessments and interviews. Their behaviour is likely to regress after interviews and when they face the offender.

If child victims demonstrate overtly sexual behaviour, reassure them that they no longer need to do such things to please adults. Confirm that safe hugs are available any time.

If the child loved the abuser, make it clear that it is OK to love someone and still hate what they did.

Therapy for victims

Therapy may be necessary to alleviate any feelings of guilt engendered by the abuser. Therapy is also helpful to explore the feelings of disabled children who often assume they were abused because of their disability. Don't try to convince them that they are wrong; however, start with their reality. Offer suggestions as to why abusers generally select children for sexual misbehaviour. Place the problem wholly on the abuser, making no excuses. There is no need to postulate why a particular child is chosen, because it is usually that they were young, less powerful or in the wrong place at the wrong time.

Explore issues of trust to help the child to regain trust in adults.

Provide basic information about normal sexuality because your child has already learned about abnormal sexuality firsthand.

If necessary, discuss homosexuality issues with boys. Remember that boys often fear that they were chosen because they must be gay, not because they were young, uninformed and possibly curious. Assure boys that they were chosen simply because they were there, not because they are effeminate or weak. Boys who have been victimised need opportunities to talk about their concerns. It is hard for parents to do this if they have had no relevant experience.

Parents often deny the need for outside help, insisting that victims are alright, which means that the children don't get an opportunity to talk about what happened. It is never easy for a parent to take a child for assessment or therapy because it brings back painful memories; feelings of guilt and shame can be prominent. For parents of children with disabilities, there may be additional guilt lingering from the child's birth. Parents almost always experience grief when they learn that their newborn has a disability and there is grief felt again when that disabled child is abused. This is in addition to the grief associated with the loss of a child's innocence.

When the abuser is in your family

The most traumatic abuse, for the victim and everyone else in the family, occurs when the abuser is a parent or parent-figure or a close relative. Sadly this is all too often the most common form of child sexual abuse. When a child makes a disclosure involving the parent's intimate partner, a myriad of intense emotions are involved:

- Disgust and horror that the child has been violated.
- Anger relating to the deception and breach of trust involved.
- Fear that the economic future of the family is at risk, especially if the abuser is the sole income earner and the protective parent isn't employed.
- Guilt — invariably there are memories of occasions when the non-offending parent handed the child over to the abuser and unwittingly made it easy to offend.
- Embarrassment if there is a court case; relatives often blame, criticise or condemn the non-offending parent, assuming that s/he was an accomplice or an inadequate sexual partner.
- Pressure from the offender who denies the offences or blames the child and promises that it will never happen again if the protective parent doesn't go to the police. This is very appealing to mothers who don't want to believe the allegations.
- Pressure from the abuser's relatives who, in ignorance, blame mothers or the children themselves.

Mothers are most likely to disbelieve children when their abuser is their own partner or a priest. They are often left with the harrowing choice of protecting their partner or protecting their child.

It is all too easy to put your own needs and the preservation of the family ahead of the psychological wellbeing of a child abuse victim. When this happens, the child ends up hating the non-abusive parent (usually the mother) as much as s/he hates the abuser and that hatred can last a lifetime. The lack of support adds further to the psychological damage caused by the abuser.

How mothers react depends on their relationship with the victims, their relationship with the abusers and whether or not there are other siblings to support. The mother's coping skills and resilience may also depend on the level of support she receives from her own friends and relatives. The most significant factor in the recovery of the victim is the supportive reaction of family members. For that reason, it is a good idea for the non-offending parent to seek help from support services.

Additional reading:

Developing Personal Safety Skills in Children with Disabilities, by Freda Briggs, published by Jessica Kingsley, London (1998).

Teaching Children to Protect Themselves, by Freda Briggs, published by Allen and Unwin (2000).

The Silent Crisis — Simple ways to protect your children from sexual abuse, by Amanda Robinson, APTI Perth (2007).

Chapter 9

Hints For Safe Student Travel

Would you send your car to Europe, the USA, India or South America and trust strangers to look after it for a whole year while you stayed at home? Would you send your kids to live with strangers, whether on the next street or the next suburb, while you went overseas for a year? Probably not!

So why is it that, every year, countless intelligent, well-educated, middle-class parents think they are doing their children a favour and, at considerable expense, send them to live with strangers in faraway countries with vastly different cultural values and where different languages are spoken? Parents place their trust entirely in the school, sports organisers, choir director or other exchange agency to keep their children safe. These young people have invariably been well-protected and are naïve youngsters who are ill-equipped to protect themselves if things go wrong.

Overseas youth exchanges are advertised as providing life-changing experiences. If the student is sufficiently mature to travel alone and deal with all the issues that arise, it can indeed be beneficial but, for some, it is a life-changing experience of the worst possible kind.

Since the 1980s, most Western countries have made efforts to create a safer world for children. One group slipped through that net, however, namely, the children who stay in other people's homes with visiting choirs, sports teams and student exchanges.

Governments took no interest in them because the student exchange industry is international, while the governments and police responsible for handling complaints are regional and national. Furthermore, there has been little research into students' experiences, given the difficulty of accessing participants without the cooperation of the agencies responsible for their safety.

While most students return home with fond memories, some report exploitation of all kinds. Students have been made vulnerable by the sheer size of the industry and the agencies' reluctance to make home inspections or subject hosts and coordinators to criminal record checks. Successful students are welcomed back and give talks to their sponsoring clubs, while members pat themselves on the back, whereas those who lodged complaints about their overseas experiences have been ignored.

Furthermore, the police appear to lack interest in prosecuting offenders when it takes one to two years for a case to reach trial, by which time the central witness has returned home. The result has been, not surprisingly, that paedophiles have moved into the home-stay scene and students have been placed unwittingly with known sex offenders throughout Europe, Thailand, India, South Africa, Japan, Canada, Brazil, Germany and the USA. When a serious complaint or an allegation of sexual abuse is made, the most prestigious organisations have put their own interests first, supporting sex offenders while discrediting and heaping psychological abuse on victims. In hundreds of reported cases, rape victims have been denied access to police, medical checks and counselling. Instead, the typical agency labels the victim as a troublemaker responsible for the breakdown of the placement. Students have then been returned home with neither a monetary refund nor prior communication with their parents. Others had their passports and return tickets seized and were prevented from leaving. They were also prevented from contacting their parents.

Victims have been accused of concocting allegations of misconduct, being ungrateful to their 'generous' (abusive) hosts and poor ambassadors for their country.

Some former exchange students are still in therapy years after reporting sex offences. Some had their complaints ignored while offenders were permitted to continue hosting other students. Victims confirm that the mishandling of allegations contributed substantially to their subsequent post-traumatic stress disorder.

Agencies accept more students than they have hosts available

Student exchanges are big business, especially in the USA. Some 1,450 American agencies claim to facilitate the entry of more than 275,000 exchange participants annually. This doesn't include organisations that have managed to remain outside the influence of governments. Some pretend to be not-for-profit but accounts often show that some directors — often members of the same family — paid themselves millions of dollars in alleged travel expenses.

When you arrange for your children to go to the USA, you are told that a caring family and school await their arrival. You may be asked to provide private family background information and photographs, ostensibly for the new host. Although it is contrary to regulations, some agencies habitually advertise for additional hosts because they have accepted up to one hundred more students than there are beds or school places available. They resort to all sorts of unethical means to find hosts. Competitions are held rewarding coordinators who place the most students. Wal-Mart vouchers have been presented as prizes for recruiting new hosts.

American agencies blatantly make emotional pleas, indicating that, if readers don't respond, the students will be returned home. Their photographs and personal details are used for publicity, placed at bus stops, on lampposts, in letterboxes and even on the Internet, bearing phrases such as, "Will you take me into your home?" A host convicted of rape told the court that he was attracted to the photograph of the girl and offered to take her into his home specifically to use her for sex. Although students can pay up to $20,000 US for their board and schooling, quite frequently we hear of them being housed in impoverished homes where they have to buy their own food. Some students have been placed in filthy trailer homes in disreputable trailer parks. Two recently received vermin bites that became infected and had to be hospitalised. Needless to say, parents were not informed.

Typically, students and parents are not informed of the risks and young people are totally confused when they experience inappropriate sexual and other behaviour involving host family members, coordinators or other authority figures. A New Zealand lawyer convicted of sex offences was allowed to remain in a Rotary club that continued to be involved in student exchanges. Two students were placed with an American family that belonged to a group that worshipped snakes. Some have knowingly been placed with convicted criminals including paedophiles, one with the approval of the US federal government official responsible for youth. Many report being housed, contrary to regulations, for months at a time in hammocks in coordinators' garages, cheap motels, caravans and disreputable trailer parks. Some Australian and New Zealand children have been placed with such impoverished families that they had to buy their own food, only to have it stolen by family members. Some have been exposed to porn, domestic violence, alcohol abuse and drugs.

What needs to be done?

The reason given for neglecting student travel in Australia at a government level is that Australian states are responsible for child protection whereas the federal government is responsible for travel warnings. Regulation of the industry is clearly the responsibility of state education departments but the federal government should demonstrate leadership to ensure that states implement uniform, tough regulations.

Thousands of young Australians leave the country every year and groups of vulnerable young children with only a smattering of English are arriving from China, Japan and Korea to live in Australian homes. To cater for their safety:

- Criminal checks must be required for all those involved in housing student visitors to deter convicted criminals from becoming hosts.
- Host homes must be inspected to ensure they are clean, there is decent food in the fridge and that students will have privacy in bedrooms and bathrooms, and will receive emotional support in caring families.
- Hosts must be made aware of mandatory reporting legislation and sign an agreement that they will comply with requirements.
- Students must be given realistic warnings and information about inappropriate, reportable behaviour and how to handle it, written in their own language and signed by the student.
- All students should be surveyed by someone other than the sponsoring or host agency when they leave the host country to return home.
- Responsibility for distributing surveys, collecting and storing data should be with a government department, not the sponsoring or host agency.
- Agencies should not be allowed to advertise in a country unless they have been examined and meet certain criteria.

It seems that it is hard to move away from that comfortable, glowing view of exchanges that the industry has created. And, given that the US-Australian relationship has been in such good shape, foreign ministers could and should have made representations to the US Government for the reform of criminal statutes relating to child sexual abuse as happened in Australian States and Territories.

There have been no high-profile, foreign, student-related court cases in Australia compared with the large numbers of them in the US. But there is a very high likelihood that foreign students have been sexually assaulted in Australia and that Australians are being abused overseas right now.

Child-Safe

The risks in student exchanges and home stays were first brought to international notice by Avon and Somerset Police (UK) Chief Superintendent Christopher Gould, who undertook research resulting in 2,000 cases of travel-related abuse. Gould found that, in Europe, as in the US, students who had been led to believe that homes and schools awaited them, were being hawked around shopping centres looking for hosts. Child-Safe was created as a result of Gould's findings. This is a charity attached to Avon and Somerset police headquarters near Bristol.

A series of Travel-Safe guides are available, offering practical advice and guidance to a wide audience, including young people, parents, schools, host families and commercial agencies. They cater to choirs, sports teams, Scouts and Girl Guides travelling to major events. For more information about the content of the booklets, see www.child-safe.org.uk/about/cs_travel_safe. aspx. Child-Safe incorporates a wide range of safeguards in its products to reduce the risk of unsuitable people working with children. There is a strong emphasis on helping organisations produce effective vetting and barring systems. The charity also provides systems for those who want to report abuse or neglect. Through partnerships with international law enforcement agencies and other statutory child protection organisations, Child-Safe facilitates appropriate early intervention, which may lead to timely and effective investigations. Prevention of abuse and staying safe are the key objectives and outcomes of the charity.

Chris Gould highlights the need for safe travel for children in sport. He acted as consultant to London's Tottenham Hotspur Football Club, which brings in many young, international players, age 15 to 18, who are hosted in London homes from anywhere from two days to three-and-a-half years. The football club had no policies in place regarding home-stays until several scandals erupted. As a result of Gould's research, he was invited to talk to host families and undertake similar work for the Football Association (FA) and the Premier League (PL), targeting all soccer clubs in the UK. Gould retired from the Avon and Somerset Police in 2007 to work full-time with Child-Safe.

Children's choirs frequently stay unsupervised in private homes when they travel overseas. Westminster Abbey brought 20 boys to Australia in 2007. Visiting six cities, they probably stayed in 120 different homes. When the director was asked whether the boys received any information for their personal safety, there was no reply. By contrast, when Wellington Girls' College Choir (NZ) toured Australia and had home-stays, they completed the national "Keeping Ourselves Safe" school programme before they left.

Think Smart! Travel Safe! is a booklet that provides practical tips for young travellers. The *Travel Safe Book for Parents and Guardians* advises how to prepare your child, what you need to know, what questions to ask and what you should expect from the organisation responsible for the travel. Booklets for hosts, schools and organisations responsible for children are also available. Products are available from www. child-safe.org.uk/products or email them at childsafe@ avonandsomerset.police.uk.

International Committee for Safety
of Foreign Exchange Students (CSFES)

In 2004, a California student exchange coordinator, Danielle Grijalva, resigned in disgust when she discovered that another coordinator in the same agency had knowingly placed two boys from non-English speaking backgrounds in the home of a pederast. This abuser immediately began grooming them with homosexual pornography (which constitutes a crime in California), offered them alcohol (also against the law) and deprived them of bathroom and bedroom privacy. This was the eighth time that he'd been allowed to host boys.

Mrs. Grijalva was appalled when she discovered that neither the police nor the agency responsible was interested in the boys' predicament. For drawing public attention to the situation, the agency director sent her a one-line email accusing her of bias against homosexuals.

The agency refused to provide a different placement and accused the boys of theft when they attempted to retrieve their passports and airline tickets in a failed attempt to return home. In common with many others placed with inappropriate hosts, they were forced by the agency to sign a statement admitting responsibility for placement breakdown with the threat that failure to sign would ban them from re-entering the US. The boys were too young to realise they were being blackmailed. They signed.

When Grijalva wrote to inform the overseas agencies that sent these boys to the US, she received aggressive responses indicating that they didn't want to know about the problems. When she persisted, she received a single sentence reply: "When we told you we didn't wish to hear from you, we meant it."

In the months following, Grijalva received so many complaints from parents and students that she created a website which attracted more and more horror stories. She then established the International Committee for Safety of

Foreign Exchange Students (CSFES) enlisting the support of others who were aware of the risks. CSFES became a registered charity in January 2007, by which time its filing cabinets were full of complaints from parents, along with newspaper reports of exchange students having been raped, molested and exposed to every type of extortion. Unfortunately, CSFES has no power other than its ability to support parents and students; publicise the actions of unscrupulous agencies using the media; lobby politicians; and lodge complaints with government and exchange agency officials who invariably blame the victims.

USA regulations not enforced

In 2005, complaints of abuse and extortion were so prevalent that Grijalva and I separately contacted American Secretary of State Condoleeza Rice who, in turn, informed President George Bush, who personally announced the impending introduction of new regulations. The US federal government introduced them in April 2006. Criminal background checks are now required of host families, including all household members who are aged 18 and older.

The regulations state: *"Accordingly, all officers, employees, representatives, agents and volunteers acting on the sponsors' behalf must not only be adequately trained and supervised but, if they have direct personal contact with exchange students, must also pass a criminal background check."*

The Department of State was not specific about the type of criminal background check to be undertaken and there are concerns that police records are unreliable and FBI fingerprint checks are necessary. The Director of the Bureau of Educational and Cultural Affairs in the U.S. Department of State, Stanley Colvin, dismissed police checks as unnecessary on the grounds that agencies, some of which charge up to $20,000 US per student and pay hosts comparatively little, could not afford to pay for them.

The new regulations state that all sponsoring agencies must, before departure, provide exchange students with "age- and language-appropriate information on how to identify and report sexual abuse or exploitation". Students travelling to the USA a year *after* the new regulations came into effect confirmed that this information *had not been provided to them.*

The US Department of State Rules and Regulations 62.25(d) (3) states: *"Ensure that no organisational representative acts as both host and area supervisor for any exchange student participant."* And yet, as CSFES records show, when agencies accept more students than they have hosts, some area supervisors routinely take large numbers of students into their own homes and even house them in hammocks in their garages.

Regulation 62.25(f)(2) states: *"Under no circumstances may a sponsor facilitate the entry into the United States of an exchange student for whom a written school placement has not been secured."*

Again, there is evidence that students continue to arrive in the US without a school enrolment, are unable to attend any school for weeks or months as a result and some are sent home (with no reimbursement) when parents complain.

Regardless of the regulations, agencies have blatantly advertised for hosts using newspapers, the Internet and posters *after* the students have arrived in the host country, ignoring the Council on Standards on International Educational Travel (CSIET) Standard 4: Promotion B:

"The organisation shall not publicise the need for host families via any public media with announcements, notices, advertisements, etc., that:

    a.   are not sufficiently in advance of the student's arrival

    b.   appeal to public pity or guilt

    c.   imply in any way that a student will be denied participation if a host family is not found immediately

d. *identify photos of individual students and include an appeal for an immediate family. It is not permissible to identify the specific student as needing a home."*

Not only do some agencies continue to do all of these things but, in their advertisements, some blatantly state that, if there is no response from readers, students will be sent home.

Is that what you would want for *your* child?

Convicted criminals can act as hosts to students on overseas exchanges

A man serving an 11-year parole period for robbery with violence (having, allegedly, previously been charged with rape), was allowed to host four foreign students in succession, seemingly without the knowledge of his parole board.

His criminal history included:

1986	Charges of sexual battery and rape
1987	Burglary of a house: 3 years probation
1990	Arrested for the possession of a short-barrel gun: 6 months in prison
1994	Entered a Food Mart and stole $1,160
1997	Convicted of burglary: imprisoned and subsequently paroled, July 23, 2006

(Source: Department of Corrections)

On querying the placement I received the following email response:

"The host father was convicted of burglary and served his time. The local school officials and police found no issues and the natural family has no objections to the placement. I am at a loss to understand why you think you should substitute your judgment regarding the bona fides of this placement for that of the local authorities and family."

The agency's only concern was how we learned about their host's history. This demonstrates that people who would not pass police checks could become your child's host.

Is this what you would want for *your* child?

Parents discouraged from contacting their children

When you go to a student exchange agency to sign up your son or daughter, you are invariably treated with great respect. All your questions and concerns for your child are heard with sympathy.

Once the contract is signed and your child has left your care, the agency takes full control. If you try to maintain contact, you may receive an abrupt email from the area representative ordering you to desist because you are affecting your child's ability to adjust to the new environment. They argue that students feel more homesick after long conversations with relatives. But if you ask the agency how your child is coping, you are likely to be told that your behaviour is unacceptable, you are not allowing the agency to do its job and must stop interfering. Thus, your child is deprived of parental support and the agency has complete authority. Furthermore, your "unacceptable behaviour" may be used against you if, later, you have cause to make a serious complaint.

Unscrupulous agencies concoct fictitious laws to increase their power over students

CSFES has received many reports that students arriving in the USA are told that they will be breaking international law if they speak to anyone outside the organisation about any concerns they may have. This is blatantly untrue, designed to keep problems of abuse and exploitation in-house. Students have been forced to sign a Code of Conduct which states that they may speak only to their area representative about concerns and to do otherwise will result in deportation in disgrace. This, of course, is blackmail but students alone in a foreign country, often with minimal language skills, are unaware of their rights and, in these circumstances, lack support. Thus, child abuse by hosts, coordinators and others has remained hidden until comparatively recently.

When students reported sexual offences or lodged serious complaints, some were forced to sign statements admitting responsibility for the placement breakdown. They had no access to parental support. Students of non-English speaking backgrounds are especially vulnerable to tricks.

Some students are moved from home to home

While you may have been given the impression that your child will have no more than three hosts in a year, some students are moved from home to home irrespective of their wishes or the wishes of their hosts. It is not uncommon for students to have lived with nine host families and attended three different high schools in a six-month period and still expected to maintain excellent grades. The agencies accept no responsibility for the effects of frequent moves on schooling and anything less than excellent progress results in a warning letter, behaviour agreement or probation letter. If the problem continues, the agency may order immediate repatriation with no refund of the fees paid by parents.

Some parents arrange exchanges to resolve their own problems. That isn't a good idea. The kids travel reluctantly and this increases their vulnerability to exploitation. When a student is placed in a bad situation, the lack of support from natural parents will give a corrupt exchange agency a distinct advantage. Some parents choose to believe the fictional explanations of unscrupulous agencies when their children have reported that something was seriously wrong.

Agencies involved in complaints have accepted no responsibility and these problems are likely to continue until regulations are enforced. It is no surprise that cases of abuse have been making headlines in newspapers when there was only one compliance officer at the US Department of State. In 2007, it was reported that four new positions would be created but, given that there are more than 1,500 agencies (as well as others which manage to escape the scrutiny of the Department of State), they are unlikely to create any significant impact in the foreseeable future.

TIPS FOR PARENTS

While the vast majority of travellers have exciting and invaluable learning experiences, there are still some who suffer physical or sexual abuse, psychological cruelty or physical neglect at the hands of those who organise or host exchanges.

So what can you do to maximise your children's safety?

- *Ask to see child protection policy, protocols and guidelines before you make a booking.* If they can't produce them, go elsewhere. Any agency that does not recognise the vulnerability of these students and seek to protect them is irresponsible.
- *In the USA, ask for evidence that host families have undergone fingerprint and background checks.* In Europe and Australia, you may have to be satisfied with police checks. Bear in mind that they only expose people with criminal convictions and most offenders are not prosecuted.
- *Test out responses to emergencies.* How well does the exchange organisation respond to calls during the evening, weekends and holidays? Obtain their emergency phone number and call after office hours to see if there is a response. This will indicate if this is a responsible organisation.

- *Review student profiles on the Internet.* Check what controls are in place to prevent easy access to students' profiles. Is personal information easily accessible? Are students' photos displayed to be seen by anyone around the world?
- *Is the organisation seeking homes for students after they have arrived in the host country?*
- *Ask yourself,* is this how you want *your* son or daughter to be treated?

Check out information about the host family:
If you have progressed to receiving your son or daughter's prospective host family information package from the student exchange organisation, verify that the host family really exists. Check that the family's interests and background are similar to those of your child. Ensure that, if your child has allergies or asthma, s/he is not being placed in a home with animals or people who smoke. (Sometimes this information is ignored.)

> Be very concerned if, shortly prior to your son or daughter's departure, you are notified by the agency that there has been a sudden change and your child's host family is no longer available, due to a divorce, ill health or unforeseen circumstances. There is a chance that there was no host family in the first place.

In the US, you may be told that a Welcome Family (in lieu of the host family) will await your son or daughter. In other words, someone may have been persuaded to look after your child temporarily or the coordinator may, contrary to regulations, be housing your child. Being met by a Welcome Family can result in your child being passed from family to family before a permanent host is found. This is very distressing for students because it usually deprives them of schooling and socialisation with young people in the interim. Enquire whether the organisation pre-screens its Welcome Families, including finger-print and background checks.

The US Department of State Regulations, Section 62.25(d)(3) states: *"Ensure that no organisational representative acts as both host family and area supervisor for any student participant whom that organisational representative may host."*

In Rotary exchanges, no club member can be both the host and the student's counsellor or a friend of the counsellor because, in the event of a complaint, your child is less likely to be supported than if there is an independent party involved. Your son or daughter should not be placed in a home where his or her host is also the organisation's supervisor/coordinator, area representative or regional director. There is no neutrality if a young person has concerns or is involved in an emergency.

Is There a Secure High School Placement?

Do you have a letter from the high school confirming that your child can attend? Students often find there is no school place although they have paid the agency for their education. This is despite the US Department of State Regulations, Section 62.25(f)(4), which states: *"Under no circumstance shall a sponsor facilitate the entry into the United States of a student for whom a school placement has not been secured."*

Student Identification Card

As per the US Department of State Regulations, Section 62.25 (g)(4), your child requires: *"An identification card which lists the student's name, United States home placement address and telephone number and a telephone number which affords immediate contact with both the Department of State and sponsor in case of emergency. Such cards may be provided in advance of home country departure or immediately upon entry into the United States."*

You should make certain that your son or daughter has this information before leaving home.

If your child is not provided with a Student Identification Card complete with the above-referenced information, prior to departure or arrival into the United States, please notify the CSFES website immediately.

Ask who has the final say in the selection of your child's host family. If told that you have to accept any family chosen for your child, ask more questions.

In addition:

- Ask for a guarantee in writing that the home of the host family has been inspected and that the privacy of the student in bathroom and bedroom is ensured. Bathrooms should have locks.

- Ensure that your child is aware of what constitutes sexual harassment, given that most rapes are preceded by touching the thighs or breasts, accompanied by comments about the sexual attractiveness of the student, introducing sex talk, etc., which, if ignored, leads the perpetrator to think that it is acceptable to proceed further. If the student objects, the perpetrator usually pretends that the touching was accidental and embarrasses the student. Remind your child that being embarrassed is better than being raped.

- Ask the agency to provide telephone numbers to call if abusive behaviour occurs (police, rape crisis centres, etc.). If this is refused, do not use that agency.

- Make certain your child will be able to access his or her passport and return ticket in case an unacceptable situation is encountered. Most agencies seize them and they can't be accessed until students return home.

- Ensure your child knows how to phone home from overseas.

- Ensure that your child knows how to contact your consulate in case s/he encounters problems that the agency ignores.

- Ensure that your child is well informed about the culture if different from your own.
- Ensure that your child has a basic knowledge of the language if it is different from your own.
- Believe and support your child if s/he reports problems.
- Remember that boys can be sexually abused by both males and females (including host mothers) and they need to be as well informed as their sisters about recognising and handling inappropriate behaviour.
- Bear in mind that the United States is one of only a few countries that have not ratified the UN Convention on the Rights of the Child and that reforms to sexual assault legislation have been much slower than in other developed countries.
- Don't allow your daughter go to a patriarchal country that is known for treating women as second-class citizens.

Precautions for Exchange Students
Students:
- Should never leave their home country without having contacted and having some knowledge of the properly screened host family awaiting their arrival.
- Should know before they leave whether they will be attending a public or private school and be apprised of a completed High School Permission Form prior to leaving their home country for the US.
- Must not live in the home of their area representative or coordinator while waiting for a permanent family.
- Should never be placed in the homes of convicted criminals or persons charged with criminal offences.
- Should not be expected to live in homes lacking basic standards of comfort and cleanliness.
- Must know how to contact local police and child protection services.

- Must know how to contact the US Department of State and sponsoring agency in an emergency. Confirm that the numbers you are furnished are correct before the child departs, because some agencies have misinformed their clientele, making it difficult to lodge an official complaint.
- Need to be fully aware of their rights as visitors in the country.
- Must know how to contact their nearest consulate in case of problems.
- Must be educated on all aspects of child protection, such as the grooming methods used by sex offenders, what constitutes sexual harassment and the importance of stopping inappropriate behaviour in the early stages to avoid rape.
- Must never sign agreements admitting guilt for something they didn't do or sign documents they do not fully understand.
- Cannot be banned from a country by not signing a statement produced by the exchange agency.
- Investigate the culture and what might be expected of them; no culture requires students to provide sex.
- Should never be sent home early without good cause and a review process.
- Must not be afraid of being sent back home for voicing concerns. Being returned home should not be regarded as shameful. It may just be an indication that the organisation lacks integrity.
- Who are unfortunate enough to experience sexual misbehaviour, must not believe an agency that tells you that, if you report to the police, you can be sued for defamation.

Schools and communities can help to keep students safer by:

- Confining exchange schemes to students who are at least 17 years old at the time of selection and have completed years 12/13. This is important because selection at ages 15 to 16 disrupts the educational progress and friendships and younger students are most vulnerable to exploitation and abuse.
- Schools that ensure agencies do not oversell international student exchanges as 'the experience of a lifetime'. It is a very challenging experience for all.
- Making selection committees gender-balanced, including at least two high school teachers and a former exchange student.
- Establishing selection processes that will sift out emotionally vulnerable teenagers, e.g., those trying to run away from home or escape school or bullying problems and those who have difficulty expressing their feelings or have suffered a mental illness. There should be many hypothetical questions at the first interview, such as:

    You're home alone with your host father. You have been in the country for four weeks. You're feeling very homesick. What would you do if your host father squeezed you gently on your thigh and said, "You're not homesick, are you?"

    Let's assume you accepted an exchange on the basis that you would be staying with two families. Your first family has two children your age. You settle in and everything's going really well for the first month, then your host parents tell you they have to move away for work reasons. How do you think you would cope?

    Your host is driving you home. He (or she) stops the car, puts his/her arm around you and says his/her marriage is a sham and s/he has fallen in love with you as you are the sexiest, the most attractive guy/girl s/he's ever seen and wants to make love to you. What would you do?

Difficulties Experienced by Students in 25 Different Countries

In 2006, James Cook University Professor of Psychology Russell Hawkins and the author surveyed more than 400 students after their return home from a year spent in Australia, Japan and Europe. Ninety per cent of students said that, overall, their exchange had been helpful to their development. Some said that host families were fantastic. Sixteen said they had difficulties adapting back to family life; their own families and schools seemed boring and their former friends had moved on. While most students believed that the experience was worthwhile and some didn't want to return home, they listed the difficulties they experienced as follows:

1. Loneliness and homesickness in the initial stages — missing friends and family

2. Inadequate knowledge of the language, which limited conversation, comprehension and participation in school. One student was threatened with repatriation because she didn't learn Danish fast enough. One school was described as 'filthy'. Several said they didn't get on with other kids in the class. Some said their schools didn't know what to do with them, given that they were at different levels from the rest of their class.

   "The biggest problem at school was I didn't know what was expected of me and I also found that I was unable to talk to a number of staff about issues as I did not have the language skills."

3. Host clubs and/or host families were disinterested in students. Rude members taunted and mimicked students' accents and belittled their home countries. Several experienced inappropriate behaviour by hosts:

   ▸ *"It was awkward and uncomfortable in my third host family because they were getting divorced and fought all the time."*

- *"Just that one host father who told me all his problems and said that he loved me."*
- *"One of my host fathers didn't seem to understand me at all (there was no language barrier in this case). He had extensively visited the US and, he often came off as arguing with me about my country as if he had authority to do so. That was difficult and I felt like he couldn't hear me without having his pre-judgments already placed on me."*
- *"Inappropriate behaviour from my host father."*
- *"Harassment by a host father who asked obscure questions about Australia and when I didn't know the answers, would laugh at me, belittle me and tell me I was a terrible exchange student for not knowing about my country. This went on daily at the dinner table and would only stop once I was in tears. Then he would laugh again. I complained after three weeks and was moved within a day."*
- *"Host family treating me disrespectfully, not respecting privacy and harassing me."*
- *"My host mother didn't seem to like me or even want me in the house. They treated me poorly. And the father was interested in me sexually, but I avoided it."*
- *"Being neglected by my host father — to the extent of having my host family forget about my birthday and go on a holiday without me, leaving me with my host father's ex-wife who he no longer spoke to. Complaint about third host family — sexual harassment (dismissed by counsellor as accidental and not important), lots of internal family issues (making me an outsider and uncomfortable around the house), organising for me to stay with family friends for weekends without my knowledge (this all led to an argument in which I was painted as the troublemaker both by some members of the Rotary club, the host district and previous host families). I didn't tell my sponsor/ counsellor at the time because I wasn't encouraged to,*

didn't have access to a phone in which I could have a private conversation and was afraid I would be sent home if I made a fuss (a perception given to me by my host district coordinator)."

4. Used as unpaid domestic servants:
    ▸ *"They had different expectations about an exchange student, like I should stay at home and take care of the younger 7-year-old sister. Couldn't go to friends, places, etc.; that was horrible, too. But I got through that. The other four-and-a-half hosts (one without the dad) were absolutely AWESOME!!!! Thank you!!"*
    ▸ *"In my third family, I ended up doing everything from the laundry, to the dishes, to cooking and cleaning the house, because my host siblings couldn't be bothered."*

5. Australian and New Zealand students resented having to adapt to strict house rules:
    ▸ *"I only had problems with one family. All others went out of their way to make me feel welcome and were better than I could have ever hoped for. The family that I did have a lot of problems with imposed a lot of rules about what I could and couldn't do, both outside the house and within it...They also made a clear distinction between the rules that their children were given and the ones I was given. This situation left me feeling very stressed as well as unwanted and as though I was really putting them out by living there."*
    ▸ *"My first host family wouldn't let me out of the house alone unless I was going to school, period."*

6. Too many host families:
    "I had six host families which were a bit much to contend with but they were all nice people."

7. Placed in unsuitable homes: some students were placed in inappropriate, occasionally dirty and impoverished homes where hosts could not afford to feed them adequately and their own food was stolen.

- *"In my third home, the house was really dirty. The bathroom wasn't clean at all. I won't tell you everything but it was really disgusting but I didn't say anything when I was there because I liked the host family."*
- *"Lack of privacy, in relation to having my diary read, room searched and belongings stolen by first host family."*
- *"One set of host siblings didn't want me there and they made it very obvious."*
- *"My third host father was abusive, my fourth host mother was an alcoholic and I was given the job of being her carer. My school was my saviour, but more as a chance to escape, because they couldn't do anything to help me with my living arrangements."*
- *"My third host family was never there and as a result I had to pay for everything."*
- *"My host sister told other exchange students she hated me and her family did, too."*
- *"My fourth host family was completely nuts. My host mum would tell me how horrible I was on a daily basis. My host dad was also my counsellor."*
- *"My second host family was simply never there and the mother was over-controlling and complained about me. She just happened to be one of those big personalities who had previously been known to cause troubles within the community. My counsellor later told me that he had had doubts about putting a student into that family and he certainly wouldn't be doing it again."*

Quite clearly, much depends on the personality, maturity and social skills of the student. However a prior knowledge of the language would seem to be essential when students travel to countries with languages other than their own.

Overseas gap years can be very rewarding but parents must realise that student exchange agencies are businesses and some are not as reputable as they claim to be. Great care must be taken in their selection and in the preparation of your son or daughter for this experience.

Chapter 10

Protecting Children In Cyberspace

By Richard Beach, Nancy Groh, Lee Chisholm

New Zealand Cybersafety Consultants
netsafe.org.nz

There are four important points about children and technology:

1. Children are now growing up in a world where technology, electronic gadgets, and the Internet are an integral and familiar part of their everyday lives.
2. You can't prevent your children from going online because the Net is everywhere. Young people can access the Internet through gaming consoles, smartphones, at friends' houses, at school, at public libraries and more.
3. Teenagers may not consider a parent or any adult to be the first port of call for support and advice; they are more likely to rely on friends for guidance about cyber issues.
4. Keeping the lines of communication open with your child about online activity is vital so you can provide effective guidance.

This first point is probably already recognised and accepted by most parents. You are faced with the evidence every time a child picks up the newest mobile phone, helps solve a computer problem or sets up the latest home electronic device with ultimate confidence. Accepting all of these points, however, will do more to help you keep your child safe online than any amount of rule-making, enforcing, prying or surveillance.

Most people in developed countries have some experience of the Internet. Children born since the mid-1990s have grown up with an ever-increasing array of online tools and devices. They accept that using these modern technologies and being online is just a normal part of life.

Being online can provide access to a world of fantastic resources, but there are some challenges involved. Many of these challenges may at first appear to be new, created by the unrestricted, unmanaged nature of the Internet. But by looking more closely at some of the issues, it becomes apparent that parents can take a role in protecting their children in cyberspace by applying and passing on the wisdom, common sense and experience they already have in dealing with other challenges and problems.

Being Online

Australian research findings (2007)[64] revealed that children 8- to 17-years old spend an average of 75 minutes per day online. This dropped to 30 minutes per day for those 8- to 11-years old.

A Canadian study[65] found that 8- to 12-year-olds spend around 10 hours per week online. Similar studies in the UK showed that one-third of 9- to 12-year-olds are online for an hour or more each day, while a study by the New Zealand Broadcasting Standards Authority in 2008 showed one in five 4- to 5-year-old children use the Internet.

Computers are still the most common way to access the Internet, and children also go online using other devices, such as mobile phones and game consoles.

Mobile phones can access web pages, chat rooms and instant messaging sites which are common places for children to "hang out to communicate with friends". Many new model smart phones come with preloaded applications designed to access social networking sites like Facebook and Twitter.

The current generation of videogame consoles is designed to allow players to play either against or in cooperation with one another over the Internet. A component of this play involves the facility to chat, by text or voice, with others in the same game. All that is needed is an Internet connection. Many of the portable versions of the game consoles, such as Playstation Portable (PSP) can access web pages wirelessly. This makes it possible to get online from wherever there is a wireless network available. The use of Web-enabled game consoles in continually growing.

Most Internet safety organisations advise parents to locate the computer in a family space, such as the living room. Centrally locating the home computer or other devices will help establish technology use as a family activity. It makes it easier to explore the Internet with young children, managing what they do and where they visit. It can provide opportunities for older children to take a mentoring role with younger siblings and for all family members to discuss cyber-safety. Older children will of course want more freedom and they will likely be online outside the home. It will also help you monitor the amount of time they spend online while at home. This only allows supervision over one of a number of Internet access points that might be available to a young person. It is not possible to supervise them all.

Every now and again, the topic of technology addiction gets highlighted in the media. Stories of young people spending days without eating or sleeping while immersed in online games, or of parents neglecting children while they battle in some virtual environment, make for scary reading.

Overuse can be a problem for children if it comes at the detriment of other social interaction, exercise, homework or spending time with family. Late-night sessions will be difficult to monitor if the computer is in the child's bedroom.

From an early age, children can be taught when to turn the computer off, and helped to manage their time spent online. A simple kitchen timer can be useful and new computers have parental controls in their operating system which can be set to shut down or log off users at certain times. Encouraging and helping children to self-monitor their own use from the outset is likely to be the best strategy in the long term.

So children *are* online. What is useful is to know is what they are doing, and how they are interacting.

How are children interacting with technology?

It is tempting to think about all the 'new' technology that is around nowadays. To children, none of it is new. Youngsters already regard email as out of date. In time, even the word 'Internet' may seem quaint, as personal and multiple devices around the home interconnect with others around the world seamlessly and instantly. Knowing how to connect a computer to the Internet may eventually become as irrelevant as knowing how to wire up the house to the city electrical grid. In fact, by the time many adults had figured out how to find a webpage, or check their bank balance online, along came something called Web 2.0.

Web 2.0 became a popular term for websites that enable users to publish their own images, stories, diaries, video recordings, thoughts, music, and so on. Typically, a Web 2.0 environment allows a person to create and control their own content on a website. The key in this is the idea that others will visit the page or space, and share *their* ideas, images, thoughts, etc., with that person. Groups of people with similar interests find each other, and in this way networks of people form and grow. Often these social networks consist of people who are already known to one another in a face-to-face situation, but it is just as likely that this will be the first forum in which many have met.

You don't need any special equipment to explore Web 2.0, just a computer with Internet access. But if you talk about Web 2.0 to teenagers and children, you'll likely just get a blank stare. It is the one and only Web they have always known.

A New Zealand project, CensusAtSchool 2007,[66] surveyed over 25,000 school children aged 6 to 19 and came up with a list of the ten most popular websites for boys and girls. At that time, the social networking site Bebo topped the list for both sexes. Over half of the sites would be considered Web 2.0 websites, facilitating chat, message boards, online multiplayer gaming, trading or creating online pets or personas. Although the Bebo user base has steadily declined since 2008, the use of social networking sites by young people, most notably Facebook, continues to grow.

While the Web was about finding and viewing information, Web 2.0 is about participating. Growing up involves learning about yourself and learning to get along with others. The Internet is a fashionable place for young people to socialise, and to test out their emerging personalities. Studies show that between 55 and 70 percent of teenagers have web pages on social networking sites. Girls in particular favour these sites; 70 percent of girls aged 14 to 17 years have an online profile compared to 50 percent of boys in the same age group.[67]

Social Networking

A social networking page is a modern-day version of a friend-ship book. Instead of listing likes, dislikes, friends, and thoughts in a book, however, today's youngsters are creating profiles of themselves online. Social networking sites encourage personal information sharing. They allow users to post photographs and videos of themselves and their friends, write notes, keep an online diary, run a quiz or poll, and chat about their daily activities. Many users also list their email address, instant messaging address, and their mobile phone numbers.

Facebook, with over 500 million active users in 2010, has clearly won the lion's share of users interested in social networking. Created originally for students at US universities to network with classmates, it became available to the general public in 2006. Users create their page by listing details: name, birthdate, location, hobbies and so on. The site is very interactive, with programmers able to create applications that can be plugged into a user's page. One example is the 'Countries I have visited' map. There, a user tracks international travel destinations and this information is stored on the site. In the photo sharing section of the site, users can list the names of everyone in the photos. Users are also regularly encouraged to share or 'invite' other friends to participate and join common interest groups.

Many sites restrict membership to people by age, (e.g., Facebook terms and conditions require users to be age 13 or over.) New members are usually asked to self-verify that they meet this age requirement, so it is relatively easy for those under the prescribed age to create a public profile. Facebook has a facility to report underage users.

There are a growing number of game sites designed for users as young as 5 years old that also allow restricted forms of social interaction. Many of these sites have built-in security settings that only allow the parent to register a child. Some will allow parents to set age-appropriate parameters related to the child's online activities while others send daily reports to parents about their child's online activities. Club Penguin, Moshi Monsters, Neopets, Poptropica and Disney's Toontown have been growing in popularity. The popularity of sites can change very quickly, however.

There are a number of websites that are commercial brand sites and interactive virtual worlds, often dubbed 'virtual playgrounds'. The distinction between these types of sites, product brands, virtual worlds and online games is rapidly blurring.

Many sites for younger users have facilities for young people to interact in pre-defined ways with other users on the site. Disney's Toontown, for example, limits interaction to a specific menu of greetings, questions, statements and actions. An additional feature allows players to type their own messages to other users but only if they share special passwords outside of the site. This is designed to ensure the children have a real-life relationship with each other before they are allowed to communicate more freely. Every message is filtered to allow only pre-approved words and phrases and blocks attempts to communicate a phone number or other personally identifiable information.

Barbie™ also has an online social site at BarbieGirls.com. The site gained almost three million members in its first 60 days. The Barbie site uses methods to control the chat possibilities. It uses a 'whitelist', which is a list of allowable words. Rather than trying to block inappropriate text (blacklist) or use clever technology to try and identify when users are typing in their personal details such as their email address, a whitelist only accepts words which are on the allowable words list to be entered, This list of allowable words is determined by the site administrators.

The best way to understand social networking websites is to take a look. Generally, they are free and no detailed personal information is required in order to explore the site's features. Once you've signed on, you will want to explore a number of the site's elements, including privacy settings, commercial branding and messaging, common activities and user interactions, as well as the site's terms and conditions. It's useful to your child's capability and skill when you compare the safety information, policies and level of monitoring on the site. You know your own child best.

If your child is already using a site you should consider sitting alongside them as they use it to gauge their level of understanding about whom they are interacting with and the messages they are receiving.

If you are surprised by what you see, it is important not to overreact. Remember this is your child's social space. Just as you might be a little shocked at a conversation your child might have with friends out of adult earshot, you might have the same reaction looking at their interactions on these websites.

For the most part, what you are seeing is your child expressing their current online persona, which may or may not be the way you experience your child. On- or offline, a child can be a football fanatic one day and a poet the next. A young person's persona can change with different environments. This is a space your child might consider private. Children view their webpage conversations as their private property. Without education, children may not realise that, once information has been sent electronically, the sender has lost control of it.

It is possible to restrict access to a social networking page to people who are identified as friends, however some young users do not take the time to 'lock down' their profile or do not understand the importance of doing so. Their personal details, information and photos may remain open to the general public. In a recent New Zealand case, a number of girls received harassing text messages from an unknown cell phone number. Initially it was thought that a clever hacker had used some special wireless technology to steal the girl's phone numbers. However, police investigation revealed the common denominator. All had placed their mobile numbers on their social networking pages.

For parents, it is important to help young people think critically about what information they make public and why. Once a person posts their address, phone number or photo online, it is impossible to totally control who sees that personal information. Even with privacy settings on Facebook, a 'friend' could copy a photo or information and pass it on without the user knowing or approving. Sites continually make changes to their features and settings to stay competitive, so managing an online profile is an ongoing commitment.

Social networking is not just about young people and teen-agers. Eighteen- to 25-year-olds dominate the user statistics for Facebook but there is steady growth among users ages 26 to 44. The Facebook user base topped 500 million active users (users who have returned to the site in the last 30 days) in July 2010.

Meeting Up Online

Many parents are concerned about online predators. Their fears can be fuelled by sensational news stories that perpetuate myths, exaggerate the risks or oversimplify the solutions. Online predators who trick people, use fake personas and have effective strategies to gain the trust of their victims do exist. Children and adults have become victims in some very serious cases. Keeping the lines of communication open with your child about online activity and interacting with strangers or acquaintances is crucial.

There is no shortage of stories indicating that very large numbers of young people meet strangers online, and then arrange to meet them in person. Some publicity can be misleading, however. The online world is as much a part of children's social space today as other more traditional environments. Most children's online friends are probably known face to face, either through school, sports teams, or some common activity. Through these known friends, children meet others and sometimes this happens online. Eventually there can be an offline meeting.

Just as adults may meet a friend of a friend at a dinner party, young people now meet friends of their friends online. Quality research in this area is lacking so there is little to counter some of the media stories and sensational accounts of a meet-up with an online friend that went horribly wrong. Taking the stories that use scare tactics to heart can have negative implications on the trust relationship between a parent and child. Overbearing parents who pry or place excessive restrictions on children's use of technology may simply force their children to stop talking about their online activities and go elsewhere for advice and support.

Parents and Technology

Young people come across a range of different material when exploring the Internet. While a lot of this material will be fun, educational or informative, some of the content they view may be upsetting or cause them confusion or distress. It is important to reassure your children that you will help them find a solution to problems they may encounter.

There are many programmes parents can use to limit access to specific material on a computer. These are typically known as 'filtering' programmes. Filtering aims to minimise the risk of accessing inappropriate or illegal material. Generally Web filtering software blocks a default set of content categories, i.e., adult material, gambling, file sharing. The categories in turn determine which sites will be blocked. Some users of filtering software have expressed concerns about how categories are defined and how specific sites are categorised.

As new sites are identified, they are added if necessary to the filtering software. But continuous growth and changes in online content can have an impact on the overall effectiveness of filtering software.

Filtering software may be most useful for very young children, but as children grow older they will be capable of circumventing filtering programmes with relative ease. Not all young people will have this skill or knowledge but step-by-step instructions can be easily shared on the Internet. Websites abound about hacking, breaking, and generally beating technological security measures.

In July 2008, Australia's *Choice* magazine reported that 15 Internet filtering systems had been tested to compare freeware, government-funded and commercial products. *Choice* found that some of the free software performed as well as commercial products that carry a cost. The products recommended were NetNanny, Integard, ParentalControl Bar, CyberPatrol, and Safe Eyes. New filtering software comes on the market regularly, some offering free trials.

These test results showed that all filters were effective in blocking pornography. Thirteen out of the 15 filters tested blocked 90 percent or more. University of South Australia Professor of Information Systems Paula Swatman confirmed that, whatever filter programme you choose, it will never be 100 percent protective and some material can slip through. "The only really effective solution is to talk to your kids — explain why it is not a good idea to look at certain material."[68]

A common method of beating filters is to use websites called 'anonymous proxies'. Think of these as websites that act as a go-between (proxy). The user, instead of trying to access the blocked website directly, goes to the proxy website, which then fetches the desired pages from the blocked website and delivers them under a different name. This new name is usually a random combination of letters and numbers, and therefore isn't on the filter's list of sites to block. Eventually the proxy site will become known and will be added to the blacklist. The user then simply chooses a different proxy site, and there are many to choose from.

Stealing the password needed to disable the protection is another way to circumvent blocking or monitoring software. Passwords can be stolen or harvested by using keystroke loggers. Keystroke loggers are software or hardware devices that record every single key pressed. Criminals often use this technology to steal passwords used on public computers — a good reason never to use a public computer for online banking or other financial transactions.

Technology companies use parental concerns to sell their safety products. Software companies may try to make you feel that their software is essential to prevent your children from being exposed to online risks. No technology solution, however, will be as effective as regular interaction with an understanding and trusted adult who genuinely knows, cares and supports a child's safe online activity.

If you intend to use filtering tools it is important to choose one that suits your family's unique situation. One place you might start is the website of Common Sense Media at www. commonsensemedia.org. This is a San Francisco-based non-profit organisation that provides independent information on software, including filtering software, websites, games and a wide range of digital media.

Parents can also assist young children to develop effective searching skills that will help them avoid viewing inappropriate material accidentally. In particular, help your child think carefully about the keywords they use in a search engine and how to look critically at the results of a keyword search before clicking on links.

Gaming

Today's parents may have encountered videogames first in a games arcade. Others will remember the first home videogames that plugged into the TV and allowed two people to battle it out by bouncing white blocks back and forth with sticks. Those games consoles have evolved into amazing devices that are vying to become the media hub of the home. The latest version of the Sony Playstation, for example, not only plays games, but can play high definition DVD movies, record television programmes, store and play thousands of music tracks, allow video and telephone calls over the Internet, and connect wirelessly to the Internet and other devices such as computers and other games consoles around the home.

What often drives the emergence of each generation of console is increased graphic power and functionality. As computer chips become smaller, faster and capable of performing many more millions of calculations per second, the level of detail and realism they can bring onto the screen increases, too. Computer-generated characters, vehicles and explosions can look decidedly realistic, immersing the player into an absorbing, lifelike reality.

Many games available for computers and modern game consoles allow the player to log on to a central server on the Internet and pit their skills against other players from anywhere in the world. Sometimes this can be in a simple game of cards or, at other times, controlling a vast army against another human foe.

Many online games encourage players to join teams or clans and fight against other groups or computer-controlled characters. Often the setting for these battles is a fantasy world of goblins, dragons, elves or beasts. One online game, World of Warcraft, reported 12 million subscribers in October 2010. Multiplayer Online Role Playing Games (MORPGs) can also take place in a futuristic outerspace (Eve Online), or in historical contexts like World War II, (Battlestations) where players command an entire naval fleet, recreate famous battles, and even dictate their own rules of engagement as they go. Many online games provide chat room facilities for players to discuss strategy.

A popular environment for young children is Club Penguin, owned by Disney. Club Penguin users personalise cute cartoon penguins, choosing a colour, name and accessories. Accessories include MP3 players and pets. Each player's penguin has its own igloo, which can be furnished using coins earned while playing games. Players are free to roam the penguins' Arctic environment, including sports stadiums, ski runs and pizza parlours. Players can also chat with one another. There are two types of chat available, 'safe' and 'ultimate safe'. Staff at Club Penguin moderate safe chat and may censor inappropriate comments. Ultimate safe chat allows players to choose phrases from a preset list. Players using ultimate safe chat can only see comments posted by other players also using ultimate safe chat. The chat system is chosen when a user is signed up to the service.

Young children can make friends with other players by sending e-cards (postcards within the game), and that new friend can then be added to a user's buddy list. Buddy lists can grow quickly, filled with penguins with which the child has had only the briefest of interactions.

Anyone with a basic level of literacy can interact on Club Penguin. It is common for 6- to 7-year-olds to be members and parents are expected to be involved in the signup process. A child expresses interest in joining the club and an email is sent to their parent explaining what Club Penguin is and how to approve a child's membership. This consent process is designed to inform and involve parents. However, this process can be easily circumvented if a child uses their own or an older sibling's contact email address instead of their parent's.

Mobile Phones and Young People

Mobile phones companies are targeting younger and younger customers. A mobile phone designed for users younger than 8, the Teddyfone, is shaped like a teddy bear and has four programmable call buttons. Parents can programme the buttons so the child can call only four specific people, generally, Mum's and Dad's cell phones, home and perhaps a sibling or caregiver. Although it looks like a toy, the Teddyfone has some powerful functions. A parent can send a text message, which will turn on the microphone and allow the parent to listen in to what is happening around the child.

For teenagers, mobile phones are now an essential part of their social lives. It is the tool whereby friends keep in touch 24/7, social events are organised, and relationships are formed, maintained and ended. Many parents may not realise the importance of this mobile communication to their children and may react to episodes of bullying or other perceived misuse by banning access to the technology. This, coupled with a perception by many young people that parents simply don't understand how the technology works, can lead to reluctance on the part of teenagers to share issues when they arise. If parents take too hard a line or overreact to an incident, they may find they are soon the last port of call in a crisis situation.

Harassment via mobile phones, especially using the text messaging functions, can be a serious problem for some. Most mobile phone companies and teen support organisations now provide online and printed information to give young people strategies to manage unwanted calls or texts.

SO WHAT SHOULD PARENTS DO TO MAKE KIDS SAFER?

• Talk with Your Children

Discussing possible issues before they arise is an important strategy. You need to remain engaged with your child, not through overt or covert monitoring, but through conversation. Young people face many issues as they grow up. Most children actually *want* to talk about issues and wish they could discuss them with parents. Asking about a teenager's online life in a genuinely interested manner is more likely to elicit an honest result. Today's children will easily find other ways to get online, so confiscation and blocking access is a very short-term and ineffective solution.

If your child faces an issue online, and comes to you for help, try to work out a solution together. Part of the solution may involve using technology to block contact from a bully or harasser. If your child wants this to happen, provide support for them to research and implement it in the most effective way. Let them explain and show you how the technology operates. A technological solution on its own may not completely eradicate a problem, but it can be part of the solution, allowing breathing space to work on the root of the problem.

Sometimes the online issue may be a symptom of a wider problem. For example, a young person engaging in risky behaviour online may be facing a number of personal issues. Adolescents will be curious about more adult topics as they become increasingly socially aware and encounter more complex relationships. Websites and online groups cover death, drugs, sex, religion, and other concepts of interest to young people. Parents or other responsible adults who know the child can provide a supportive and responsive environment for their exploration of the wider world. Young people will look at sites you may deem inappropriate and it can be useful to discuss your views and values in relation to these.

Online sexual solicitations can and do occur. Young people are often very savvy about blocking or ignoring anything that seems dodgy however some may be at risk. A predator may work hard to obtain a child's email address or mobile number, which creates an opportunity to send inappropriate material or propose further contact. Parents have a vital role in helping young people think clearly about what personal information they share and who they share it with, both online and face to face.

Most social networking or interactive websites have a button or link to report abuse. This allows the user to report inappropriate behaviour or material to the website for investigation. Content found to breach the terms and conditions for use of the site, which invariably include harassment, bullying and sexual content, will be removed. Inappropriate behaviour can also lead to the perpetrator being banned from the site.

Child pornography is illegal in most countries, but is accessible via the Internet. There are a number of ways to report illegal content on the Web. There are links at the end of this chapter.

Computers, mobile phones, MP3 players, computer game consoles or USB drives can be storage devices for all types of digital content. An unprotected computer, that is, one without up to date anti-virus software, anti-spyware, or a firewall, can fall afoul of any number of malicious elements from the Web. Viruses, spam email, and instant messages can all be responsible for depositing inappropriate or malicious content onto a computer's hard drive. Finding such material won't necessarily prove someone's guilt. How you will deal with a potential problem like this is worth thinking through before you talk to your child. The goal of your response needs to be about keeping the communication open, even if the situation alarms or upsets you as a parent. Young children can end up in places online that they never intended to go, so working through those issues calmly and blamelessly is important.

- ## Set Clear Expectations

You can set clear boundaries and expectations with your children that are specific and appropriate for your family situation. Some families draw up contracts, which they post next to the computer. Providing a list of a few simple rules may be a useful start.

These rules serve as reminders for being responsible, and guidelines on what to do if there is an incident. Three good starters for young children might be:
- Always ask a parent before logging in.
- Tell a parent if anything happens online that confuses or upsets you, or if you need help.
- Set the timer to 'x' minutes and log off at the end of that time.

The rich and varied growth of online content and your child's changing interests means that regular discussion is an essential component of keeping your child safe online.

- **Install Electronic Security**

Although filtering software can minimise exposure to inappropriate and harmful material, every computer that connects to the Internet also needs security safeguards to prevent unwanted and malicious files from infecting it and compromising the security and privacy of your files.

Security safeguards include:
- Up to date anti-virus software.
- Up to date anti-spyware software.
- Up to date firewall.
- Regular installation of operating system updates.

These tools are designed to help protect Internet users from exposure to many of the tricks and traps criminals use to take advantage of their victims. Online scams and organised crime syndicates are adept at using the Internet to steal identities, launder money, harass the public and defraud. Your own common sense and a healthy dose of cynicism are invaluable tools to have when interacting online. Believing the simple adage, 'If it seems too good to be true, then it probably is' will go a long way to preventing the success of social engineering strategies employed by unscrupulous and criminal elements online.

NetSafe provides a resource called the Netbasics to help you learn more about computer security.[69] Software and hardware alone cannot provide all of the solutions to computer security. Human behaviour plays a significant role in creating a secure computing environment. The Netbasics has excellent examples of why electronic security is useful but not sufficient on its own to protect people from harm online.

www.netbasics.org.nz

- **Teach Children to be Good Digital Citizens**

As a parent, you have undertaken the responsibility to keep your children safe and help them grow into responsible members of society. As the offline and online worlds converge, children now must learn to become good digital citizens. Digital citizenship encompasses all that is positive about regular citizenship: contributing, caring for fellow citizens, and following the rules, but it also requires levels of resilience and competence when interacting in the online environment.

Good digital citizens manage their online interactions with integrity and confidence. They follow the guidelines, understand the challenges and have strategies for managing them. Through their actions, good digital citizens promote healthy, online communities and provide positive role models for others.

When should we start teaching our children digital citizenship? As soon as they show an interest in using technologies. A young child's first interactions with technology are likely to be firmly controlled by their parent or caregiver. This is the time to get a young child used to concepts such as limiting time at the computer or console and modelling the use of a password. If you have safety tools especially designed for young children, such as the Hector's World Safety Button™, then teach the child how to use these tools early on.[70]

One of the most useful tools a parent can use to teach children to be safe online is the online environment itself. Although it may seem worrying to have a 6-year-old interacting with strangers online, some sites provide a number of safeguards for young users. They often provide detailed information for parents about the site's features and strongly encourage parental involvement. If a site does not provide you with adequate information about its policies and safety features, shop around for comparable sites that are equipped with better safeguards and security policies.

Exploring sites with your children and talking to them about a site's features and your expectations will give you the opportunity to strongly influence your child's development of safe online practices. You can be your child's most important digital citizenship role model. Children will adopt your strategies, particularly if you let them know why you use them. You do not need to be the technology expert to help your child stop and think before acting online.

Summary

Children today are growing up in an age where convenient, fast, and open communications enable people from around the world to interact with each other to share their ideas and their creative efforts, to unite under worthy causes, and to keep in touch with those who are dear but far away. All the while, it is essential to remember that this communication is two-way.

As parents, we are responsible for creating safe and secure environments for our children — environments where children understand the challenges and the boundaries; where safeguards and protection systems are in place; and where we support our children with love and understanding. More important than ever, children need to be taught skills to effectively manage their own activity in cyberspace. They need to learn how to avoid or deal with situations where they are faced with those who do not follow the rules and where the protection systems are ineffective.

In these circumstances, all a child has to rely on is what they have been taught: the ability to be critical, to question what they see and hear, and to follow the strategies they have been shown. Fostering these skills and strategies is an essential part of 21st century parenting.

TIPS FOR PARENTS

- Position computers and other devices in a family room and make technology use part of family activities.
- Talk to your children regularly about their online activities.
- Let your children know your expectations.
- Model secure practices to help children learn safe strategies.
- Keep your computer security up to date and operational.

For Younger Children

- Use filters to limit accidental access to unsuitable and inappropriate material.
- Use family-friendly search engines designed for children; Google SafeSearch is a good option.
- Help your child create and use a password to access those websites and applications appropriate for their development level.
- Work and play alongside your child when they are using technologies.

For Older Children and Young Teens

- Help children understand the concepts of privacy, personal information and personal safety and how they relate to online activity.
- Help children weigh the benefits and risks of online communication including chat rooms, instant messaging and txt/pxt messaging.

You can find out more about the risks to children online at www.australia.gov.au/netalert or call 1800 880 176 (in Australia).

NetAlert (Australia) Tel 1800 880 176 and NetSafe (New Zealand) are both government-funded organisations to help keep you and your children safe on the Internet. To report information to Australian police, contact Crime Stoppers on 1800 333 000 within Australia.

Report online material you think should be prohibited:

Australia
Australian Communications and Media Authority (ACMA)
www.acma.gov.au/hotline
New Zealand
The ORB
www.theorb.org.nz

For more information:

Australia

www.cybersmart.gov.au/Parents.aspx

New Zealand

www.inmyday.org.nz

http://hectorsworld.netsafe.org.nz/parents

Endnotes

Chapter 1

1   '1000 youths go on the rampage,' *The Dominion Post*, Wellington, 5 March 2001, p. 1.

2   S. Van Den, Administration Support Officer, New Plymouth Police, personal communications, 23 January 2008.

3   S. Mossman, 'Plaudits and put-downs for infamous wild child and the Editorial,' *The Advertiser*, 19 January 2008, pp. 46, 76.

4   C. Lashlie, *He'll be OK: Growing gorgeous boys into good men*, Harper Collins, New Zealand, 2005.

5   'Violence on the rise in Generation Y,' *The Gold Coast Bulletin*, Southport, Queensland, 21 January 2008, p. 14.

6   M. Russell, 'Net blamed as 10,000 kids turn to crime,' *The Age*, 3 August 2008, p. 3.

7   P. O'Callaghan & F Briggs, *Report of the Board of Inquiry into past handling of complaints of sexual abuse in the Anglican Church Diocese of Brisbane*, May 2003, p. 76.

8   F. Briggs, *Children's views of their world at the beginning of the 21st C*, University of South Australia, Magill Campus, 2001.

9   J. Lepper, 'Children cite family conflict as main cause of unhappiness,' *Children & Young People Now*, 26 January 2010.

10 T. O'Connor, 'Work together for the kids: separation,' *The Australian*, 20 February 2010.

11 D. Warne-Smith, 'Cry Babies,' *The Weekend Australian Magazine*, 15-16 March 2008, pp. 2–9.

12   M. Potegal & R.J. Davidson, 'Temper tantrums in young children: 1. Behavioural composition,' *Journal of Developmental & Behavioral Pediatrics,* vol. 24, no. 3, June 2003, p. 140.

13   D. Chalke, Australia SCAN survey for Quantum Market Research, 10 April 2008.

Chapter 2

14   G. Abel & N. Harlow, *The stop child molestation now book,* Xlibris Corporation, 2001.

15   F. Briggs & R.M.F. Hawkins, *A comparison of the early childhood and family experiences of incarcerated convicted male child molesters and men who were sexually abused in childhood and have no convictions for sexual offences against children,* Report for the Criminology Research Council, University of South Australia, 2004.

16   F. Briggs & R.M.F. Hawkins, *An evaluation of "Keeping Ourselves Safe" with children of five to eight years,* A report for the Commissioner of Police, New Zealand and Minister for Education, University of South Australia, Magill Campus, 1990.

17   ibid.

18   P. Kervelaz, 'Childcare centres failing on safety,' *The Australian,* 3 September 2007, p. 3.

19   ibid.

20   S. Hewitt & P. Rolfe, 'Sex creep's green light to work with kids,' *Sunday Herald Sun, 14 February 2010.*

Chapter 3

21   D. Olweus, *Bullying at school: What we know and what we can do,* Blackwell, Cambridge, MA, 1993.

22   R.E. Winter & R.J. Leneway, 'Terror in the classroom: What can be done? Part 4,' retrieved 13 November 2010, www.schoolcio.com/showarticle/1040.

Chapter 4

23 E. Lawrence, 'Safety warnings a new chapter for fairy tales,' 13 July 2008, retrieved 13 November 2010, www.bubhub.com.au/community/forums/showthread.php?s=7 1f46543d9e8f066429eba6cbee089c8&p=2846474.

24 P. Weekes & M. Westwood, 'Parents deluded on teen sex lives,' *The Australian*, 31 August 1993, p. 3.

25 N. Bita, 'Morals blurred by sex acts in the noughties,' *The Australian*, 18 September 2008, p. 6.

26 ibid.

27 American Psychological Association Task Force on the Sexualisation of Girls, *Report of the APA Task Force on the sexualisation of girls,* Washington DC, 2007.

28 Australian Psychological Society, *Submission to the Inquiry into the sexualisation of children in contemporary media,* Senate Standing Committee on Environment, Communication and the Arts, 2008.

29 Adapted from the American Psychological Association's Tipsheet, "What parents can do," which, in turn was adapted and adopted by the Australian Psychological Society for its Tipsheet for Parents.

Chapter 5

30 B. Watson, *Sexual abuse of girls and adult couple relationships: Risk and protective factors,* PhD Thesis, Griffith University School of Psychology, Mt. Gravatt Campus, 2007.

31 W. Glaser, 'McDermott's interview with Dr. Bill Glaser,' ABC Four Corners, 23 May 2005 and W Glaser, 'Paedophilia: The public health problem of the decade' in M James (ed.), *Paedophilia: Policy and prevention,* Australian Institute of Criminology, Canberra, 1997.

32   UNICEF, *An end to violence against children*, 2006, retrieved
      13 November 2010, www.unicef.org/violencestudy/1. World
      Report on Violence against Children.pdf.

33   M. Taylor, G. Holland & E. Quayle, 'Typology of
      paedophile picture collections,' *The Police Journal*, vol. 74,
      2001. See also, E. Quayle & M. Taylor, 'Child pornography
      and the internet: Perpetuating a cycle of abuse,' *Deviant
      Behavior*, vol. 23, no. 4, 2002, pp. 331-362.

34   T. Vermeer, 'Internet operation to trap paedophiles,' *The
      Advertiser*, Adelaide, 7 August 2005.

35   F. Briggs & R.M.F. Hawkins, *An evaluation of 'Keeping
      Ourselves Safe' with children aged five to eight years*, Report
      for New Zealand Police and Ministry of Education,
      University of South Australia, 1991.

36   F. Briggs & R.M.F. Hawkins, *Personal issues in the lives of
      young people with severe learning disabilities*, Report for the
      Commissioner of Police, New Zealand, University of South
      Australia, 2005. *See also*, F Briggs, 'Safety issues in the lives
      of children with learning disabilities,' *Social Policy Journal
      of New Zealand*, no. 29, November 2006, pp. 4–9.

37   F. Briggs & R.M.F. Hawkins, *Keeping ourselves safe: A
      survey of New Zealand school children aged ten to twelve
      years and their parents*, A Report for the Commissioner
      of Police and Ministry of Education, New Zealand,
      University of South Australia, 1996.

38   M. Kennedy, 'The abuse of deaf children,' *Child Abuse
      Review*, Spring Edition, 1989, pp. 3-7. *See also*, M. Kennedy,
      *The deaf child who is sexually abused — Is there a need for a
      dual specialist?*, National Deaf Society, 1990.

39   M. Hunter, *Abused boys: The neglected victims of sexual
      abuse*, Fawcett Columbine, New York, 1990.

40   F. Briggs, R.M.F. Hawkins & M. Williams, *A comparison of
      the childhood and family experiences of elderly incarcerated,
      convicted male child molesters and men who were sexually
      abused in childhood and have no convictions for sexual
      offences*, A Report for the Criminology Research Council,

University of South Australia, July 1994. *See also,* F Briggs (ed.), *From victim to offender: How child sex abuse victims become offenders,* Allen and Unwin, Australia, 1995.

41   S. Leiblum, *The long-term aftermath of men sexually abused by clergy vs. men sexually abused by non-clergy perpetrators,* Paper presented to First World Congress for Sexual Health, Sydney, 19 April 2007.

Chapter 6

42   A. Bentovim, 'Evaluation of a comprehensive treatment approach to child sexual abuse within the family,' Paper presented to the Third European Conference on Child Abuse and Neglect, Prague, 1991.

43   G.G. Abel & N. Harlow, *The Stop Child Molestation Book,* XLibris, 2001.

44   G.G. Abel, J.V. Becker, M.S. Mittelman, J. Cunningham-Rathner, J.L. Rouleau & W.D. Murphy, 'Self-reported sex crimes of non-incarcerated paraphiliacs,' *Journal of Interpersonal Violence,* vol. 2, no. 6, pp. 3-25.

45   G.G. Abel & N. Harlow, op. cit.

46   University of Georgia, 'Study: Most female child molesters were victims of sexual abuse,' 13 May 2008, retrieved 13 November 2010, http://esciencenews.com/articles/2008/05/13/study.most.female.child.molesters.were.victims.sexual.abuse.

47   N. Evans, P. Cosgrove, B. Moth & J. Hewitson, *Adolescent females who have engaged in sexually abusive behaviour: A survey for the STOP Adolescent Programme,* STOP Trust, Christchurch, 2006.

48   L. Barker, *Protecting your children from sexual predators,* St Martin's Press, NY, 2002.

49   F. Briggs, R.M.F. Hawkins & M. Williams, op. cit.

50   M. Smith & C. Chapman, *An investigation into paedophilia,* City Counselling, Brisbane, 1999.

51 D. Grieve, Press Release, Houses of Parliament, London, 2 April 2009.

52 F. Briggs, R.M.F. Hawkins & M. Williams, op. cit.

53 ibid.

54 C. Van Dam, *Identifying child molesters: preventing child sexual abuse by recognising the patterns of the offenders*, Haworth Press, NY, 2001.

55 F. Briggs (ed.), *From victim to offender: How child sex abuse victims become offenders*, Allen and Unwin, Australia, 1995.

56 S. Leiblum, op. cit.

57 T.P. Doyle, A.W.R. Sipe & P.J. Wall, *Sex, priests and secret codes: The Catholic Church's 2,000-year paper trail of sexual abuse,* Volt Press, 2006.

58 V. Violante, 'College "ignored" claims of sex abuse court told Marist brother kept working with boys despite abuse,' *Canberra Times,* 22 February 2008.

59 L. Parker, 'Former SA Magistrate sentenced to 25 years for child sex crimes,' *PM Archive,* 07 September 2001.

60 L.D. Cromer & J.J. Freyd, 'What influences believing child sexual abuse disclosures? The roles of depicted memory persistence, participant gender, trauma history and sexism,' *Psychology of Women Quarterly,* vol. 31, no. 1, March 2007, pp. 13-22.

61 F. Briggs & R.M.F. Hawkins, *Keeping ourselves safe: A survey of New Zealand school children aged ten to twelve years and their parents,* A Report for the Commissioner of Police and Ministry of Education, New Zealand, University of South Australia, 1996.

62 D. Howitt, *Paedophiles and sexual offences against children,* John Wiley & Sons, UK, 1997, cited in Smith & Chapman, op. cit., p. 37.

63 P. *O'Callaghan & F Briggs, op cit.*

Chapter 10

64 Media and Communications in Australian Families 2007, Australian Communications and Media Authority

65 Young Canadians in a Wired World — Phase II, Media Awareness Network

66 CensusAtSchool 2007, www.censusatschool.org.nz

67 Media and Communications in Australian Families 2007, ibid

68 Larkin, N, Keeping internet dangers at bay. *The Advertiser,* Adelaide, 21 July 2008, p 31

69 www.netbasics.org.nz

70 www.hectorsworld.com

Smart Parenting for Safer Kids
Professor Freda Briggs AO

Published by JoJo Publishing
First published 2011

JoJo
PUBLISHING

'Yarra's Edge'
2203/80 Lorimer Street
Docklands VIC 3008
Australia

Email: jo-media@bigpond.net.au or visit www.jojopublishing.com

JoJo Publishing

Editor: Julie Athanasiou
Designer / typesetter: Chameleon Print Design
Printed in China by Everbest Printing

National Library of Australia Cataloguing-in-Publication data

Author: Briggs, Freda
Title: Smart parenting for safer kids : helping children to
                make smart choices and stay safe / Professor Freda Briggs ;
editor: Julie Athanasiou.
Edition: 1st ed.
ISBN: 9780980871005
                (pbk.)
Notes: Includes bibliographical references.
Subjects: Children--Life skills guides.
                Self-confidence in children.
                Self-actualization (Psychology) in children.
Other
Authors/
Contributors: Athanasiou, Julie.
Dewey Number: 305.231